CW0045163

inside the Kray family

THIS IS A CARLTON BOOK

Design copyright © 2001 Carlton Books Limited
Text copyright © Peter Gerrard, Joe Lee and Rita Smith
Illustrations copyright © Peter Gerrard, Joe Lee and Rita Smith
unless otherwise stated

This edition published by Carlton Books Limited 2001
20 Mortimer Street
London
W1T 3JW

A CIP catalogue record for this book is available from the British Library.

ISBN 1 84222 350 X

Printed and bound in Great Britain

inside the Kray family

the twins' cousins tell their story for the first time

Joe Lee & Rita Smith
with Peter Gerrard, bestselling author of *The Guv'nor*

The Lee Family Tree

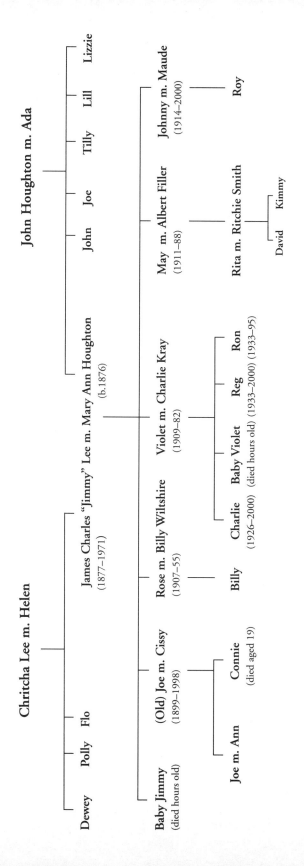

Dedication

RITA SMITH – *In memory of my mum and dad, May and Albert Filler and for my children, David and Kimmy.*

JOE LEE – *To The Lee family who I've been proud to be a part of and my wife Ann. She probably kept me on the straight and narrow.*

PETER GERRARD – *To my wife Shirley whose honest criticism, editing skills and encouragement make my half of our partnership the easier option.*

Contents

Introduction
Peter Gerrard

Ronnie Kray never tired of telling anyone who would listen that he was descended from a mixture of nationalities: Gypsy; Jew; German; Austrian; Irish; Dutch. No doubt he would have loved to add Sicilian to the list but this would have stretched an already overstretched truth. Reggie was more indifferent to the past but to Ronnie this colourful patchwork of ancestors set him apart, which was a state of affairs he strove for from an early age.

If he had had the inclination to study the past, he would have found that rather than set him and his family apart, these mixed-race origins were shared by most other East-Enders around him. For that part of London that lay to the east of the Tower had been first base for incoming communities since the 1700s.

Separating fact from romantic conjecture, it is family knowledge that Krays and Lees were in east London during the mid-nineteenth century. The great great grandparents on both sides seemingly arrived in the "land of plenty" around the late 1840s, which would fit into the history of what was happening in Europe and elsewhere around that time.

The London they disembarked into, from the decks of tall sailing ships, would barely change for at least another eighty years as far as social conditions for the working classes were concerned. Overcrowded streets seething with traders aside, the most powerful impression that would strike them would be the smell. As a boy fifty years ago I can remember days when the stink from the Thames at low tide was unbearable, and that was when the river was comparatively clean and I was some two miles away. A hundred and fifty years ago it was not only the river that polluted the air but the very streets. For at that time London had no system of underground drainage whatsoever and it would be another ten years before this was rectified. Until then Londoners continued to pour every conceivable type of waste into the open street-drains where it found its way into larger open channels before discharging into the

Thames. Small wonder it was known as the "Venice of drains". Many if not most of the stinking waterways that were turned into fetid drains were in earlier days rivers and streams, though people of the time might have been hard pressed to imagine them as anything other than the way they were. Though they have now disappeared inside brick culverts these medieval courses are still flowing under the feet of unknowing Londoners.

For those fortunate enough to have piped water in their homes or at least access to a standpipe shared by perhaps ten families, the advantage was tempered by the fact that the supply was only turned on for a couple of hours every other day. With no public services – and city government not to be established until 1888 – water was a commodity sold by a few private companies with no other thought than profit. For most, without this intermittent trickle, the alternative was to take all their liquid needs from those drains and small streams that carried the sewage. The only precaution taken against the filth and unimaginable debris that floated in the water was to fill a barrel one day and leave it overnight, by which time all the sediment would have sunk to the bottom leaving "clean fresh" water ready for use. Most must have been so immunized by this daily intake of microscopic disease that they were able to shrug off the worst effects of the contaminated water. But London's other nickname, "Cholera City", suggests that not everyone escaped so lightly.

The first thing our families would have to do, even before registering as aliens, would be to find some sort of accommodation. Now, when you allow that in Whitechapel, as an example, on each acre there lived in excess of 270 people, while in Hampstead one person per acre was the norm, they were going to face a problem. Their choice would be between a room in a common lodging house or a room in one of the hundreds of inadequate houses situated in courts, closes and blind alleyways.

At the turn of the nineteenth century the population of London was around the one million mark. Only fifty years later it touched two and a half million, with the highest proportion of inhabitants living in the east. Overcrowding was made even worse when thousands of residential properties within the city were torn down to make way for commercial outlets like offices and warehouses. To meet demand jerry-building outside the limits became rife, as London was cut up by new road and railway tracks.

Businessmen and artisans left their neat houses and fled to the suburbs. These inner-city properties were then divided and sub-divided to the extent that, instead of sheltering one family, they became the single-roomed homes of ten families. But demand still outstripped supply so, without any planning or quality controls being in place, below-standard housing was thrown up on every available space, turning many areas into little more than shanty towns. Houses that were once airy and well ventilated became hemmed in and overshadowed by new buildings that began to deteriorate as soon as the last brick was laid.

Such was the value of every square foot, that the single entrance to perhaps twelve houses would be a narrow alley leading to a dark and sunless centre court that might never feel a breath of moving air. This area of twelve metres by nine would have three or four "privies" for the use of some sixty families, or between two and three hundred individuals.

Through no fault of the tenants these "rookeries", as they were known, were manufactured slums from day one, and as such were mirrored throughout east London. A room for your family in such a place would set you back 8d. per night. A basement cellar, though it was illegal to let them out, could be had for 4d. However, since they lay six or seven feet below overflowing drains, the streets might have been seen as a preferable option. The fact that there were laws against letting out cellars shows that the authorities at least tried to keep standards up. Overcrowding too was illegal, and constables would regularly check out lodging houses to make sure the law was upheld. But there were many ways, not least a shilling for the "peeler" every now and then to look the other way, of avoiding the law, which most must have done because little changed for over a hundred years.

So why would any family wish to settle in an area that was the lowest sinkhole of poverty in England? The simple answer was that the alternatives were far worse.

Ireland, where the Lees came from, was suffering one of the worst human disasters of the nineteenth century – famine. Totally reliant on the potato for their staple diet, when the crop was wiped out by the blight, two million people died of starvation. The main meal of the Irish day was a pan of boiled potatoes placed in the centre of the table with a side serving of salt and a loaf of "boxty" bread, itself made from the humble "murphy". Children took a baked potato to school in their pocket, and working men the same for their midday break. As the crop rotted in the fields and famine took hold, the British government turned a blind eye as the hundreds of dying turned into thousands, stating with reference to an earlier blight during 1841: "Once is an accident of nature – twice is your own folly."

Faced with a bleak future or none at all, great-grandfather Lee, showing a fortitude that would be passed down through the generations, left behind his troubled homeland and set off for England.

The journey may not have been unfamiliar for, as a drover, he might often have been employed to take cattle to the English market by way of sailing ship over the Irish Sea. Even at the height of the great hunger English landowners were still exporting cattle out of Ireland. Once disembarked on this side of the water, he and others would drive the cattle into the city along the wide drove road of Whitechapel, an area he was perhaps familiar with, was the ideal place to escape to.

Europe was in turmoil in the early 1800s due to persecution and pogroms. These applied – as would be mirrored a hundred years later – to Gypsies, Jews, Poles, Russians and, for religious reasons, many Germans. Why the German family of Houghton were forced out of their homeland is not known, but one can assume that it was the possibility of death or displacement that saw them headed for England.

As happens today where ethnic groups congregate together in a strange land, the Houghtons settled in the German quarter of the East End.

The Kray origins are somewhat more obscure. The name is possibly the anglicized version of Krae or Kragh, both common

German surnames, so one might assume they emigrated for the same reason as the Houghtons. Unless, of course, local conjecture about the Krays many years ago is true and they were in fact Roma or Gypsies. The dark and swarthy looks that were handed down to a lessening degree might have been the reason for suggesting this, but then as great-great-grandfather Kray married a Jewess this would also account for the looks.

Incidentally, the Christian name Reginald is from the old German and means "Power Force", while the name Ronald is Norse, meaning "Decisive Ruler". Knowing the character of the twins I think these names should have been transposed, though either way they would turn out to be extremely apt.

So these families, who would eventually merge into one and produce two of the most infamous people London had ever known, were settled into a new land, into a new city and into an area that contemporary outsiders saw as a place to fear, populated by the poorest of the poor – thieves, anarchists and criminals – but better this and life than the alternative they had fled from.

That these settlers raised families, who went on to produce the grandparents of the Krays and Lees, was a miracle in the face of statistics. Of all West End children born, 18 per cent would die before the age of five. In the polluted slums of the East End 55 per cent would die before the age of five, although in areas such as the Nichol it was not at all uncommon for 50 per cent of all children born to die before their first birthday, with 25 per cent of those who survived their first year dying before the age of five. The reasons for such a high infant mortality were many and varied.

Brought forth from mothers themselves weakened by malnutrition and disease, many babies were sickly from birth and had no resistance to the periodic waves of disease that were endemic in these living conditions. Cholera, tuberculosis, diphtheria and meningitis were some of the serious illnesses they succumbed to. But, for babies that existed in an atmosphere so foul that the air was marginally fresher with the windows nailed shut, who never saw a shaft of sunlight, who shared their packing-box cradle with flies, bugs and vermin, the common cold was enough to snuff out their tentative hold on life. Those children who did manage to pass the five-year benchmark were often underweight, stunted by rickets and mentally backward.

People talk of "Dickensian" conditions to conjure up vivid pictures of the mean courts and alleyways inhabited by Oliver Twist and Fagin, as though that period when our early family might have passed the great man in their local streets was an isolated time, more fiction than fact. Yet as late as 1902, when the American author Jack London lived as one of the East End poor to write his *People of the Abyss*, nothing had changed. The two writers could have interchanged passages from their books and you would not have seen the joins.

One face of Victorian London, that sumptuous period so loved by BBC drama producers for its very visual sense of fashion, is represented by lofty dining rooms with tables groaning under the weight of excessive foods and wines, over-ornate draperies and fine yellow brick houses that all appear to front on to immaculate parkland. Yet only an imaginative stone's throw away from the top hats and silk crinolines lay the obscene contrast of London's East End ghettos.

Tower Hamlets is the collective name given to what were the separate hamlets of Whitechapel, Spitalfields, Bethnal Green, Mile End, Poplar, Limehouse, Radcliff, Stepney, Shadwell, Wapping and the Isle of Dogs. What in the late eleventh century were separate villages inhabited by no more than seven hundred peasants and effectively segregated from London by the city walls had become, by the eighteenth century, one unified mass, as housing extended from each until they were shoulder to shoulder.

These areas housed one third of the population of London. Their factories, docks, artisans and craftsmen serviced the city. Necessary but stinking trades – slaughterhouses, glue factories, rendering works and tanning yards that polluted the air and made life intolerable – were carried out within the residential areas of the workers, all overlaid with the sweet and sickly smell of yeast from the hundreds of breweries. Small wonder that those outside the boundaries of this stinking mass of humanity generally accepted that the only way its inhabitants could sink any lower was by dying. (Which, by virtue of their existence, they did with a regularity that made little difference to the overcrowding.)

There were no rich people in the East End, only levels of poor, and which category our families fell into we can only guess at.

In the late 1860s we know that great-grandfather John Houghton was a butcher, though it's certain that he didn't ply his trade from a tiled and chromed double-fronted shop. His workplace would have been in Aldgate and no more than a converted dwelling-house that would serve as both slaughterhouse and shop. The early morning scenes outside such places must have been chaotic. Terrified sheep waiting their turn until they were beaten and harried through the door toward the butcher's axe, would mill frantically under the legs of cattle, passers-by and crowds of gawping children. Blood and urine would flow across the pavements, but apart from perhaps a lift of the skirts to avoid the gore, little notice would be taken. It was part of everyday life. Though if local vicar Samuel Barnett from St Jude's had had his way, these "open peep shows" of horrible cruelty to dumb beasts would have been closed, to protect children from the moral consequences of witnessing such brutality.

Great-grandfather Lee would have added further mayhem to the streets, for as a drover his job was to drive the long-horned cattle from the docks or from further up country. Either way the latter part of the journey would be through the thronged streets of Whitechapel towards the abattoirs of Aldgate. Too often these semi-wild cattle would run some unfortunate down or overturn carriages as their horns, at two feet long, became entangled in the spokes.

Their contemporary on the Kray side would have trodden these same roads into the East End as he followed his business as a horse trader – something which adds weight to the local suggestion that he was of gypsy stock, for this was traditional work among gypsy folk. As the main and only form of transport, good horses were in great demand. Even so, work would be intermittent with perhaps too many dealers vying for business.

Droving too was very lowly paid, but with a fortitude and an aptitude for extracting the most from any situation – a trait that seemed to pass down through the genes – these branches of the family would rank simply as poor.

John Houghton and his family, because of his trade if nothing else, would have eaten better than the average, though the fact that he lived and worked around the East End would have meant that until he bettered himself, as we know he did, he would initially not have lived any better than his neighbours.

At least our families were working and apparently in reasonable health. Take these two things away and the spiral downward would be swift and sure.

After the poor, who might have been classed as "well off" by those below them, came the very poor. And below them came a stratum of people who lived their lives from crust to crust, too lowly even to be categorized. These people subsisted by carrying out tasks that only those on the borderline of starvation could consider. Like collecting "pure", a Victorian euphemism for dog faeces, from the streets to sell to local tanneries for use in the tanning of hides – at one farthing a bucket. Scavengers paddling through drains and gullies often knee- or waist-deep in raw sewage searching for anything saleable; be it a coin, a bottle, rags, old iron or firewood – everything had a resale value. Mudlarks, as they were known, were the young boys and girls who scavenged similarly in the stinking mudflats of the river, eyes sharp for anything saleable. Dredgers or rivermen would haunt the shoreline and piers for the ever-present corpses of the drowned then, by dragging out these bloated bodies, secure themselves a small reward. Common practice then, and even up to present times, was that corpses found on the eastern shoreline would be boated across the river to where the southern authorities paid a few coppers more.

As a last resort there was always prostitution to fall back on and figures from that period show that in Whitechapel alone it was estimated that 2,500 women were earning their living in this way. Though, given the private nature of the business, one can assume that these numbers were much higher. Child prostitution was rife and generally known as the white slave trade. Strange, when you think what the term "Victorian values" conjures up in our minds, that nothing was done about this until 1875 when the age of consent was raised to thirteen.

This obviously had little effect, for in 1885 William Stead and Bramwell Booth, who was to found the Salvation Army in Whitechapel Road, were able to purchase Eliza Armstrong from her father for the sum of five pounds. They did this to highlight how easy it was to procure young girls for prostitution and published what they had done. Some time later Stead, but not Booth, was charged and imprisoned in Holloway for unlawful kidnapping of a minor. Subsequent publicity forced parliament to raise the age of consent once again, this time by a further three years to sixteen, where it remains today.

Those people who were able to seek work from an employer laid themselves open to exploitation of the worst kind. Casual labour was plentiful and job security non-existent.

Frail men, their strength sapped by hunger, would attempt the heaviest unloading work in the docks for pitiful daily wages – many of them would have to seek a "sub" at midday so that they could eat just enough to give them the strength to finish the day. With no union behind them these men could be hired and fired at will, paid slave wages and treated inhumanely. Fatalities would mean the man's family heading for the workhouse and those injured in the accidents, that happened daily, received no compensation or sick pay, just the pittance of parish relief – and that only if they could satisfy the means test inspector.

Girls and women might work for the matchmakers Bryant & May in Fairfield Road, Bow. Wages again were farcical, while the very nature of handling match-head phosphorous every day was in many cases a death sentence from day one. Though this dangerous chemical was outlawed in America and other parts of Europe, the British government refused to ban phosphorous on the grounds that to do so would interfere with private enterprise. By taking this stance they allowed many, many East End girls to be disfigured before dying of jaw and face cancer. Girls on the shop floor with the job of carrying heavy boxes on their heads could expect to be bald within the first year. Fourteen hours a day, six days a week should have given them a take-home pay of six or seven shillings. But with a harsh fine system in place this was often drastically reduced. Being ten minutes late would cost them half a day's pay. Singing, talking, dropping matches or even going to the toilet, without first asking the forewoman, meant fines of from tuppence to ninepence, with no argument or appeal. Conditions only changed after the well-chronicled match girls' strike in 1888.

The worst exploitation was suffered by out-workers under contract to various businesses, such as the clothing trade or again Bryant & May, for their product was in demand everywhere. One tends to put communism and Russia in the same sentence, but it was only after witnessing for himself the poverty and working conditions of the masses in the East End that Karl Marx went on to found his political philosophy.

Typical of outside matchbox-makers would be a mother with perhaps two young children as helpers, turning out five gross of boxes a day, huddled over a table in the half-light of a barely furnished room. There was no health danger in this type of work but at two pennies per gross it makes one think of that saying about feeding a horse on nothing but hay: "More energy is needed to chew and digest it than can be gained from it."

Take away the cost of fuel for a fire to melt the glue and dry the boxes, the raw glue itself, plus string to tie them with (as per contract), take away the all too common rejection of perfectly sound matchboxes, often amounting to 20 per cent, and for her fourteen-hour day the worker could expect to clear six pennies daily.

Elsewhere this little army of mothers, the old and the sick would turn their living quarters into mini factories just to exist day by day, and be pleased they were able to earn a few pennies. Sack making, shirt making, button and button-hole sewing, waistcoat finishing – monotonous, eye-straining, finger-aching work, with the only goal being able to earn enough to buy daily food and face the rent man every Friday.

Food cupboards or larders were non-existent and unnecessary because, apart from keeping a paper twist of tea and perhaps a drop of milk indoors, all food was eaten almost immediately it was bought.

After food was taken care of – and often before – the rent was the main priority, for to be put out on the streets was the fear that hung constantly over the heads of East-Enders. This would mean the workhouse for the whole family, a spectre that haunted most – as it was intended to. This was no soft option like some might consider going on the dole to be today. The whole system was designed to deter would-be entrants. A man on his own, or to a lesser degree a woman, could feasibly get through each day and night living on the streets. Between begging for food they could catch up on their sleep under an arch or park bench for the law then said you were not allowed to sleep in a public place during the hours of darkness. After sunrise you could get your head down for the rest of the day, but as the light faded a constable would forcibly rouse you and force you to move on.

A mother with perhaps five children and a sickly husband could not consider living on the streets as an alternative so would apply to the parish for a place in the dreaded workhouse. The separation of the family would be the inevitable result, but what else could they do?

Imagine a family as they contemplated the bleak prison-like façade of perhaps Bethnal Green workhouse. Everything about its exterior was designed to crush the spirit and repel those inadequates who, through sloth and idleness had brought themselves to its door. They would not have gazed at its featureless bricks until they were inside the high walls that cut off the inmates from the outside world. Once behind the oak doors that would not have been out of place at Newgate, the family would be segregated. Children of whatever age would be taken from their parents, and husband and wife would be separated to remove them from any temptation to breed. After the statutory cold-water wash and the indignity of delousing, their clothes would be taken away and all would be kitted out in clothes suitable to the station they had been reduced to. Females, including children, were given ankle-length shapeless dresses, coarse stockings and knee-length underwear. No tailoring service here – everything fitted where it touched, and had to be tucked, pinned or tied for any semblance of dignity.

Males were given convict-style striped shirts, which matched the dresses of the women. Trousers were adjusted to length by a piece of string (supplied) tied round the knees. Vest, drawers, socks, neckerchief and jacket completed his transformation from freeman to workhouse inmate. Well, not quite. Hobnailed boots were handed out to all, but the final touch was reserved for the ragged crop of a haircut they would be given, protest or not, that would mark them as fallen outcasts until they left the workhouse and grew it out.

The time of day they arrived would determine whether they ate or were sent straight to work. Men and older boys of seven upwards would be put to oakum picking. Here they would reduce old, often tarry, two-inch diameter ropes back into an original hempen state, which would eventually be used as caulking for boats. With no conversation allowed and a daily target of at least three pounds in weight there was little chance for skiving. Allowing that these places were not prisons, infraction of the rules could mean a beating, solitary confinement or both.

Stone breaking was just as monotonous – the daily quota having to be pushed through a measured grill at the end of the building. Less painful to the fingers and arms was driving the corn mill that turned out the flour for the bread, but you needed a strong pair of legs because to drive the mill the inmates had to walk round and round a treadmill as if in some medieval dungeon.

This work was carried out on a diet barely above sustenance level and in two shifts of five hours each. Women and girls worked equally hard and long, mainly scrubbing stone floors and steps, endlessly polishing brassware – in fact, every domestic chore necessary to running the place.

Children too young to work were supervised but given nothing to do but gaze at blank walls and cry for their mothers.

The day's work ended at 6 p.m., but with stomachs gnawing at backbones they would have to endure one hour's prayer before being served a meal of bread and gruel, washed down by weak sugarless tea. Bed at 8 p.m. brought little comfort, for their resting places were rough wooden boards covered with thin horsehair mattresses. Two blankets per person were thought more than adequate, even in winter, while extravagances like sheets and pillows were considered unnecessary for such people. As a matter of course it was expected that two inmates should share each bed.

The dormitory was furnished with stools and a couple of tables, while the view was of painted walls broken here and there by uplifting biblical quotes. All windows were six feet from the floor, the same as throughout the workhouse, no doubt to save the inmates from being distracted from their self-induced misery.

Total lunacy or mental illness was no bar to being housed in such a place, so one can imagine that the 5 a.m. bell for more prayers could be a welcome relief from a night hideous with the cries of the insane and the mumbling moans of your bedfellows, who were being driven the same way by such conditions.

In this merge of prison hospital and madhouse a very heavy price was paid simply to have a roof over one's head. It would be as late as 1930 before changing conditions made Bethnal Green Workhouse redundant and it was put up for sale.

Much of what is perceived about the character of cockney East-Enders is a myth. The cheeky chappy, how's-your-father, diamond geezer was a music-hall invention and something that has been perpetrated ever since. One could draw a simile with that of American gangsters. Before filmmakers invented their style on celluloid no doubt villains and criminals dressed like everyone else of the period. Once immortalized in films such as *Public Enemy* and *G Men,* all self-respecting gangsters had to wear the uniform of wide shoulders, crombie overcoat and snap-brim fedora, and it's no surprise that with Ronnie's insatiable appetite for such films, his dress sense would eventually mirror those of his screen heroes. What is no myth is the general view of East-Enders being loyal to their "own", strong on family values and with an ability to get back up on their feet no matter how many times they are knocked down.

It is not difficult to see that with abject living conditions that were not to change until well into the twentieth century "East-Enders" had little incentive for grinning every hour of the day nor dancing with thumbs in braces at the drop of a hat.

What this way of life did was to unite all those within the boundary of Tower Hamlets against all those outside. That suspicion of people "not your own" until proven otherwise still hangs on today, as does those strong family bonds. In the popular television soap *EastEnders*, Pauline Fowler's daily bleating that "family is all" might be viewed with some amusement, yet as far as it can in our more mobile society, it still holds true for many

Again much is made of the fact that Reg, Ron and Charlie grew up in the closeness of grandparents, aunts and uncles living side by side in Vallance Road. But generally this was a way of life in the East End, grouping together as they had always done so that they could all look after each other. Perhaps this was an unconscious continuation of their foreign roots. Germans or gypsies, or in fact any of the ethnic minorities that are the bloodstock of the present day East-Ender, traditionally lived in tight communities and this has been handed down even when these early ancestors were forgotten.

Something else which was very common among East-Enders, at least up until the 1950s, was the practice of taking a stranger into their home to live, not just as a lodger but as an accepted part of the family. So many of the older generation recall an Uncle Bill or Uncle Fred who occupied the back room, that it must have been an accepted part of life. The Lees were no exception to this. Why whoever it was joined them in the first place might be long forgotten. A homeless child, a friend of the old family down on their luck – whatever. It says a lot about the generosity of these people that while apparently they had nothing, this nothing could be stretched enough to help someone less fortunate.

While conditions such as these paint a grim portrait to us in the twenty-first century, we have to consider how those people who lived and worked in such times viewed their own situation. While most would be aware of the enormous gulf between themselves and the better classes, that was how life was and I am sure they did not spend their days aspiring to move into the red-brick houses of St James's.

Money was short if not too often non-existent. Sweat, tears and occasionally blood had to be shed to gain every crumb. Infants died with regularity and every day had to be faced with fresh courage just to get through it. But then everyone else they associated with was in the same boat, none better or worse off than their neighbour.

Today, when even the weather has to be blamed on someone and most expect to be mollycoddled by the State when things go wrong, we are all striving upward and dissatisfied with ordinary life. Today, with work available at almost any level, blue collar or white, with some initiative or a small talent for warbling or kicking a ball, most of us can aim high: a villa in Spain, top-of-the-range cars and positions of either fame or power or both. Nothing is out of reach.

Victorian lower working classes had no such aspirations. Live, work, raise a family and die – that's about as good as it would get and it was generally accepted. But living was not only about a life-and-death struggle. At a time when you could get drunk for a ha'penny and dead drunk for a penny, pubs were on every corner, while porterhouses, beer shops and front-room drinking places filled in the gaps between.

If you wanted more entertainment than alcoholic oblivion, the streets were filled with free and colourful acts of every kind. Dancing bears, held by a chain to the nose, would be led through their paces by German-gypsy owners with a cruelty that the laughing crowd would be indifferent to. Street dancers, street singers, street organs with optional monkey, snake charmers, fire eaters, sword swallowers, clowns – the list of the talent on display is endless, each vying with the other to coerce a farthing from onlookers who had little more than themselves.

For those with a few coppers to spare, the entrance fee to theatres and music halls, which were everywhere in east London, provided a cheap respite from the summer heat and smells, and a warm refuge from winter cold and fog. There was the Garrick just off Leman Street, the British Queen in Commercial Road, the Effington in Whitechapel Road and the Pavilion nearby – not to be confused with the similarly named music hall in Vallance Road, which would be graced by Lee and Kray descendants on- and off-stage in years to come, because this was not opened until 1898.

The markets of the East End were outdoor theatres in their own right. Smithfield meat market – named after the "Smooth field" it was located on outside the city walls – was a horse market in the middle ages. This site was also a place of execution for over four hundred years. In 1666 the Great Fire of London was halted here and debris was brought from elsewhere and piled up in great mounds.

Spitalfields market took its name from the medieval hospital (Spital) and priory of Saint Mary that once stood there. Brick Lane, favourite haunt of Grandad Lee, was originally the home and workplace of Flemish brick and tile makers. Later it became a livestock market and later still a general market as it is today.

To the north was Club Row, where all manner of exotic and domestic animals could be bought. From monkeys brought in by Lascar seamen to parrots, wild songbirds and even rats caught to supply the fighting pits of local public houses.

The most well-known market by name is Petticoat Lane, yet it has not officially been known as that for a hundred and fifty-five years. With their sensitivity to any mention of ladies' underwear the Victorian authorities changed the name to Middlesex Street in 1846. In Elizabethan times this street marked the boundary of the City of London and the East End (which at one time was in the county of Middlesex). It was where pigs were sold, so was aptly named Hogs Lane.

A more macabre form of entertainment and one freely available was the spectacle of public hangings. These never failed to draw enormous crowds, sometimes reaching numbers of twenty thousand and more. It would be more than likely that the great grandparents of our present-day family would have been taken on such an outing, much as we might take our own children to Alton Towers. A brisk walk from the East End would have taken them to the docks at Wapping where traditionally those who carried out crimes on the sea paid the price of justice. Once the sentence had been carried out the corpse was traditionally left until three tides had washed over it, only then was it taken down and hung on a gibbet as a warning to others. When the famous pirate Captain Kidd met his end here, the rope broke on the first attempt and he had to wait while a new one was brought and fixed before he could finally be dispatched. Piracy was not the only reason for being sentenced to climb the scaffold steps. Mutiny at sea or arson within Her Majesty's docks were other crimes that were punished with the hempen necklace.

Further along the river and a similar distance from home was Tower Hill, where they might have watched a better class of prisoner in their death throes. The majority, and run-of-the-mill murderers, would be dispatched outside Newgate Prison, which is now the site of the famous criminal court the Old Bailey – again not too far to walk from east London.

Children as young as eight were still being publicly hanged in the 1850s, though more and more of these sentences were given but immediately overturned in favour of hard labour or deportation. Amazingly, it was not until as late as 1908 that a law was passed preventing a child under sixteen from being executed.

Female hangings were a great favourite with the men and they would wait with bated breath for that moment when skirts would fly up as the ladies took the final drop. Maria Manning, the murderess who was hanged side by side with her husband – a rare event – knew what was expected and in her final days painstakingly cut out and sewed new drawers for the occasion.

Whatever age or gender, the death throes of these unfortunates were met with cheers rather than horror – and horrific it must have been. It was not until William Marwood brought a more scientific approach to the job in hand – namely a calculated long drop, that death was instantaneous. Prior to this a short rope meant four to seven minutes of strangulation. And this is what the young forebears might have regularly watched in childhood fascination, though I like to think they were more interested in getting to grips with a large paper cone of hokey pokey (ice cream – "Hokey Pokey, penny a lump, this is the stuff to make you jump"), which would be a special treat on such a day out.

These child forebears would be ten or twelve years old before scaffolds were dismantled from public squares and erected behind prison walls. The last man to die under the scrutiny of the population was the Fenian Michael Barratt. He was hanged outside Newgate in May 1868 for a bomb attack in Clerkenwell that killed twelve and injured one hundred and twenty. The last woman was Frances Kidder in April the same year at Maidstone. It would be another one hundred years before the death penalty would be put on hold, though the gallows are still in place in Wandsworth Prison should it ever be brought back.

When Newgate was torn down and the Old Bailey built in the early 1900s, a diary was found dated 1881 that had once belonged to a convict by the name of Alfred Jones. Scribbled on one page, in an attempt at a rhyming couplet, was a note saying: "Goodbye Lucy dear, I am parted from you for seven long years." Below in a different hand was written, obviously by another con with a sense of humour: "If your Lucy is like all other gals, she'll give a few sighs and moans, but soon she'll find amongst your pals, another Alfred Jones."

Early family history being thin on the ground, years of birth can only be educated guesswork. The early settlers very likely had some children in arms when they first arrived in London. Then, by the very nature of things, they would have added to the size of their brood as time went on. It is a safe bet that the great-great-grandparents of the Kray twins were born between 1850 and 1856 into the east London described above.

As Dickens said of an earlier age, "It was the best of times, it was the worst of times." Exciting events were taking place all the time. One of the brightest points in the century was the Great Exhibition of 1851. With poverty, disease and death stalking the east London streets Britain proclaimed itself the finest nation on earth and the unchallenged leader of the industrial revolution.

A showcase exhibition hall named the Crystal Palace was erected in Hyde Park and the world was invited to see what we had to offer. Under a canopy made from a million square feet of glass, thirteen thousand exhibits of British skills and technology were displayed among water features, animal attractions of lions and tigers, tropical gardens and a circus. Blondini, the famous tightrope walker, entertained the crowds in the main foyer. Eight years later he would not only cross Niagara Falls on a thin wire, but also carry out a stove, squat in the middle and fry a pan of eggs. Rather than praise his bravery, the better quality papers of the day reported his feat as an act of extraordinary folly.

Later this vast conservatory was dismantled and moved to Sydenham Hall, south London, where it remained a popular theme park attraction until it burnt down in 1936.

The great bell of Big Ben was cast at the Whitechapel foundry at 32 Whitechapel Road, though with delays on the construction of the building it was not actually put in place for three years. An oversized clapper cracked the bell in a very short time, mirroring the fate of the famous American Liberty bell, which was cast at the same foundry.

St Katherine's dock saw the launch of the *Great Eastern* steamer, which would eventually lay telegraph cables from London to North America. King's Cross Station was built. Livingstone trudged across Africa. Florence Nightingale crept into history by tending the wounded in Crimea, and many names from the Indian Mutiny of 1857–8 would be remembered for ever as London street names.

But this was a world far removed from daily life of the average east Londoner. What they probably hailed as being worthwhile was the opening of a vast system of brick-lined sewers, linked to treatment plants and pumping stations, in 1860. At last the filth that lay in the unpaved streets would disappear overnight down modern sewers. Unfortunately, our great-great-grandparents and their children would grow up before there was a noticeable difference.

Through the 1850s, the 1860s and into the 1870s our families would be growing up in an oasis of sameness, within but not part of a changing world. When the young Lee and the young Kray chose brides to be, it is an interesting thought that one or both of the couples might have tied the knot at the Church of St James in Bethnal Green Road, for this is where Reggie and Frances would marry some ninety years later.

Church ceremonies cost money, which might have been a reason for so many couples living "over the brush" in the East End. As an encouragement against such behaviour there was always the "penny wedding" where for that sum twenty couples or so could have a collective service – the vicar at least getting slightly more than the price of one marriage, as against no work at all. Then in the face of a barrage of criticism, the "Red Church" in Bethnal Green Road, as St James's was known, began marrying anyone for free and by this act of Christian charity helped to reduce the figures of those living in sin within the parish. So it makes sense, if only in conjecture, to think that one or all of our family might have taken advantage of this bargain to start their lives together.

The birth certificate of the twins' grandfather James Lee places him over the river in one of the worst slum areas of south London in the year 1877. Why his father, Chritcha, had moved into an area as alien to east Londoners as a foreign country is again conjecture. He, as stated in the official document, was still applying the calling of his father and grandfather, namely drover, and it may have been that he was working the cattle droves from further south. On the other hand, he may have sunk so low financially that the only way to keep a roof over his family was to move into an area where rents were cheap. Lewis Street (now long swept away) was in a district named Colliers Rents, and as Mearns states in his *Bitter Cry of Outcast London*, home to convicts, thieves and prostitutes, which was no reflection on other tenants with more honest callings. For, whether east or south London, cash was the only reference needed to gain a room.

Mary Houghton, the future wife of James Charles Lee, or Jimmy as he would always be known, was born near Whitechapel in the previous year. Other than "within the sound of Bow Bells" nothing is known of where the Kray grandparents were born.

***

In 1899, at the respective ages of twenty-three and twenty-four, Jimmy and Mary Ann started a family. I was privileged to spend some time with Joe, their eldest son, when he was in his ninety-seventh year, and I could not help feeling that his memories and recollections of family and an East End past allowed me to touch history.

Highly thought of by everyone in the family, Uncle Joe was a particular favourite of Reg and Ron and they both thought that I would find it an interesting experience to meet him. Prior to this, during one of my visits to Reg in Maidstone prison, he took great pains in pointing out that I shouldn't overtire the old chap as he was getting on in years. So with this firmly in mind I arrived at his home in a block of retirement flats near Romford in Essex expecting to meet someone frail, perhaps rambling, perhaps forgetful. Instead, I was greeted by a tall wiry man, strong voiced and as mentally agile as someone less than half his age. I was made welcome from the moment I stepped in the door and once a cup of tea was in front of us, and unbidden from me, he launched into the favourite pastime of the old – talking about the past. From then on he only paused for breath when it was time to refuel with a midday meal that might have floored a horse.

Old Joe, as he was affectionately known to separate him from his son Joe, co-author of this book, died two years later at the age of ninety-nine, leaving behind him a legacy of strength and humour for all those who knew him. I have never forgotten the impression he made on me and here, in his own words, are the stories he told.

1. The Southpaw Cannonball

Old Joe Lee

I was born in Cadover Road, Mile End Old Town on the 12th December 1899. From what my mother told me and from what I saw when I was old enough to take things in, those days were rough old times for everybody. Funny though, it's only when you look back that you realize how hard it was just to get by for most people, but when you're growing up and living through it you don't know any different so you just take every day as it comes.

When I look round my little place here, with its fitted carpets, central heating, telly in the corner and plenty to eat, I can't help thinking that back then if we'd had just a little slice of what everybody's got now, we'd have felt like millionaires.

For the first seven or eight years of my life I was on my own with my mother and father. I would have had an older brother, but Jimmy, as he was named – after the old man – died as a baby like a lot of kiddies did then, what with malnutrition and epidemics from bad water. Sounds harsh but I think mothers accepted that's the way it was and just got on with it. I'm not saying they didn't grieve – that would only be natural – but no sooner was one buried than there'd be another on the way. When she first told me about this brother of mine I was only a nipper and she said he was only a few hours old when he had convulsions and died in her arms. Years and years later, long after the pain would've gone away, I'd hear her telling my sisters or her grandkids that what killed him was "looking at his ugly face" and she'd nod toward my father. Couldn't understand why people laughed when she said it.

Move around? I couldn't begin to tell you how many different rooms we lived in. You didn't get a whole house then, you got a room along with five or six other families, and made the best of it. I don't know how landlords made a living because everyone was at the same game. The first day you moved into a new place you'd have to put up the full week's rent, which could be as much as five or six shillings. The next Friday you'd keep quiet when the rent man knocked and the Friday after you'd make a dreadful excuse and promise to pay the following week. But instead of that, on the Thursday night all your bits and pieces would be slung in a barrow – I don't suppose there was hardly enough stuff to fill it – and you'd do what they called a "moonlight" and on to the next lodging.

My dad was a van driver and I don't suppose his wages were all that much even on a full week, so he'd always be looking to save himself a few shillings wherever he could. More than once I saw him have a fight with one landlord or another. They'd be asking for what was rightfully theirs and the old man would take exception to their tone of voice, "up them", and we'd be packing our bags.

It's funny when I mention to youngish people that my dad was a van driver because I can see what they're thinking. But what I'm saying is the vans he drove were pulled by a pair of shire horses, and it was a job that took a strong man with his wits about him to keep things straight in the crowded lanes. He had both these qualities and on top of that he had a way with horses, which was just as well because a lot of times he had to sleep in the stables with them.

When we'd been kicked out of our rooms and had nowhere else to go Mum would have to swallow it and go knocking on her mother's door. Of course the Houghtons would take us in for a short while, but no way would they entertain the old man. Mum's family, particularly my grandfather, were a bit on the posh side and they couldn't take to the old man's ways and his swearing.

At that time of life mother never used a bad word, but me being a small boy used to try out what I'd heard the old man saying without realizing there was a time and a place. One of the times we'd moved in with Nanny and Grandad we were all sitting round the table having our tea when their neighbour called in. He was asked to sit down and we all carried on. But I was fascinated by this man's wispy straggly beard and I couldn't take my eyes off him. I looked and studied and thought and the wheels were going round in my head. In the end I couldn't contain myself and said out loud, "Mum, that man looks just like a fucking Billy goat," looking round to see if anybody else agreed with me. Grandad's face went as red as the table cover. He stood up, pointed to the door and said to mum "Mary Ann, take that child out of this house and don't bring him back until he's learned some manners".

Going back to Dad and his horses, in days when people weren't too particular about how an animal was treated, he looked after his like they were mates and not just something that earned his living.

One day he was delivering tea down at Hayes Wharf when his offside horse that was known as a biter, took a snap at a carman walking past. This bloke was a bit of a flash bastard from over the water and he just picked up a lump of wood and belted the horse across the head. My dad shouts, "Oi, when I get off this rig I'm going to do the same to you". But before he could the other fella's run round, grabbed his leg, given him a pull and Dad's fell off the van down about five foot and bashed his face on the kerb, knocking him spark out. A load of girls and a woman who was coming out of a factory over the road because it was finishing time, see him lying there, carried him back inside, fussed around him and brought him round. I bet he loved every minute of it because he always had an eye for the ladies.

Anyway when we saw him later he had a terrible face but that didn't stop him wanting to go and pay [hit] the bloke there and then, but my mother wouldn't have none of it and he gave in. But he did say, "If that bastard's there on Monday I'm going to have a fight with him". Well he was and Dad carried out his threat and beat him dreadful. But that wasn't enough. Every time he saw him after that he laid into him until the bloke couldn't take no more and gave the job up. Altogether they had about ten one-sided fights.

A long time afterward I saw this fella down Borough Market working one of the stalls and even then his face was all lumps and bumps. He didn't know who I was so I said nothing to him, but I didn't tell the old man where he was because I knew he would go after him and I thought he'd paid handsomely enough for what he did.

All I can think is that the man had never heard about my father or else he wouldn't have got involved. He might not have been very tall but he was wide, as hard as nails and like most blokes out of that part, he loved a good fight. It was always the way, even when I was growing up and into the days of the twins, and we all know they could have a go. Then it tailed off after the sixties when the law came down hard and you couldn't give somebody a slap without being charged.

Back then it was different and all you had to do was bump into somebody and splash their beer or say the wrong word and fists would fly at the drop of a hat. But my father didn't only have a row when he got upset, which he did often enough, but he went out looking for it in a semi-professional sort of way. When you spend every day of your life pulling about a couple of pair of horses that weigh getting on for a ton, getting stuck into a bloke who might weigh eighteen stone would be a piece of cake.

And that was my father. Afraid of no man and willing to take on the biggest – gloves on or bare-knuckles, for money or just pride – didn't matter to him and he always came out on top. He had the most wicked left-hand punch you've ever seen. Came out of nowhere just at the right time to finish the other fella off. They gave him the name of "Southpaw Cannonball" and you would've thought that would give the game away, what with southpaw meaning left-hand puncher, but none of the blokes that squared up to him ever took this on board until up it came and the lights went out.

Like I said, for a lot of years I was on my own in the family so I spent a lot of time with my mother, what with going here and there to the markets and all that. They talk about congestion and traffic jams in London today like it was something new but, as I recall, you could hardly cross the street for hansom cabs, carriages and vans, all horse drawn, flying up and down. If you were a rose grower then, and not many were, you'd never have gone short of a bit of fertilizer as they call it.

So what with the old man's job and seeing all these vehicles every day, never mind train driver like kids later on, I couldn't wait until I was old enough to climb up behind a pair of horses and get my hands on one of those lovely whips they all carried.

Reminds me of a time my mother took me to have my photograph taken. If the truth is known Nanny Houghton put the money up because they weren't short of a few bob and we had nothing. I was all done up in a sailor suit that was very popular, and to crown it off Mum bought what they called a cup-and-saucer hat to go with it. Now, ordinary people never owned a camera so we headed for a photo place in Stean Road, the same road the twins would be born in years later. I was a bit of a case in them days and when we got in the shop I refused to wear this hat. Short of clipping me round the ear, which mother wasn't prone to do anyway, the only way she could get me to do what she wanted was to promise to buy me something afterward. That's all it took. Bang, the hat's gone on my head so fast it made my ears stick out.

Picture taken, we ended up outside a shop that had all the gear hanging on the front like they did. I've sorted through a box of spinning tops, had a bang at a drum and tried out an iron hoop, then I spotted a toy whip and nothing else would do – cost about a penny. Then I'm off, cracking this thing and in my mind driving a pair-horse van through all the people on the pavement. As we came down Kingsland Road there was a long line of carts with the horses in the shafts and every one with its head in its nosebag. What do I do? I gave the last one in line a crack across the arse. Its head came out of the bag like it had been shot. It gave a squeal and bucked right up in the air, tipping all these pans and kettles off the cart, then it took off down the road and half the line went with it. You've never see nothing like it. Stuff all over the place and people diving out of the way. They reckon my nephews caused a few problems in London, but I was there before them that day.

Mum slipped us down an alley and nothing more was said, but she held on to that whip all the way home.

I didn't really know my grandparents on my father's side. Well I wouldn't expect to know my grandad because he was locked up in the madhouse at Epsom for over seventeen years. My own father took me to see him one time and I must have been small because I remember that when we got inside Long Grove Asylum and went into this room where he was, the first thing he done was grab hold of me and fling me right up in the air about five or six times. Frightened the life out of me and I wouldn't go back again. Strangely enough this was the same place where young Ronnie was certified when he took a bad turn after a spell in prison.

To be fair to the old boy it wasn't madness that made him chuck me about like that and I've seen it many times; some adults don't know how to show affection to a little child so they rough them up playful like.

They tell me people put in books and what have you that he was a drunkard all his life and that's why he went off his head, but Mother told me that he'd had a bad accident at Aldgate and was never the same after it. He was driving or riding on the back of a tall wagon, and as it went under an archway he struck his head on the brick wall and fell clean off. After that he had no end of fits and I don't suppose they knew what to do with it in those days so he had to get on with it.

By this time in his life he'd moved on from droving cattle and into the meat trade and I suppose that would make sense once you got fed up traipsing all over the country. I understand that at some time there was a plaque on the wall at Smithfield Market that said LEE & CODY. What that was all about I don't know. Might have been that him and his partner was the first shop in the new part in the early 1900s. Again it makes sense to me that he was in with somebody else, because a few bob must have trickled in over the years from it, or else he couldn't have left a tidy sum when he died. Stands to reason he couldn't have earned a brass farthing stuck in a madhouse all them years.

What got him put away in the first place was one night he woke all the family up by standing over the bed with a big knife in his hand. He must have had one of his turns and what with being a butcher and slaughtering all day, he got everything mixed up in his head and it was a close thing that he didn't cut their throats like they was bullocks. My mother said they were all terrified and screaming but Helen, my grandmother, had seen this sort of thing before and got him a tea with brandy and managed to calm him down. After that she couldn't take the risk no more so the police came, took him away and he never came home again because he was to die in that madhouse.

So what with him going like that and his son Dewey ending up in the Claybury mental place, then later on young Ronnie – they might say there's a streak of madness runs right through the family, but I don't know about that. You can't deny what's fact and staring you in the face, but to my way of thinking each one of them had his own different reason for going on the turn. A bang on the head or too many drugs doesn't mean there's an illness in the whole family.

As for my Nanny Houghton – in later years I'd hear my mother telling people that she was a spiteful old cow. I don't remember seeing too much of her when I was a child, but when I did she was either going in or coming out of a pub and she'd say, "Come over here, Joe luv". And then she'd give me one of them arrowroot biscuits they sold in the pubs. Other times it might be a penny, so I thought she was the best Nan in the world.

But Mother, she wore a bandage on her wrist all her life and when she took it off to do the washing or whatever, you'd see a hole in her wrist that you could put your finger in. What it was, when she was little she was buttering bread at the table and her mother said, "That's enough, girl, don't do no more". Well, being a kid she either didn't hear or she must have cocked a deaf 'un and carried on, because next minute old Ada's picked up a knife and stuck it straight through her arm. Temper, see – and that's something that did run through part of the family. That wrist played her up for the rest of her life and I must have heard the story a million times. Yet when she was in her nineties and some young doctor noticed the scar and asked her what it was, she pretended she didn't have a clue. I think she was ashamed to say to a stranger that her own mother did it.

By the time we moved out of Hackney and into Bethnal Green our family had grown a fair bit. I'd never done a day's schooling in my life and I was coming up to my twelfth birthday. As it turned out, when Mum thought I should have a bit of education at last, every school was full up except a Jewish one, so I ended up there. The only boy in the place that wasn't a Jew. I didn't mind though because it didn't last, what with the First World War breaking out less than two years later. Never held me back though because you learned all you needed to know from the family and by taking in everything you saw.

After me came my sister Rose in 1907. She was a pretty little thing – dark skinned and dark haired, taking after our grandmother. She should have been a boy, that one, because she was into everything. Always ready for a fight and never changed the rest of her life.

I remember one day she was up and down the street wheeling one of those pram things you could put your foot on – pushchair. Next thing she's run into the back of some woman's legs and a right row went on. That's not enough; the woman's husband came out and stuck his three ha'pence in, just as the old man comes up the street. I knew what was going to happen. He has a go at the woman, her husband tells him to fuck off and Dad knocks seven bells out of him. While he's doing that a big fella that's going with one of this bloke's daughters steps out of the house, hits the old man over the head with a lump of wood, then goes back in and shuts the door. Dad gave such a roar, goes after him, kicks the door open and beat him up. All that because of little madam Rose who stood there like butter wouldn't melt in her mouth.

After that came our Violet, who we've always called Violi. I can see her now. When she was little she had a chubby face and real rosy cheeks. Most of the time she seemed to be in a world of her own – a proper dreamer. I've seen her be sent to buy a bowl of salt herrings and come back with just the bones because she'd stood on the corner and eaten all the fish. Perhaps that's why they nicknamed her "Doodle". May, who turned up two years later, could have been Violi's twin, because they did look alike, what with the blond hair and blue eyes. That came from the German side and my Joe and young Charlie picked those looks up as well. May was always singing or larking about and they all called her Dinah, though don't ask me why. There might have been an actress with that name on the music halls. Johnny was the last-born and that was about the same time the 1914–18 war broke out. I didn't know it right then, but a couple of years later I'd find myself volunteering for that war and end up in the cavalry, what with knowing about horses and that – but that's something else entirely.

If ever anyone mentioned my mother's German background she always said, "Ah, but they weren't none of them bad ones".

By now we were all living in Hemming Street, just through the arch from where we'd all end up in Vallance Road. This place was just a little two-up, two-down.

When the old man was after renting the two upstairs rooms he took me and my mother along and swore to the landlord who lived downstairs that I was the only child. Course once we were in, up pops the three girls and his missus said, "What's all this? Whose are all these kids? We ain't going to stand for it, you wait till my 'usband gets in." But when he did come in and raised his voice too loud with his wife egging him on, my father settled it by giving him a good hiding at the bottom of the stairs, which was a shame really because after they let us stay and we got to know them, they turned out to be nice people.

I don't think we were in those rooms more than a few weeks, when one afternoon while I was outside talking to a couple of little mates, there was this almighty bang. We all jumped and looked round but other than that didn't take too much notice until the landlady came flying out shouting, "Get a policeman – something's happened upstairs". I've jumped the stairs as quick as you like and run into our living room and what a mess. The window was knocked half out and there was broken bits and pieces all over. Mum was white faced, the three girls were crying and little May had blood running down her face. Turned out my mother had left the gas on while they were all out, then when she came back, lit a match for the kettle. Cooker was blown to bits and it's lucky they weren't killed.

There was always something or other going on. I don't know if we were all that different from other families, but there was a story every day that went on all our lives – and I'm not even counting what those boys got up to later on.

A lot of people, and that's people all round the world, think they know what my father was like because of that film they called *The*

Krays. I was nearly in it myself but Young Joe can tell you more about that. I saw the film and didn't recognize no one, least of all my old man. The fella that played the part of my old man did a good job and I'm not knocking the film but when they put over that this old geezer was a bit soft – a figure of fun if you like – I felt it was letting down the real Jimmy Lee. Dad was comical but that was more to do with the things he did that didn't turn out right, and the things he said that didn't come out like he meant them. What I'm saying is he wasn't a joker and he took life serious. But he was an entertainer and a good one at that, else he wouldn't have toured all the local theatres and music halls like he did.

Sometimes he used me as a prop in some of his stunts. I'd only be a nipper but he'd get one of those big glass bottles they call carboys, stick me on the neck and balance the lot on his head. But that wasn't all. Without the bottle he'd put me up on his shoulders, do a couple of turns, then slowly balance his way along the tops of a line of beer bottles. When he got to the end of the line he'd climb up a pair of stepladders that had bottles on every tread. Then stepping on the necks again until he got to the top, he'd jump down into a barrel with me still clinging on. Brought the house down. I've never heard of anyone else before or since who could do that. In fact he was so confident that nobody else could match him he would stand on the stage and offer a tenner to anyone who could. Just as well it wasn't taken up because he wouldn't have paid out anyway.

He used to practise by jumping out of our bedroom window into a barrel over and over again. Mother stopped him using me in the end in case there was an accident, but I was never worried.

Licking a white-hot poker was another of his stunts and you'd hear the people in the audience gasping when he did it. He told me that as long as you had plenty of spit on your tongue it would throw the poker off before you got burned, but he never would let me try it.

He would sing, dance and play the squeeze-box and I don't think he was all that but at different times in his younger days he was on the same bill as Marie Lloyd, Charlie Chaplin and Old Mother Riley. This was before they made names for themselves, and at the time I don't suppose they was much better than he was. The thing with my old man was he'd have a go at anything, whether he knew what he was doing or not.

In his mind the big chance to break away from grafting all day and ducking and diving to make ends meet was when his father died in Long Grove asylum. Now my Grandad Lee hadn't worked for seventeen years what with being locked up, so I don't know how he managed to get any money together. But wherever it came from he left a good lump to be shared out.

One of my aunts had married a man with a bit of a head on him – good with figures and what have you. So he got hold of this money and said to the rest of the family who was involved, "Now it's your money but I'll invest it for you. If you need some just come and see me and I'll sort it out." So like a lot of sheep them that was due a share would go to him every now and then with cap in hand like he was doing them a favour and ask him, "Please can I have five pounds," or two or ten – doesn't matter. Then he'd make a big fuss about signing their names in a little book "to keep it legal, like" before he weighed out.

Father swallowed this for about a month then I remember him saying to my mother, "Mary Ann, fuck this. I'm going to get my money," and off he went. He came home that night and poured, and I mean poured nigh on a hundred gold sovereigns out on to the kitchen table among the brown sauce bottle, the milk jug and all the other bits and pieces. I didn't even know what they were, what with only ever being used to coppers and tanners. Never seen such a thing in my life. My mother stood there with her mouth open and he laughed and said, "He wasn't all that keen, Mary Ann, but he saw sense in the end," and knowing Father we knew what that meant.

Turned out this uncle was cheating the family anyway. What he would do was when any of them signed for say five pounds the crafty old bastard would stick a one in front of it. Dad found out about this but like he said, "That ain't my worry. I've got mine and we're going up in the world."

He couldn't boil a kettle or fry an egg, so in his mind the obvious business to put this found money into was to do with cooking. He got himself a fish shop, had hundreds of handbills printed up and delivered round the doors saying fried fish, herring, soups, dinners and everything. He didn't have a clue. Five or six weeks later the money and the shop was gone – all down the pan. But he never accepted that it was down to him. As far as he saw it "them fucking Jew bastards" had put him out of business by opening shops near his. Daren't mention fish to him for months after.

Next thing he'd be buying sacks of peanuts up the market and then sell them off in little bags. If you was lucky you got a big bag – if not a small one, because he never thought of measuring them out. No. Chuck them in, give the paper a twist and that was that. For a while he had my mother selling them off the back of a barrow outside the Regal until she got fed up with it. These things were down the backs of chairs and crunching under our feet for weeks until he moved on to something else. But he never gave up trying because in his mind every new thing he tried was going to be the winner.

Fruit and veg was another caper. By this time we were living down London Road before the council changed its name to Dunbridge Road. He kept a lot of his stock in a big old tin bath out in the yard, filled up with water so he could wash it and keep it fresh. Same bath as we washed in every week funnily enough. What he never knew was our Rose, who lived upstairs, used to come down with a bucket that had a cloth over it. If he wasn't looking or wasn't about she'd help herself to a nice lettuce, a few bits of greens and a couple of apples then shoot back upstairs again. Thing is he'd have give her them if she asked but she just loved the devilment of it.

Anyway, when he set up in this game he got himself an old barrow – bought not hired. But his pride and joy was a pair of gleaming white Avery scales. They were "on the book" for about ten bob a week and as far as he was concerned they set him apart from all the other traders and made him look a proper businessman. Same as always a few months down the line it all went pear shaped and he gave it up. Them posh scales must have been worth near enough a hundred quid or something like, but whatever, I do know they were expensive. So what does he do? He sells them off for practically nothing. Trouble was he'd never made one single payment for them.

Time went by and the firm where he got them from was sending letters first, then blokes knocking on the door chasing him for the money. But all he said about them was "Fuck 'em – I ain't got 'em no more". So they took him to court. When he came up at Prescott Street Magistrates Court and was stood in front of the magistrate he said, "I'm ever so sorry, your lordship, but somebody nicked them off me barra". The bloke says, "I have every sympathy with you but nevertheless they must be paid for". Well the old man's gone green at that but told them that if he suffered terrible hardship he could just about find a shilling a week and would they accept that. They did, but same as the scales, he never made a payment even though we had all kinds of people and a copper one time banging on the door. They gave up in the end.

Years later when he was pushing on a bit he'd always tell people: "I ain't never took what wasn't mine an' never owed a penny to any man." If I was there I'd say, "What about them scales then? They nicked you over them." And he'd give me a dirty look as if to say, "Oh yeah, the big fella knows all the answers," sarcastic like. That's what he called me then when he had the hump. What it was, he didn't like me pointing out faults with jobs he'd done at home, and he'd come in and say to my mother: "Has he been in today? The big fella? Everything suit him – did he find any faults?" One time he put a light up and my mother told him it was too low, so he said, "I know, and when the big bloke comes round he'll bomp his head and make a complaint". It wasn't that I was picking on him but the stunts he got up to could've killed the pair of them. Didn't have a clue about electrics and I'd call in and find he'd strung all lights around the room, and outside, with nothing but bare wires.

He went down the lane one Sunday morning and came back with one of them old blow-lamp things. He's no sooner got in than he's crazed to find a use for it, so he decides he'd decorate the front room. He filled it with paraffin, fired it up and there's flames shooting out about two foot long. Now we all know that you get wallpaper off by soaking it with water – not him. "Nah, you watch, it'll be burnt off in no time." Next thing the curtains are alight. Mother's gone running over to Burns' timber yard shouting, " Over 'ere quick, he's fucking well set the house on fire". Course they've run over and put it out. But when I see him next morning I said, "That was a bit of a do you had yesterday". And he said, "Weren't my fault, that bastard down the lane sold me a dodgy lamp".

When he wasn't trying to earn a few bob (and that wasn't very often) he was a keep-fit fanatic. There were always old bikes knocking about because he'd buy half a dozen old wrecks and make one or two good ones out of them. He said to me, "Come on, boy, we'll have a ride to Southend and get a bit of fresh air". Thirty-five miles. I was about fifteen and as strong as a man but halfway there going up Bread and Cheese Hill nearly done me in – and he's nearly at the top.

The First World War had only just started and I can remember seeing all these wounded soldiers in the grounds of the Palace Hotel that they'd turned into a hospital.

We got to Southend, took three breaths and he said, "We'd best get back". I was dreading it. I was riding a fixed-wheel bike and never gave it a thought, and as we got to the top of Cheese Hill ready to go down he said to me, "Whatever you do, don't take . . ." But I'd already taken my feet off the pedals for a minute and on their own they was going round at a hundred miles an hour. I'd no brakes and couldn't get on the pedals. If it was today I'd have been killed, but I didn't come to no harm. All I prayed for was a puncture so we could have a rest but we never and I had to struggle to keep up all the way back to Bethnal Green.

We'd only be home for five minutes and he'd want to get the gloves out and have a spar in the backyard, and he must have been nearly forty then.

Somebody bet him ten bob that he couldn't push a barrow to Southend so next day he's gone and hired one from the coal shop and told the bloke he only wanted it for half a day to do a carting job – fourpence a day or something. I'm not talking about a wheelbarrow but a little flatbed with those big wheels. Well, I never thought he'd do it what with Bread and Cheese hill and all them miles, but he did. I don't think the bloke who laid the bet thought it could be done either, because he kept well away from the old man and never did pay up.

Only thing was, he never pushed it back. He'd had enough, I suppose, and left it where he finished up. A week or so later the man from the shop came banging on the door looking for his barrow. "Ain't you finished with it yet, Jimmy?" "Course I have," said the old man. "Well where is it then?" He's said, "I dunno, last time I see it, it was on the front down at Southend". The geezer was livid but he couldn't say nothing because he knew the old man could be a bit fierce if he was upset.

Funnily enough it was another time he'd just come back from Southend when he had a terrible fight with his brother. All I know is that it was something to do with their sisters but I don't recall what. Must have been serious though because as my father was taking off his bicycle clips outside the house, Uncle Tom came marching toward him effing and blinding. One of the neighbours must have clocked what Tom was up to because she called out of an upstairs window, "Look out, Jimmy, he's got an iron bar behind his back". I suppose that upset Dad more than anything, so before Tom even swung this lump of iron the old man knocked him into the gutter – then he payed him unmercifully. And that was his own brother. He was knocked about so bad they thought he was dead but lucky he wasn't. They never spoke for years afterwards. Fiery tempered my family and it's led to a lot of trouble one way and another.

He was a case, my Uncle Tom Lee. I remember him telling me a funny story, though he didn't think it was at the time. This was before that fight. He was a foreman at Pool Wharf in Upper Thames Street, and he had about six blokes under him. One day this man turned up – smart looking and a good talker. There were a line of warehouses in the dock and he's took Tom to one of them and told him that he needed to stock-take his furs that were inside, but had mislaid the padlock key.

As a carrot he's thrown in that if Tom could help him out of a hole, once he got inside he'd want to hire some men to help him shift some of this stuff. In those days all it took was a suit and a posh voice to get respect from the average working man – like they knew their place if you know what I mean – so Uncle Tom's already hooked.

On top of that was the chance to earn a couple of shillings, so he's agreed. The man said, "While you're getting the doors open I'll go and get a van to put the furs in". An hour later he came back and Tom and his six men carried out whatever he pointed at – and there was hundreds of these furs. When it was all done he put a new padlock on the door to replace the one they'd smashed off, lined all the blokes up, shook their hands and told them what a great bunch of lads they were. Tom got two pounds to share out and that was that.

A few days later another fella comes to Tom, what with him being the foreman, and said he couldn't seem to fit his key into what looked like a new padlock on his warehouse. Tom acted a bit vague until the police turned up, then his memory came back a bit sharpish and he had to admit that him and the other blokes had helped to rob the place.

Nothing came of it but none of them ever lived it down. Mind you, he could be a bit slippery himself if the chance came up. There was a local mob of flash geezers who were into everything and I suppose to get themselves into favour with Pedlar Farmer, who was a British Champion boxer, they got him a load of expensive shirts. Knowing Uncle Tom lived just round the corner from Pedlar they asked him to drop them off to him. Does he? No. He says to my father, "What's he want shirts for – he's got loads of money?" So he flogged them and hung on to the money. This mob was after him for a long time after that and word was he could expect a right doing over, but like I said he was a bit slippery and kept out of the way.

I think he was a bit wrong anyway because I don't suppose Pedlar had two ha'pennies, champion or not. None of them did and my old man knew them all, what with his own boxing and fighting.

Later on I know the twins rubbed shoulders with the likes of Joe Louis and Sonny Liston, but that was different. The boxers I'm talking about were just ordinary working blokes who made a name for themselves in the ring and the old man knew them all on the way up.

There was Solly Mendehof, a Jewish boy who changed his name to Ted "Kid" Lewis, one of the best fighters ever to come out of the East End. I suppose he changed his name because a lot of people had feelings against the Jews. Don't know why because half the people around those parts had a bit of Jew in them somewhere down the line.

Jackie "Kid" Berg came out of Whitechapel and he was known all over as the "Whitechapel Whirlwind". He could have a fight and took the world junior welterweight championship off of Mushy Callahan in 1930, I think it was. When my old man first knew him he was living with his parents over a fish shop in Whitechapel Road, and his name was Judah Bergman, but later on, like Ted he changed his name to save any problems. There was hundreds at the game from around our way – they didn't all make champions like these two but they had a good name. Yes, these fellas would drop in for a cup of tea and it wouldn't be long before the old man got the gloves out and we'd take turns sparring with them. Even my sisters would have a go. It was only a lark but you could say that over a time my family squared up to some of the best names in British boxing history.

Later on it was only natural that my sister's boys would get the gloves on because they never heard nothing else from my old man. Reg was a boxer, proper like, but Ron was a fighter and would get up to some dirty tricks if he could get away with it. We went to Manor Place baths over Walworth when the twins were on the card as amateurs. Ron was fighting this fella and I saw him deliberately bite him on the neck when they got in a clinch. I think I was the only one who clocked it. I said to old Charlie, "Did you see Ron sink his teeth into that other bloke?" And he got a bit annoyed and said, "My boy wouldn't do a thing like that." And I thought too fucking right he wouldn't, except I saw the little bleeder do it with my own eyes. He wouldn't have it that one of his own was breaking the rules, but if that Ronnie could find a dirty trick to help him win, then he took it every time.

Reg was different altogether. He had a good style and was a clean fighter – in the ring anyway – and if he'd stuck at it and never got mixed up with the likes of that Bobby Ramsey and all that mob, he had the makings of getting somewhere. But Ron just flung his arms all over the place and tried to flatten the other fella with nothing but aggression. Don't get me wrong, he was lucky most of the time and came out on top, but you can only go so far with that style – if you can call it that. What I didn't agree with was when they were the only two left in the schoolboy finals and they had to fight each other. Three times they did it and of course neither one of them wanted to lose so they really hurt each other. I mean, they were only kids and it should never have happened.

Looking back, it seems like every young fella was either an amateur, semi or professional boxer – that's the way it was. Nobody had nothing and the way out was to try and follow in the steps of all those that were local heroes. They'd say, "Look at 'im. He was only a barrow boy; now look at 'im." How else were kids with cardboard in the soles of their shoes going to better themselves? Speak to anyone of a good age and they'll say, "Oh, my father or grandfather was a boxer". What they don't say is "So was everyone else's".

On top of that there were fighting men who had most of their bouts on the streets. My father was one of them and about the same time so was old Jimmy Kray. A long time before him and his mob became part of this family by marriage, these two come across each other a number of times. I'm talking bare knuckles here, but he never bested my old man – not once.

Some of these fellas got a lot of respect because they were what you called the guv'nors – tough blokes but fair with it, like Jimmy Spinks, who was related to the McLeans out of Hoxton. Then there was others like Dodger Mullins and Wassle Newman and these two were right bastards and got respect out of fear, which ain't the same thing. Of course, we had nothing to worry about because them and others like them were always in and out of our house, though my old man did keep them at arm's length when it came down to getting involved in their capers.

Funny really when you think of what my sister's boys got up to later on (and I don't know the half of it), their grandfather, my dad, wouldn't have no truck with them people they call gangsters now.

He passed the time of day with them and mother gave them cups of tea, but that's where it stayed.

No end of fellas we knew ended up on the rope or doing hard labour on Dartmoor, but you didn't take a lot of notice. One of these blokes, Nipper Osbourne, got in a fight and cut this other man's throat from ear to ear. Five or six weeks he was on the run and one of those he spent hiding in our house. In the end I think the old man talked him into giving himself up because by then his hair's gone white what with worrying about taking the drop – hanging that is. He was lucky and only got time but his head was all gone by the time he came out. He said to me, "They might as well have topped me 'cos I can't take it any more". But I said, "Well, you didn't say that when you was hiding in our back room".

Nowadays when you see kids coming out of school they're all six foot tall, even the girls, but in my day all these tough men I mentioned were about five foot seven or eight. Mind you, most of them were as wide as that as well. So when a geezer like Tommy Brown came along he stood out a bit. What with his size and his reach he was a bit tasty in the ring, but he never made champion or nothing. Still he must have had what it takes because when Tommy Farr was training to take on Max Baer he was hired as a sparring partner. Farr wasn't an East End boy, he came out of Wales and they called him the Tonypandy Terror and he was as well. Anyway, he was paying a pound a round to his sparring partners and that was good money at the time. Only trouble was Farr's manager, Ted Broadribb, was a bit slippery and didn't want to part with the cash. Kept making excuses – Tommy this and Tommy's a bit short and what have you.

There was about four or five sparring partners, so Tommy Brown said to them, "Fuck this. We don't fight until we get squared up." Later on when Farr jumps in the ring Tommy's leaning on the ropes with his coat on. When he was asked what was going on he said that he thought they was being cheated and they wouldn't stand for it. Farr never said a word – got out of the ring, went to his dressing room and came back with a bundle of notes. He paid what was owed and a bit more. After that he paid them at the end of every day.

I was at Devonshire Hall with Tommy Brown one afternoon when two plain-clothes detectives came into the gym. One of them said to Tommy, "Excuse me, could we have one or two rounds with you because we're in the police boxing team and we're training for a fight?" Tom came over to me and said, "What do you think, Joe?" Like most people in the East End I could spot the law a mile off, so I said, "I don't see why not, but you know they're both coppers don't you?" He said, "They already told me, now watch me mark their card". The biggest one climbed into the ring and squared up. Now sparring is what it says and not a world title fight, but with one punch Tommy went through his guard, broke his nose and put out his front teeth. I suppose the copper thought he didn't need a gum shield. Of course, Tommy apologized and all that so they were never sure whether it was deliberate – but it was.

In later years people had him down as a minder for the twins, but he never was. He idolized those boys and wanted to look after them. They called him "The Bear" because he was so big, but he was never a bully. If somebody got out of order his favourite trick was to up end them, hold them by the ankles then put his foot on their chin, gentle like, and say, "Be nice".

2. Mother Lee

Old Joe Lee

I don't seem to have said too much about my mother and as she was the one that held everything together, like most women then, I suppose I should. Because she married my father it turned her into the black sheep of the family. Her father, John Houghton, had made something of himself and was the manager of a gum factory. Where this gum stuff came from or what it was I don't think any of us questioned, and I still don't know to this day, but it was hard, yellow and the lumps came in all different sizes. Out in the factory the girls sat and graded it into different batches.

With him wearing a suit and making regular money they was better class than the Lees. Posh but not stuck-up posh. Him and his wife Ada had six children and they were Mary Ann (my mother), John, Joe, Till, Lill and Lizzie. Funny enough later on Aunt Till had twins as well, so it must have been in the family on that side.

This side of the family came out of one of the worst parts of the East End and their background was no different from anyone else's, but my Uncle John became what they called Royal Toastmaster to the Mayor of London. One minute he'd be standing right behind Neville Chamberlain or Winston Churchill the next, or one or another of the Royal Family at some state banquet or other. Never went to his head though. He'd do the business at one of these posh dos, rubbing shoulders with heads of state, and the next day he'd turn up at our house with the left-overs. That was one of the perks and we'd have a right old knees-up.

One of these nights him and me were standing at the door and coming down the road we saw a bloke with an organ– the sort where you had to wind a little handle on the side, hurdy-gurdy they called them. It was quite late and I should think the fella was on his way home, but next thing my Uncle John's called over and asked if he'd come in and give us some music. He agreed and between the three of us we managed to squeeze this organ indoors, then away we went and all had a lovely night. Didn't have such a thing as a record player then. Next day Uncle John would be back among the toffs again.

When people lump all the family together as villains and gangsters – and I know that's what they're thinking – I feel like saying, "You're only looking at a small part of the picture," but I don't.

When Mum and Dad got together they must have been like chalk and cheese. His language could strip paint. Like I said, it was so bad his father-in-law wouldn't have him in the house, but Mother wouldn't even say "damn". As time went on though she got just like him, and later on still she got worse. Don't know what straightened him up but when they were in their eighties and the old girl was effing and blinding he'd say "Mary Ann, did you have to say that?" Didn't stop her though. She'd just flick a duster at him and tell him to mind his own fucking business.

Like I said, for the first six or seven years I was on my own and Mother used to talk about when she was a girl, and when we went here and there she'd be saying, "See this – see that," and be showing me places where all kinds of things went on. She said there was beggar kids all over – hundreds of them. What happened was if the old man died or run off, the mother would keep the girls and sling the boys out to get on as best they could. If the mother died, a convent or something might take in the girls but again the boys would end up on the streets.

Funnily enough she took in a pal of mine and he ended up living with us for years and years. We must have been about fourteen then and it's so long ago I couldn't begin to tell you why it come about. All I remember is that Jimmy Cornwall had no family and nowhere to stay so I took him home with me and that was that. I do believe my parents legally adopted him in the end. He was a case and a trial to my mother but it was all in fun because he did think a lot of her.

One time this old gypsy woman knocked on our door and asked if she could use the privy. Now if it was a bite to eat or a drink of tea she would've got it gladly, but mother had just got a new toilet and she wasn't having no stranger sitting on it. So when she said no, this woman said, "Right, you old cow, I'm coming back tonight to shit on your doorstep". Jimmy's overheard this and next thing he's made up a little pile out of brown putty stuff that looked just like the real thing and put it on the step. Blimey, if you'd heard the effs and blinds the next morning from my mother, it was enough to wake the dead. He was a nice fella and part of the family, but the fact that he was taken in when he had nothing wasn't unusual because everyone did it in the East End in those days.

A story my mother told me happened one summer when she was about ten years old. Her and all the family were in bed and the window was wide open because it was so hot. About five o'clock they heard the lamplighter coming up the road putting the street lamps out and he was shouting: "Don't go out – Leather Apron's about ... Apron's dunnit again." And her dad jumped up and shut the window. This was that Jack the Ripper, but he wasn't called by that name then. When they were up and about they found out one of those girls had been found all cut up near Dog's Lane, just round the corner. They never did catch him and for years she was worried that he might jump out from one of the alleys and get hold of her.

After that if kids played up or wouldn't go to sleep their mothers would say, "Jack'll come and get you". She used to say it to me because don't forget it was only ten years before I was born. Years and years later when that Elephant Man got well known, when they made a film about him, she told me she remembered seeing posters on a shop opposite the London Hospital in Whitechapel Road showing him with a big long trunk and flappy ears. They were showing him off inside and she wanted to go in and see him but her mother wouldn't have none of it.

My mother was a bit of a looker when she was younger, and the old man always had a bit of a jealous streak in him. A lot of blokes were like that back then. They did what they wanted to do but the woman's job was to look after the home, the kids and run around after them.

Mum and me went to the pictures one night to see a film with an actor by the name of Milton Searles. Bit of a heart-throb and all the ladies went for him – tough guy and all that. On the way home Mum got herself a small jug of beer, and when we got in the door the old man's just going to get stuck into a plate of fish and chips he's bought himself. Straight away Mum started going on about this actor. "Isn't he lovely? Handsome. Real romantic." The old fella got quieter and quieter, then he jumped up shouting, "Milton Searles, I've heard enough about that fucking bloke". And he took up her beer and tipped it on the floor. Now Mother wasn't one of these women that jumped when the husband said so. She said, "Oh, so I can't have me beer? Right you ain't having no dinner." And she flung his fish and chips in the fire. Then there was fireworks.

There was another fella – and I think he had a fancy for Mother – Bill Elcot, an old-time fighter and a saucy bastard when he wanted to be. He got himself a job with an undertaker as a driver for one of those horse-drawn carriages that carry the coffins. He drove up our road and seeing Mum at the door reigned up outside. Thinking the old man's at work he said for a lark, "Now then, Mary, have you got him laid out or shall I come in and box him up myself?" She said, "Come in and get him, he's having his tea". The old man was sitting just inside the door and he'd heard what was said and wasn't very happy. So he came flying out shouting, "I'll box you up when I get hold of you, you flash bastard". Old Bill didn't hang about – he gee'd up the horses and flew off.

Father didn't have a drink. Couldn't stand the stuff and didn't agree with anyone else taking it. My mother said that was because he blamed "gut polish" for seeing his own father off. Though another reason was that he'd had a nasty bang on the head same as his own father. He came off a van and fell head first between the shafts and after that the slightest drop of drink made him come over all dizzy. There was just one occasion when he did have a drop, but that was medicine and it done him up proper.

By this time things have moved on and he was driving lorries for a firm at Spitalfields by the name of Miles & Hyams. They sent him all the way up to Lancashire to pick up a lorry and he had to drive it from there to a body-building workshop in Whitechapel. Now this is the middle of winter and he's got no cab or nothing – just the bare chassis, engine, wheels and all that. By the time he got to London they had to lift him down because he was frozen. The guv'nor got him in the office and gave him his wages and a glass of whisky to thaw him out. On the way home he's collapsed in the road and just laid there for an hour or more. Somebody must have come across him, but instead of helping him to get out of the frost they nicked his wages and left him.

In the washhouse we had one of those bricked-up copper boilers with a fire under it. When he eventually came to and got himself home he stuck his head in the hole where the hot ashes go, and stayed there all night. Mother said, "Just leave him. He'll be all right unless his head catches alight." I suppose whoever robbed him thought he was just another drunk, but he could've died. So don't talk to me about them days when the East End was a safe place and you could leave your door open day and night. It's a fairy story. The only reason people left their doors open was because they had nothing worth nicking. But if you did you could bet your life someone out there would try to take it off you.

Another time he cycled all the way up to Manchester to see some of the family who had a business that way. This was the middle of winter and when he was having a bit of blow – resting like – he fell asleep and lay there all night. Gave himself pneumonia over that and was lucky it didn't kill him. He had to stay up there for weeks after until he was fit enough to cycle back.

Even when I was a nipper Mother used to send me round to "Auntie's", that was the beer shop, to fetch her a jug of stout. She'd say, "Don't let your father see you". Then when I'd get back she'd have a poker waiting in the fire and she'd pull it out red-hot and stick it in the beer – warmed it up and made it frothy.

Later on she got all the grandchildren on the same game. My Joe, the twins, young Rita – they all got a turn but by then it was in bottles and they'd have to tie a string round the neck, then when the coast was clear their nanny would pull it up into the bedroom.

Whisky? I'll tell you – all the time someone else was buying she was their best friend. There was a Jewish man called Davis who took to drink after his wife died, and he'd go in the Standard in Hemming Street and treat all the women, so of course she latched on to him straight away. He was another one who fancied my mother. I think she liked him more than she should have, but with the way she treated him when he wasn't buying, it didn't always show. If the old man had known they had this bit of a spark going he'd have upped the pair of them.

One night I was there and see her taking glass after glass of the stuff, then next morning I was talking to her outside the front door (she spent all day there) and along came this Davis. "Morning, Mother Lee," he said, all friendly, and she said, "Fuck off out of it, you one-eyed Yiddish bastard. I don't want to see you." I said to her, "Cor, fancy you saying a thing like that to 'im after the way he treated you all night." She said, "Oh, he's all right, he don't mind". Same night she's in the pub and emptying his wallet for him. She was like that.

She did the same with Dodger Mullins' woman, not his wife because she'd died, but some other woman. Swaby, I think her name was, and she was in a gang out of the Elephant and Castle that they called the forty thieves, so you can guess what she was up to. On top of that she used to lend out a bit of money so when my mother see her in the pub she became her best friend because this woman stood her whisky all night.

She could be a trial even without a drink inside her. She followed me into the pub one night. She had a mate with her – both of them done up to the nines. She asked me to buy them both a whisky but I had to tell her no because we were in a beer house which meant they only had a licence for beer and couldn't sell spirits. Well, she wouldn't have it and thought I was being a bit tight. In the end she said to me, and this is her son she's talking to, "Fuck you then – we'll go to the pub on the corner". And they charged out.

On the way out in such a hurry they've nigh knocked over one of the Starkies, a right mob of a family. As they've gone out one of this family said, "Bleedin' made-up dolls – want sorting out". I thought if anyone gets sorted it won't be my mother. I got myself over a bit smartish and we had a right argument. Now, my sister Rose was in there as well but right over the other side standing by the piano – place is packed out being a Saturday. As us lot are having a barney one of them must have raised a hand behind my head and Rose has clocked this. I heard a shout and looked round to see my sister scrambling over the heads and shoulders of people to get to my side and she's screaming, "You bastards ain't going to touch my brother". I was a big fella then and like my father could have a fight with or without gloves, but I honestly didn't think it was going to come to that – not until Rose arrived. She's into a couple of these fellas like she was a man herself, belting them this way and that and the air was blue because she took after her mother. Course they weren't going to have a go at a woman and thought twice about taking me on, so it all finished up quiet in the end. And my mother never knew what trouble she caused, what with her going out in a huff.

When I got home Mother and her mate was already indoors and this mate was trying her best to eff and blind because she'd lost her teeth somewhere, but she couldn't get the words out proper. I was a bit mad and I said to my mother, "Don't you ever come in my company again – every time you show your face in a club or pub there's nothing but trouble". It got so that I never told her when there was going to be a do on because I knew she would follow me.

Another time she was caught stealing in the dairy opposite. This thieving was regular with her. She'd take two jugs in but only have milk in one. Seems funny now when you think what London's like, but then this dairy had its own little herd of cows – and funnier still when I recall them being taken for a walk around the streets. Then if there was something that took her fancy she'd pick it up and pop it in the jug. The owners were nice people but they told her not to come in any more.

When she told Rose that she'd been chucked out and banned I don't suppose she gave the whole story, so Rose's gone flying over to give them what for – always ready for trouble. The shopkeeper put her right and she knew it was true so she apologized and went back to Mother who's standing there going, "Well? Well?" as much as to say have you told them off. Rose says, "Don't give me that 'Well?' They was entitled to chuck you out, you've been nicking all their stuff." Mother just said, "Fuck 'em then – I'll go somewhere else," like it wasn't her own fault.

Trouble was she was running out of shops she could go in because she pulled the same stunt in every one of them.

I just came out the door one afternoon and one of the neighbours said, "I've just come back from the shops and your mum's having a right go round there". I thought, what now? But shot round there quick like. I could hear her before I got to the bakers. She was effing away like a good 'un. I opened the door and she was chucking bread rolls and bagels all over the show. The rolls are all the same but it turns out she's been picking them up one by one and giving them a squeeze to make sure they're fresh. Course the woman in the shop has told her to get out so Mother's turned the place over.

You couldn't reason with her and once I got her home she told all the others that the effing baker woman was trying to palm her off with stale rolls.

Just before one Christmas the old man brought home a goose he'd got down the lane and put it out the back. I didn't know because I'd been at work, so as I'm going out there to have a wash in the old bath my mother said, "Mind how you go, there's a fowl loose out there". Well, to me a fowl's a chicken so I don't care, but I'm no sooner out the door than this bloody great white thing is chasing me all over the place, pecking and flapping.

Anyway, come the time to kill it for the dinner it was nowhere to be found. We searched all over but no, it's run off or someone's nicked it. When Johnny, I think it was, went to the outside toilet there was this bird, head first down the pan, drowned. Now this pan must have been a hundred years old, all cracked, and Mother could never get it proper clean, so you can imagine. Still, the old man done the goose all up and Mum cooked it, but when it was ready for the table none of us could look at it. Except father. He was rubbing his hands together and saying, "I ain't wasting good grub, if you lot are too fussy then it's all the more for me". And over the rest of the week he ate the lot.

A little story after that was my mother put into the landlord for a new pan and not long after it was fitted. From that day on, for months and months she left the privy door wide open and the back gate as well, so anybody passing could see this gleaming porcelain toilet.

I suppose when you've lived through times like they did, with money short and wondering where the next meal was coming from, you're not too fussy about what you eat. And apart from that goose, as far as Mother was concerned food was food, however it was dished up, and she did stick some rubbish in front of the old man. He never turned a hair but the years must have taught him something because the first thing he'd do before sitting at the table was take a bite out of the whitening stone women used for doing the front step. Chalk? Pumice? I don't know. He reckoned it was good for the digestion, but it's a wonder it didn't kill him.

On a Thursday she might come across a lump of Yorkshire pudding left over from Sunday. It's all curled up and rock hard, so Mother would pour a bit of boiling water on it and he'd get it down him without complaint. No doubt the pudding would've been a lot bigger but by the time she came across it the rats and mice had most likely chewed off a fair piece because we were overrun by these things.

First thing she'd do when making a cup of tea was get the cups off the hooks and blow the droppings out, or if they ran along the shelf she'd just say, "Get out of it, you little bleeders".

She was tidying around one day and when she lifted the cushions off the old man's chair she came across two mice all flattened and mummified. She said to Dad, "Look what you've gone and done – you've killed them little things". He just looked and said, "Oh that's Bernard and Aubrey. I thought I hadn't seen them for a while". Didn't care, see – it was just part of life and all the houses were the same because of the railways and factories.

Spiders frightened the life out of him, as tough as he was, but show him a big rat and he'd corner it and pick it up by the neck. I've seen them screaming and trying to bite him, but he'd just take them outside and bash them on the kerb.

Sounds like we lived a bit rough, and I suppose by standards people have nowadays we did, but Mother kept the house tidy. Don't forget these places were old and falling to bits, but she brought all us kids up well, especially my sisters who she always turned out nice.

They was all lookers and it was only natural that sooner or later all the local boys would be hanging round our door. The old man was pretty easy-going with young Johnny and me, but he kept an eye open where the girls were concerned. They knew they couldn't take liberties but they was never frightened of him because he never lifted a finger against one of them.

We had a big mirror over the fireplace and before he went out he always stood in front of it and done himself up. He was like a lot of blokes then, very vain. He'd stand there combing his hair and tying the white scarf round his neck, and all the while he's got his tongue poking out the side of his mouth – like he did when he was concentrating. I can see it now. Rose would stand in the doorway behind him, stick her tongue out and mimic everything he did. This would go on a bit and we're all trying not to laugh, then without turning round the old man would say, "Go on, take the piss," because he could see her in the mirror, and he'd make out he was annoyed but we all knew he wasn't because he could see the funny side.

My sisters could twist him round their fingers. I've heard it said that our father was real hard on those girls and perhaps that's how they saw it, what with being young and wanting to be out all hours, but from what I remember as long as they were indoors at a reasonable time he didn't say too much.

At the time I'm talking about Rose and Violi were always out – over Victoria Park with the lads or dancing at Tottenham or that place up Mare Street. May didn't go out much because she was only about thirteen or fourteen, and our Johnny was only a nipper.

One night Rose told me that Violi was seeing one of the Kray brothers and I wasn't too best pleased, especially when I learned it was Charlie, because he was about the same age as me [twenty-six] and she hadn't even reached sixteen.

We knew the lot of them – flash mob really, like travelling people and our family didn't have time for any of them. The old man Jimmy had a stall up the lane selling suits and whatever he could get hold of. Then there was five boys who we had a few run-ins with over the years, and three sisters who was nice enough. The only one out of the family I could make any sense of was Jimmy and he was nothing like the others. He worked steady down at Woolwich arsenal and later on the twins got him working in one of their clubs because they did think a lot of him.

I said to Rose, "You better not let the old man know what's going on else there'll be murders. I'll have a word with that Charlie myself, see if I don't." But before I could, my Violi's brought him to our house one Sunday. I can see him now. Bit gyppo looking, but suited up with his hair all plastered back with macassar oil – same as Ronnie wore his years later. I was civil but I didn't say too much because I didn't think he was all that. He gave Mother some old flannel and turned on the charm because that was his game, what with him being on the knocker and talking old girls into parting with their dead husband's gear.

Violi was all over the place, giggling and fidgeting about, and I could see that though she was a bit brave, what with bringing this Charlie home, she was worried about father coming home from the market where he went every Sunday. Of course he did turn up and things got a bit frosty. The old man never even spoke to him. He asked for a cup of tea, sat himself in the armchair and stuck the paper in front of his face.

Give him his due, Charlie kept smiling, but he left after about ten minutes and I wasn't far behind him because I knew it was going to go off. Later Violi told me the old man went up the wall. "He's old enough to be your father. He ain't no good. You keep away from him," and so on. She told him she wouldn't see Charlie no more but she never meant it. I mean from a young girl's point of view he was the business – good looking, bit of a joker and he had a few quid in his pocket – nothing else mattered.

So with Rose and May making excuses for her and Mum turning a blind eye, she carried on seeing him behind the old man's back. Things got a bit strained because the old man wasn't daft and was always asking where she was going and where she had been. Mum and my sisters didn't know where it would end up or they wouldn't have gone against the old man. None of us did. We thought it would all blow over, knowing what young girls are like. Then it all went wrong.

I came in and Mother said, "Our Violi's gone". I said, "What do you mean, gone? What's been said?" She said, "Nothing. Her stuff's gone out the bedroom and she ain't been to work." You didn't have to be too clever to work out where she'd taken off to and word came back very quick that her and Charlie had slipped down the registry in Kingsland Road and got married. Wasn't even legal because she lied about her age and said she was eighteen, so it could have been stopped with her only being sixteen, but nobody took it up.

The old man took it all inside and was hurt very badly. Being the man he was, we half expected him to go after Charlie, but he never did. At first he shouted and swore she was no daughter of his and she'd never set foot in the house again, but that didn't last and he went all quiet – like the spark had been knocked out of him.

We all missed having her at home because she was always laughing or singing around the place, but we had to get on with it.

When Christmas came round it must have got him thinking because he said to me, "Joe, let's go and get our Violi back." He must have forgotten she was married and there was no bringing her back, but he was so keen I didn't have the heart to say anything. We went down to where she was living in with his parents, and as we stopped outside we could hear a party going on. He banged on the door and some bloke I didn't know stuck his head out and asked what we wanted. We told him and at the same time Jimmy Kray's shouted from inside: "Who is it?" This geezer said, "It's Jimmy Lee and he wants a word with his girl". So Kray shouted back: "Tell the old bastard to fuck off."

I've never seen the old man as wild as he was then, and if I hadn't stopped him he would've smashed the door in and killed somebody. I didn't see no need for that, though I was mad myself. All the way home he kept shaking his head and saying "Why is she doing this?"

They say that Jimmy Kray was a tough nut and a tearaway, but I think a lot of that talk came from young Ronnie, who always did have what you might call a romantic head on him. From what I knew of Jimmy he was really a quiet sort of chap and I never did hear of him going out of his way looking for any trouble. So all I can think was that he'd had a bit too much drink when he shouted at my father.

A long time after, Violi told me she was upstairs too frightened to come down and crying because she knew her dad would be upset. What none of us knew was that when she'd eloped she was pregnant. Nothing was said right up until she had a boy, and that was young Charlie.

All the women got excited like they do when one of their own had a baby, and I thought that would bring the old man round to accepting the way things were, but he had a streak of stubbornness a mile wide and he wouldn't acknowledge anything was different. On the quiet, as though he couldn't care less, he used to ask me what the boy was like. Was he big? What colour hair did he have? Who did he look like? Because what with our Connie being five and young Joe being a year old, he knew that me and my Cissy saw Violi quite often – you know what women with babies are like. So I know he did care but he was prepared to cut off his own nose to spite his face, as they say.

Something else we didn't know and wouldn't find out until they both moved in with us was that Charlie was getting a bit handy with his fists when he'd had a skinful. Used Violi like a punchbag and she kept it all hidden – even from her sisters. Proud, you see. Didn't want anybody saying she'd made a mistake, though I think she'd realized that herself early on. Those days women accepted that sort of thing as part of married life.

Over the next six or seven years the family changed. Rose took up with Billy Wiltshire and got married. May tied the knot with Albert Filler, and that only left Johnny at home for a while because he was only eighteen.

We all moved about a bit, though stayed around Bethnal Green so we didn't lose touch. Nowadays families are all over the place, what with work and cars and all that. I'm down here in Romford, my Joe's up in Norfolk, Charlie's over Croydon way, and of course we all know where the two boys are. But then people never strayed far from where they were born; they all stuck together and helped each other out.

So there came a time when we moved into my in-laws house – the Whittingtons at 68 Stean Street. It was a big old place and we took over the two basement rooms and one on the ground floor. There was a docker and his family had a room, then above us lot Ciss's mum and dad had their couple of rooms. That left two rooms at the top and it wasn't long before my Violi said to me that she was fed up with living with Charlie's mob over in Gorsuch Street and would I put a word in for her about these rooms. Well of course I did and the three of them moved in, but it was a bad day's work on my part because Charlie caused a lot of upset with his drinking. Fortunately, he was away a lot of the time, what with travelling around buying his bit of tat – as far as Gloucester and Bristol.

My Joe said that he read somewhere that old Charlie was supposed to be earning thirty or forty pounds a week in them days, but a doctor couldn't even pick up that much, and if he was, our Violi never saw none of it. Every Sunday without fail he was on the tap looking for a few bob so he could pay his train fare and buy a bit of gear. I mean, who was right? Here was him without a second's thought for his family – Jack the Lad with his own business as he liked to call it, and us lot working hard for guv'nors every day subsidizing what he got up to. Friday you'd get your few quid back; Sunday he was banging on the door for it back again. Weekends were the worst. One, because he was home and two, he was drinking any profit he might have made.

You have to let people live their own lives and look the other way when it doesn't suit you, but when it's your own sister taking a hiding what are you going to do? Same every time. He'd come in late – voices would be raised and he'd start chucking his weight around. Little Charlie would start crying, then Violi, and I would jump them stairs and get hold of him. He never was a fighter and never would be, so a couple of right-handers was all it took to quiet him down. I was a big fella when I was younger but I never went too strong, though seeing Violi with a cut lip or a red eye made me want to chuck him out the window. But half the time she defended him once I got up there. "Don't hurt him, Joe, he's just had too much. He don't mean it." And that was it until the next time.

It seems like I've got a down on him, but I've got to say that once I did get to know him he wasn't really such a bad fella. It was that "gut polish" as my father would have said – turned him into a monster. I might have given him a slap the night before but next morning he wouldn't even remember it, so he never bore a grudge.

One incident did upset me but by the time I heard about it too much time had gone by to even mention it. Women things, if you know what I mean, are kept among the women, so I never even knew my sister was pregnant again. She must have put on weight and all that but what woman doesn't when she's married. This would be around 1932 and at that time I was driving all over the place and away from home quite a bit.

On the Sunday night Charlie had been on the piss as usual and given Violi a worse bashing than normal, probably because I wasn't around to put a stop to it. Next morning she's real bad – doesn't feel well and she's bleeding down there, if you get what I'm saying. For whatever reason the house is empty apart from that husband of hers. Connie, Charlie and young Joe would be at school, the rest of them in the house either working or shopping – whatever. Charlie's flying around getting ready to catch his train so he can go on the knocker and all the while she's asking him not to go because something ain't right with her insides. He's ignored her and disappeared out the door.

About an hour later she had a baby girl. Later on there was talk of it dropping out of her and on to the floor but I'm not sure about that. Either way with Violi giving it a cuddle this little mite died almost straight away. She had loads of black hair and big dark eyes, and sounds like she would have taken after our Rosie. The name was picked out and everything. She would've been Violet, same as her mother. Terrible thing to happen.

You know, right up until the day she died she kept a lace-trimmed funeral card in her top drawer. And beside it all wrapped up in soft paper there was a white carnation that she took off little Violet's coffin, even though it turned black with age eventually. She hid what she felt inside but never forgot.

NANNY LEE –
Wearing her favourite fur coat.
Fifty years later it had fallen to
the floor of a cupboard and was
home to a nest of 'mices', but she
wouldn't part with it.

GRANDAD LEE –
A keep fit fanatic all his life, he'd
think nothing of cycling to
Manchester from the East End.

LOUISA ELIZA KRAY NÉE TURNER (grandmother) –
Her mother was a well-known midwife in the Hackney area.
(Courtesy of Terry and Peter Steadman)

JAMES FREDERICK KRAY (grandfather) – Though given an exaggerated reputation for being a tough fighting man, he was in fact a quiet sort of person. The twins always called him 'Farvie'.
(*Courtesy of Terry and Peter Steadman*)

GEORGE AND CHARLOTTE STEADMAN (Charlotte née Kray).
(*Courtesy of Terry and Peter Steadman*)

NANNY AND GRANDAD LEE – In later life
they were rarely apart.

GRANDAD LEE – Manoeuvring a pair of these giant shires
through the streets of the East End on a daily basis gave him
strength that left him unrivalled in the bare-knuckle ring.

JOHHNY – Old Joe Lee's brother, youngest of the five Lees. Lorry driver, mechanic, part time racing driver and, with his wife Maude, owner of Maude's Café in Vallance Road.

ROSE – Feisty Aunt Rose was always a special favourite of both Reg and Ron.

MAY – Rita's mother. As a pretty blonde youngster she was nicknamed "Dinah" by the Vallance Road cab drivers who cheekily sang out as she passed by "Dinah, is there anyone finer?" and it stuck with her for the rest of her life.

OLD JOE LEE, CISSY, CONNIE AND YOUNG JOE — A family trip to the coast. Sadly, Connie was to die a few years later from tuberculosis.

VIOLET – Vivacious, spirited and full of life. Things were to change when she met and married Charlie Kray.

Mr. C. KRAY
WARDROBE DEALER.

Will call back in one or two hours time to purchase any Clothing you wish to dispose of for

SPOT CASH

Cast-off Clothing, also Bed-Linen and Childrens' Clothing

HIGHEST MARKET PRICES GIVEN FOR OLD GOLD

BEST PRICES FOR OLD SUITS

Postcards promptly attended to.   Distance no object.

178 VALLANCE ROAD, LONDON, E.2.

CHARLIE'S BUSINESS CARD – No telephones for the working classes then.

CHARLIE KRAY – Handsome, silver-tongued and dapper.
It's understandable why he turned Violet's head.

BABY RONNIE – Even at this early age he had 'those eyes'
which later on would chill anyone summoned to his presence
(8th February 1934).

BABY REGGIE – Though never dominated by his twin, throughout his life he allowed himself to be led into situations he might normally have avoided (8th February 1934).

THE TWINS – aged 2

SCHOOL PHOTOGRAPH – Despite how they turned out, the twins, enjoyed their schooldays and were both polite and normal children.

YOUNG RONNIE AND REGGIE – with friends while away fruit picking at Wisbech.

BILLY WILTSHIRE – A right little daredevil. If anyone was taking bets on who in the family would end up behind bars, money would have been placed on him – and lost.

JOE LEE (*left*) and CHARLIE KRAY – Ready to do their bit for King and Country (29th December 1943).

She was ill for ever such a long time after and I didn't really know what was wrong with her. Not ill – bedridden – more depressed and doing a lot of crying. I thought she'd had enough of Charlie, and at the time he did cut down on the booze. So to me it did look like they had problems but were trying to sort them out, so you don't say anything.

Doctors said that if she didn't hurry up and get pregnant again she'd end up in Bethnal Green Asylum. If they'd known the background to all this they'd have been better advising her to go back to her mother, but that just wasn't entertained then. You made your bed, you laid in it. In those days you did whatever doctors told you, because they knew best and so she's taken up what they suggested and just before Christmas the next year she had those twins.

If any good did come out of that it was that my father decided to let bygones be bygones and take up with Violi again. Eight years it had been and they'd barely spoken a word, and though it was his own doing, he was pleased it was all over.

The other girls had always stayed close to Violi and them and Mother was forever making their way up those stairs with a pie or a couple of tins of fruit, but it made life uncomfortable, what with pretending to the old man that they didn't come near. Those twins was going to end up being a trial to the whole family, but right then they brought everybody together, though they didn't know it.

Cissy's mother and father were good people and they'd put up with a lot over the years, but as time went on they had enough and asked Charlie and Violi to move out – polite like, but they didn't want them no more.

They took on a right dump of a place in Dunlow Court. Up an alley it was and still gas-lit even then. It was a slum really and they pulled it down not long after and the family moved above a furniture shop in Hackney Road right opposite the Odeon pictures. After that they took over a house just round the corner from my mother and father in Vallance Road and there they stayed. Later on all the families would live side by side, and I suppose you might say that's where all the capers started that would make those little babies famous — but we could've done without it.

3. "Say hello to your brothers"

Joe Lee

By coincidence the road I was born in had the same name as ours, 21 Lee Street, just off Kingsland Road in Haggerston. Obviously, I don't remember those early years and by the time I was old enough to be aware of what was going on, we'd moved just round the corner into Stean Street to live with my Nanny and Grandad Whits. Their proper name was Whittington, same as Dick, but it was a bit of a mouthful for a youngster so it got shortened down and I never called them anything else.

It was a big old house and me and my sister Connie, who was three years older, and my cousin Charlie had the run of the place. He lived on the top floor with Aunt Violet and Uncle Charlie, and we spent all our time together. One minute we'd be in his place cadging a biscuit, then down to the basement to pester my mum, then back up the stairs to Nanny's to see what we could get there. Must have driven them all mad banging up and down.

My Aunt Violet was a lovely woman and always had plenty of time for us, but Uncle Charlie could be a bit up and down, especially with young Charlie, so we kept out of his way when he was home – which wasn't too often because he worked away nearly all week.

If we caught him on a Friday before he had a drink he was always good for a penny, but make too much noise on a Sunday and he'd come out of the door swearing and shouting.

My old man was as good as gold, but a lot of grown ups were like Charlie back then so we didn't take a lot of notice. Mind you my dad could have his moments. He had this pony and trap and the pony was a lovely animal but a bit highly strung. He got hold of it cheap because it was known as a bolter. If it saw a bit of paper fly up or heard a bang, away it would go. Dangerous, really.

Now if he didn't know anything else my dad did know his horses. He'd been involved since he was a kid, so I suppose it was a challenge. He had a special pair of reins made so he could hold it back if he had to. He would take Mother and me out in this trap, and being a young fella then he'd get carried away and we'd be flying. I loved it. I'd be on the bell, ding, ding, ding, but Mum would be screaming in the back. "That's enough, Joe. Slow down – let us off," because she knew what this pony was capable of. After a while Dad would stop and say, "Go on then. Get out of it." And we'd have to get the bus home. Then she would tell my nan that he'd slung us off and all that. But he never really – it was her own making.

I don't know whether she thought it was going to be different each time we went out, but a lot of times it was the same. He took us to Dagenham one Sunday to visit his mate Boy Boy Cartwright, who lived in this row of terraces. When we got there he said to the fella, "Can I give my pony a feed in your garden?" When he said, "Yeah, help yourself," Dad unhitched it from the trap and geed it through the front door and a couple of rooms, and stuck it on this patch of lawn. I ask you, who would do that nowadays?

Anyway, big changes in the house came when I was seven years old. Charlie would be about six then, and we both went to Laburnham Street School, just round the corner. Why we was home this particular day I don't know – might have been a weekend, but I do know it was October because it was freezing out. Charlie and me were playing in his place, quiet like because Aunt Violet wasn't well, and next thing all the women turn up and we're slung out of it. Well not slung as such, but we were given a penny apiece for a lump of Indian toffee [candy floss] and told to go out and play, and not come back until we were shouted. That was no hardship and we ended up round the square chucking stones at each other.

When we got in my mother told Charlie to get upstairs pretty sharpish because there was a surprise for him. He took off and I was right on his heels. Now if they'd been out and bought a dog we might have shown a bit more interest. As it was, Auntie Vi was sitting in bed holding these two little dolls – one in each arm. She said to Charlie, "Say hello to your brothers. This one's Reggie and this one's Ronnie." I don't know about him but I couldn't tell the difference – it was like looking at one with your eyes crossed.

To a six year old a surprise is something you can eat or play with, so I think he was a bit disappointed that these two were none of them and all he could say was "What did you buy them for?" Neither of us had a clue about babies though I did have an idea they came off apple trees or under cabbages. Young Charlie didn't have a lot to say on the subject. He either had the hump with his mother or he didn't care one way or another. But if those twins didn't put his nose out of joint right then it wouldn't be long before they did and he'd eventually find that wasn't going to change for the rest of his life.

Looking at old photos now I've got to say they were beautiful babies – and a bit special because they came in a pair – but if I remember right, what was going through my head that day was they looked like a couple of little monkeys. The twins got their names because Nanny Whitt's brother Bert had a couple of boys called Reg and Ron. My Aunt Violet always thought their names sounded nice, so when her own two turned up there was no argument.

As far as us kids were concerned these twins didn't make the slightest difference to our lives whatsoever. All Charlie and me was concerned with was getting out with our mates and roaming the streets. Getting a pair of rusty old skates on our feet, kicking tin cans around, swinging on people's gates until we got told to clear off and play in our own street, in fact anything that didn't mean we was stuck indoors. Half the time we knocked around with another cousin of ours, Billy Wiltshire. He was Aunt Rose's boy and his dad, Billy, same name as him, had taken off and left them both. Nothing nasty, it just turned out they weren't made for each other. Rose liked to sit indoors with the radio on or a book and he wanted to be out dancing or in the pub, so they parted amicably.

Before that though I remember the law banging on our door one night and my father opening up to see what was going on. Seemed like my uncles Charlie and Billy were banged up down Old Street nick for fighting and being drunk and disorderly. Now they don't want to kip on bare boards all night so they've sent a copper over to ask my dad if he would go down to the station and bail them out. I heard him shout, "No, I fucking well won't. You keep 'em and chuck the key away." When they eventually turned up next day my uncles were livid because the copper had told them what the old man had said – word for word. But they couldn't kick up too much of a fuss because they knew my dad had a bit of a temper and could have upped the pair of them.

So young Billy knocked about with us and I've got to say he was a right little bastard. There was nothing that kid wouldn't do for a dare. I've seen him jump off a roof twenty foot high and then be frightened to look in case he was dead.

Another time the three of us were walking down Kingsland Road messing about like you do, then as we're going past a shop with all the stuff outside, he runs a stick down the kettles and pans – bang, bang, bang – then picks up a big tin-plate model car and makes off with it. Of course with the noise the shopkeeper's already on his way out and makes a grab for him. What does Billy do? He slings the motor straight at the geezer's head. If it had hit him full on it would've killed him. As it was, it just caught him a glancing blow. He's shouting, "Get the coppers. I've been done over." So we took to our heels. Me and Charlie are panicking because we weren't bad kids really and our arses are making buttons, because this is out of our league. Billy didn't give a toss about nobody so he just ran backward making faces until we were out of sight.

A lot gets made out of Rose supposedly saying to Ronnie that he was born to hang, but I doubt whether there was any kid didn't get that thrown at them some time or other. It was just something that was said; tear your trousers, break a window or answer back and you was headed for the gallows. But if anybody was, it was our Billy. If you was looking for odds on which of the boys would turn out as a gangster and end their days behind the door you wouldn't have got even money on him. Nothing slowed him down, not even when the backboard on his dad's trailer fell on his head and knocked him spark out. An hour later he was back on the streets and up to all kinds.

Funny thing is, later on he went in the army, done his bit for king and country in Malta and came out the other side a completely different character. He got himself a job in Covent Garden and stuck it out until the day he retired. Don't know what changed him from the little tearaway he'd always been, but I never heard of him putting a foot wrong from that day on.

Up the road from us was a coal shop, and as a bit of a sideline the bloke hired out barrows. Big old things – two wheelers. Because no one had a car then, if you wanted to move a bit of gear this was the only choice you had. They're all lined up outside the shop with a big chain running through all the wheels so they couldn't be nicked. So this geezer collared me one morning as I was passing and asked me if I'd keep an eye on these barrows and take the names and money off anybody who wanted one because he was locking up the shop and going out. It was worth a few coppers so I was up for it straight away. I was about ten then, which seems a bit young, but you have to remember that kids were older in their ways those days and some of them started proper work when they was only twelve.

I went home, had my dinner then shot back without telling my mother what I was up to. So there I am, the guv'nor. I walked up and down like I was in charge of the crown jewels. I straightened them all, brushed out the backs and fiddled with the chain just to make myself look busy. After a bit a bloke came up and said he wanted to hire one of these but he needed somebody to pull it. Was I up for it?

Now I was supposed to stay where I was but when he mentioned a shilling a trip I came over giddy and said I'd do it. Turned out he needed two barrows so I told him to hang on, I'll go and fetch my cousin. Ten minutes later me and Charlie are lugging one of these things apiece from Hackney Downs to Victoria Park. We was moving his furniture and bits and pieces from one house to another, and as one hour turned into the next the two of us are counting the money in our heads and talking about what we'd spend it on.

As time went on and his bill went from silver to note it was getting dark. As we dropped the last lot off it was half ten at night and pitch black. Young Charlie, at nine years old, was asleep on his feet and I was done in myself, but we was due for weighing out and that was all that mattered. As it happened instead of the thirty bob each we expected the fella told us to fuck off out of it, and shut the door.

I'll never forget turning into our street. Everybody was out looking for us because word had got round that Joe and Charlie had been taken away by some man. We dropped the barrows and run indoors expecting a right good hiding, but the family was so relieved they never thought of it. Charlie was put to bed but the old man took me and half the neighbours to go and find this bloke. If they had got hold of him they would have killed him. As it was I nearly got some fella murdered because I pointed him out as he came walking toward us and said, "That's him". He got a bit roughed up before I could say I'd made a mistake. My dad spent weeks going round that house but he only got the wife in and she cried every time, so he gave up in the end. But it shows you people were as aware of dodgy characters on the street as they are today.

Listen to the old ones now and the East End sounds like fairyland. They reckon old people and kids were as safe as houses and all that, but it wasn't any different really. They didn't call it mugging then but a bang on the head's the same whatever name you gave it, and kids disappeared and got murdered – but that's all forgotten now.

Talking of strange characters, there were some fellas that lived on our street that were odd. Not dangerous or nothing, but different. We'd see four men go in the house and next thing four women would walk out – all done up with lipstick and eyes blacked up. We'd look over their fence and the washing line would be full up with dresses and girls' knickers. Gave us a giggle but we didn't understand what it was all about. On the other hand we wasn't too young to know you didn't take the piss, because even though they was the other way – if you know what I mean – they'd smack you in the head quick as you like.

They'd stand at the gate talking to my mum and Aunt Violet like they were real women themselves, shaking their hair and straightening their nylons. What this mob did for a living was street dancing, but dressing up was nothing to do with it because they wasn't like a drag act or nothing, they were just naturally over the side. They'd cart a big square of wood around with them and when they was ready they'd put it down on the pavement and tap dance on it – good turns really.

They wasn't on their own because you'd see the same thing with flower-sellers. These men, dressed up like women, would stand on street corners singing out: "Who'll buy my lavender! Who'll buy my roses!" They couldn't help it and they were harmless enough.

One of these geezers in our street was called Air Ball Huggett and years after I was in the Double R Club with Reggie and I thought I recognized him. He had a proper suit on but his eyes were still done up with mascara and his face was powdered up – that's what made me think. I said, "Is your name Huggett?" And when he said yes I told him who I was, and he said, "Ooh, I remember your father. Tall handsome looking man – I didn't half fancy him." I could hardly stop laughing but I said, "That's nice. I'm seeing the old man next week so I'll tell him – he'll be right pleased."

Turn the telly on or open a paper today they're all at it. And if he took any notice at all my old man would say, "What's all that about?" Didn't understand it and didn't want to, so I wasn't going to tell him that he was some geezer's pin-up even if it was years ago. Same as with villains and delinquents. Now he's old he wants them all strung up or exterminated, but he forgets he was no angel as a nipper, and when he got older he mixed with some tasty faces.

He was great pals with the Sabini boys and they were terrors. The whole family was and had been for years and years. They ran protection at all the race meetings and had every copper in London in their pockets. They was into everything and I tell you they was the guv'nors – every one of them. They was called the Italian Mob and as far as business went they stuck to their own, so I'm not suggesting the old man was a gangster or nothing like, but there's no getting away from the fact that if he had any trouble he didn't have far to look for some heavy people to back him up. Funnily enough when the twins were in a spot of bother and up in court, the judge said to them, "Don't go round thinking you're the Sabini brothers," so it goes to show they were no strangers to the law. To be honest as far as the old man and his younger days are concerned we don't know the half of it.

There was one time though when these Italian fellas had a street battle in Vallance Road and according to the old man it was all down to him. This was when he was about eighteen or twenty and what happened was a neighbour's missus took a bit of a fancy to him. She and her old man, who was in a wheelchair, lived round the corner with their relation Mrs Doyle, the woman who Rita saw as a ghost a couple of times. Talk about making it obvious, this bird was never out of Nanny's house. The excuse being that she was a bit of a piano player and what with Nanny having one, she'd pop in and knock out a few tunes, but with one eye on my father.

I've no idea if my dad was innocent in all this caper but either way her old man got the hump eventually and came wheeling round to the house. Well he's having a ruck on the doorstep with Nanny and when Grandad shouts out to her what's going on like, she's told him that Mr Bloater's having a go. He flies to the door and this blokes raving about there's something going on with his wife and their son [my old man]. Anyway, to cut a long story short he said he was going to bring some mob over that night to sort it out. Grandad wasn't going to up a bloke in a wheelchair but he said, "Bloater, I'll give you bloater, show yerself round here an' you'll be fucking kipper – now piss off".

Course when my dad's come in and they told what's been happening he said, "Oh yeah, coming mob-handed are they, we'll see about that". And he's took off. He's back indoors that night about half seven, when – *bomp* – a brick come through the window. Now the old man wasn't scared of anyone, not even when he was ninety let alone at that age, so he's gone out and fronted this gang of about ten fellas. What they don't know is that he's already had a word with his mate Harry Boy and with perfect timing the Sabini mob turn up from each end of the street. There wasn't just blokes, they'd brought the women along as well and some of those big old Italian girls was right brahmas and built like wrestlers. What a ruck! That lot that thought they was going to belt the life out of a bloke on his own got the bollocks knocked out of them. Fists, bottles, coshes, you name it. Windows got smashed and the whole street was turned upside down, but I'll tell you what, the old man never had trouble from that lot again.

While we were in this Stean Street my Uncle Johnny got himself a big old Chrysler – American motor. First time he brought it round our place I think every kid for five miles round came to stand and look at it. Keeping them all back, Charlie and me showed it off like it was our own. As soon as Uncle Charlie clapped eyes on it, his brain must have gone into overdrive, what with always being on the lookout for something that might do himself a bit of good. I learned all this when I was older, but within five minutes he's got Johnny talked into joining his one-man business of totting, knocking or pestering – whatever you like to call it.

Basically, what he did was bang on doors and very politely ask if they had any broken watches, gold, jewellery or clothes they might want to sell. If they wasn't interested he'd leave his card because he had them all printed up, and tell them he'd call back if he was passing. Of course he's sown a seed by then, so when he's gone they start digging out the cupboards and what have you. Two hours he'd give them then "just in passing" give them another knock and get a result. He wasn't above getting the local paper of wherever he happened to be, study the death columns, then chase up the widows for their husbands' shoes and suits.

So he's roped Johnny in and off they've gone – Charlie lying back on the leather, a fag in one hand, a hip-flask in the other and his feet up on the dashboard while Johnny's driving his bollocks off all over the country.

It only lasted a couple of months, and I can remember Johnny telling my old man that it was costing him more in petrol than what he was getting out of it, so he jacked it in and Charlie was back on the train.

For some reason or other this Chrysler was laid up round Grandad Lee's. Might have been that my uncle was up north driving the lorries. Either way the car sat outside the house for weeks and weeks. When he came back he called in to see his mother and his dad stuck eight quid in his hand. Johnny was a bit taken aback because the old fella wasn't too quick when it came to putting his hand in his pocket, so he says, "What's this? You come up on the dogs?" Grandad says, "No – I've sold that motor for you," and he's grinning all over his face like he's done him the biggest favour in the world. Well, Johnny's gone fucking mad, because the car was worth forty quid or more, but it was too late as it was already a done deal. He didn't half bollock his old man. Whether Grandad was doing what he thought was a good turn or whether he was doing himself a bit of good, we never did find out.

When it came to anything on four wheels Johnny knew everything that needed knowing – you name it, he could drive it. Even did a spell as a racing driver, and he was top notch. He did all the testing for Coopers and that goes to show how good he was. One motor he took round the track no end of times was the one Jack Brabham won the world championship in. Trouble with that machine was they designed it with Jack in mind and he was well over six foot. The seat was fixed and Johnny was five seven, so you can imagine.

When the twins were small I can't say Charlie and me had a lot of time for them. Fat little things they were, and the old man said they were like their mother when she was a baby.

The Krays had moved out of our house by then, but it didn't make a lot of difference. We still saw them every day because all of us ended up at Nanny Lee's at some point or other. It was like a focal point for everybody and always would be.

A big thing that was supposed to have happened to the twins was that they were seriously ill when they was about three years old. It's reckoned that it turned Ronnie's head so that he was never the same again, and that it made both of them a bit clingy with their mum. But they were always that way right through their childhood anyway. To be quite honest I don't even remember it, nor does my old man, Ronnie himself or anyone else. You wasn't allowed to be ill and if you was, none of them took any notice. If you had a headache fresh air was the answer, and if it was a stomach ache out came the bottle of castor oil and that was so bad to swallow – the thought of having to suffer a mouthful of that stuff kept you healthy.

One year when they was only nippers, Uncle John and Auntie

Maude took the pair of them down to stay with her mother in Clacton. It was only for a week to give Violet a break, but they wished they hadn't. Johnny said they were little bastards. When they wasn't into everything they were crying to come home – complete nightmare. He said he'd never do it again, and he never did.

With young Charlie it wasn't so much that his family deliberately shoved him out and sidelined him, if you know what I mean, more that those twins took all the attention, what with being cute and a bit demanding and Charlie being so quiet, they just left him to get on with it.

One incident sticks in my mind. Young Charlie was off school with real bad toothache, and his face was twice the size it should've been. Why my aunt didn't whip him round the dentist and get him sorted I don't know. Most likely she couldn't afford to because the National Health didn't come in until after the war. So he's laid on the settee all day with a wet flannel round his jaw. Like I said, a dim view was taken of any illness or skiving over a bit of pain, so when old Charlie came home he's given him a look and told him to get off his back and go and buy him a piece of fish. A woman and a kid couldn't argue with him when he was tanked up with beer, so young Charlie's had to drag up Kingsland Road with tears streaming down his face. He's come back, put the bag on the table and the old man's opened it up, looked at the fish, then tore it all to pieces saying, "What's this fucking rubbish you've got? Get back up there and get something proper." My cousin had to set off all over again. He wouldn't have treated the other two like that, so his attitude to his oldest boy speaks for itself.

Trouble with Charlie, he was too easy-going – never caused no fuss and was always trying to please – in his own way looking for affection that never really came his way. I mean, Violet was good to him but I suppose the other two took up all of her time, and if the other one's giving no trouble, well he's going to be ignored.

They say twins are close – like one person in two bodies, but you never saw a lot of that with those two, at least not as nippers. I've seen them get their dinner stuck in front of them, then spend five minutes counting the peas one by one or measuring off the sausages with their fingers. If one had more than the other, God help us – one or the other would throw a right tantrum. If it was their brother he'd have got a bang round the ear'ole, but them two got away with it.

And fight? They'd get stuck into each other like they were worst enemies, and half the time they were encouraged. I suppose we all were really. It doesn't happen today and I suppose that's down to there being lots of other interests. But when I think about it that's all any of us did back then. Mothers don't want their kids having a punch-up now in case they turn into thugs or what have you, but I remember running indoors one time and telling my mother that a big boy had hit me. I wanted her to go out and tell him off. Instead she dragged me outside, went up to this boy, held me by the shoulder and told me to give him one. I gave him a half-hearted slap and she said to him, "That'll teach you a lesson". Oh yeah! She went back indoors and he hammered me black and blue.

Even my old man got a similar lesson from his dad. Same thing – getting bullied at school, so Grandad's taken him out in the yard and shown him how to defend himself. That was keep going forward, don't step back – attack all the time. My dad tried it and never looked back.

Years later Grandad Lee was still teaching the same moves to me, to Charlie and to the twins. If you ever saw them in the ring that was their style – keep the other fella on the run, keep after them. Perhaps we all saw ourselves as potential Kid Lewises, who was our hero, and we took it serious.

Two minutes after walking in the door at Grandad's and he'd have us out the back with the gloves on. One time me and Charlie got stuck in and by the time our mothers knew what was going on my lip was cut in two places and he had a bruised forehead and blood running out of his nose. While the women are kicking up a fuss, Grandad's rubbing his hands together and saying, "They're boys – they've got to learn".

Him and my old man had a go one day, friendly like, and by the time they're finished Grandad had a lump hanging off his eyes as big as a plum. Dad had accidentally caught him with the laces on the glove, and it had filled up with blood. Grandad didn't give a monkey's and was going to use the old fighter's trick of cutting it with a razor and draining it off, but my dad stopped him.

When he was younger Grandad used to get the gloves on his sisters and they'd do each other a bit of damage. One of the times Aunt Polly broke her arm but none of it must have done her any harm because she went on to live until she was a hundred and three.

As for Reg and Ron, they never gave us a minute's peace. Whether it was Charlie or me, you couldn't sit down for five minutes without them saying, "We're ready – we've got the gloves – when you coming out?" They was no match for us because we were a lot older, but they'd have a go. Thing is you didn't take one on, you had to take them both – like everybody would years later.

They was crafty even then. Reg would come at you from the front then Ron would sneak round behind and give you a belt. I always took it a bit steady but Billy Wiltshire would give them a right pasting if he got them cornered up – never made any allowances at all. I don't know what it was with him but he didn't know how to torment them next.

There was a big metal barrel out in the yard, and he'd get it, take it in the road and stick those two boys inside, then roll it up and down the cobbles banging into whatever got in the way. They'd come out all dizzy and covered in bruises, and he'd think it was the funniest thing in the world. If it weren't that, he'd have a rope round their necks trying to strangle them. When we went round to the local bathhouse he'd hold their heads under water until they went blue in the face. One time he nailed the pair of them up in the cupboard under the stairs. They're screaming the place down because it was dark and full of mice and spiders and Billy couldn't get the nails out, so he had to wait until Grandad came home.

Funny when you think that these two little nippers, who would grow up to be called the most dangerous men in London, were nearly being seen off by our Billy before they got into long trousers.

My Aunt Rose kept a few chickens out the back, same as near enough everybody did then, and she wanted one killing for dinner. Well, Billy and me knew as much about necking a bird as flying, so were looking at this thing and scratching our heads. Then the twins chipped in – "We can do it, we can do it" – so we said, "Go on then, get on with it". Well, they tied this bird by the feet up on the washing line and knocked the bollocks out of it with lumps of wood and all the time it's squawking and flapping. They got right excited and by the time they were done they were covered in blood and no one could've eaten this chicken because it was smashed to bits. Shameful really, and cruel, but I don't think it would be fair to make any comparison between that and what they would do to people years later, though to my mind it seemed like they got more fun out of that than was natural. On the other hand, never mind what other people say, I thought they were violent little bastards from day one, but they was crafty enough to keep that side well hidden from the women in the family.

By the time war broke out in 1939 most of the Lees were settled in Vallance Road. Last in was my Aunt May and Uncle Albert, though I think he was away by then, what with being called up. Johnny and Maude was in 172 and 174 was derelict. Rose lived next door to Nanny, just round the corner in London Road (which they eventually changed to Dunbridge Street), then she moved into 176. Aunt Violet took over 178, and of course Nanny and Grandad Lee stayed right on the corner.

May went to see the landlord about 174 but he said no chance because it had no floors or nothing. When she offered to get the work done at her own expense if she could have it, he must have thought it was his birthday and gave her the key.

Grandad was doing a bit for a local builder so he got him to do the place up on the cheap, but just your basics because these houses were practically falling down anyway. Take the wallpaper off and they'd have collapsed.

My family and me weren't too far away, but that lot stayed shoulder to shoulder for years – some of them until the houses were pulled down.

I think the East End took the worst of the batterings because of the docks, and in the thick of the bombing places all round us were being flattened every day. Sod's law, me, Connie and Mum and Dad had just moved into a lovely block of flats they were throwing up everywhere around that time, and we thought we were in paradise. Inside toilet, nice bathroom and hot running water – unheard of. Sirens went off and we made a dash for the shelters and bang. Bomb's dropped on the flats and that was the end of that. Our place was completely wrecked and dangerous really, but I can still see the old man fighting his way in there to get a few bob he'd hidden in a wardrobe. He was in there for ages and we're worried in case the place fell down on him – but no. Out he came saying, "Fucking door was jammed but I got it open". So like thousands of others we were homeless.

The family down Vallance Road took us in. We were lucky really when I think of some of the things that happened.

If you walk up Vallance Road now, there's a bit of open ground that's a playground for kids – swings, slides and all that caper. Back then Hughes Mansions stood there, which were three blocks of flats with mainly Jewish people living there. One V2 and the whole lot was destroyed and about 140 families killed. I remember going up there and watching them digging all these people out, and it went on all week. Even the queen turned up, the one who's the Queen Mother now, and I can remember she had a blue coat on and a hat with a feather in it. She couldn't do nothing but it says something that she'd come into Bethnal Green to pay her respects.

Then there was that business up at the Salmon and Ball in the new underground. What people did, and Mum and us two kids did the same was, if you didn't want to or couldn't get in one of the air-raid shelters, you went down the underground. We used to use Liverpool Street and it was no joke because they were packed full and stinking. Kids crying, talking, laughing, singing – you couldn't shut your eyes all night.

With this other place, what happened was that there'd been an air raid and it was all over, so people were all coming out. Hundreds of people. Then for some reason an anti-aircraft gun was fired over in the park – might have been a German straggler or something – and this set off a terrible panic. Thinking the planes were back, all those people that had got outside turned back and made a mad dash to get back down into the underground again. Trouble with that was the builders hadn't finished off all the work in the station yet and there was no handrails. So with crowds coming up and that lot pushing down, people were tipping over the edge of the stairs, with the result there was chaos and two hundred people finished up being crushed to death.

My old man knew a lot of the people that died that day. One of them was Dickie Corbett, a champion boxer. Another was the wife of Johnny Boxer. She was carrying her little baby, but as she went down somebody grabbed it and passed it over the heads of all the people and it was saved. Johnny was on war service at the time, and the authorities wouldn't even give him leave to come home and bury his missus.

Funnily enough him and the boy that was saved ended up living near my dad at Harold Hill, but of course they're both dead now.

Every day there was tragedy after tragedy happening right under our noses, but when it struck my family it was nothing to do with the war or the bombings. My elder sister Connie hadn't been too well for a long time and after a while they diagnosed her as having tuberculosis, something you never hear of nowadays. From what I was told the family seemed to think she probably picked it up from a boyfriend, but wherever it came from she had it bad.

After a while she was taken into a hospital over at Eltham in south London and we were backward and forward as often as we could to keep her spirits up. She was a lot like my Aunt Rose, fiery like and never took any nonsense from nobody and she fought against that illness same as Rose would hers years later. My cousin Rita was getting on for about five years old at the time, a proper little doll with her blond hair, and Connie thought the world of her and she always spoke about her. I mean, May couldn't visit because of the risks to Rita but they was always writing to each other and my sister would be saying, "How's my littlest cousin?" and, "I can't wait to get better, then me and you can go over the park with her". What it was, Rita was a bit of a novelty in the family, being a girl among all the blokes and she gave Connie something to focus on while she was having treatment and away from home.

She never did get to go over the park though because she died in the June. It should never have happened. She was on the threshold of her adult life and suddenly she was gone and all of us were knocked for six. Devastated doesn't even cover it.

She used to have my father wrapped round her little finger, like most girls with their dad, and he took it real bad – we all did. And all these years later I still think of her, but what can I say? When it's your own sister it never goes away.

The twins missed some of the worst of the bombing because Violet and May had taken them and young Rita off to Hadleigh in Suffolk. Hundreds of kids were taken away from their families and sent all over the country as evacuees and had a rough old time of it. Little brown suitcase, label round the neck and bosh – away from everything they'd ever known, so our three were fortunate they didn't have to suffer that. Charlie wasn't evacuated as such because at his age he was big enough to look after himself, but he went along anyway, mainly to keep an eye on his brothers and to help his mum out. I think he got himself a bit of a job in a local shop so he was well out of all the carry-on back home.

From what they said when they came back Reg and Ron loved every minute of it. Well, they would because I don't suppose they ever had such freedom. There wasn't too many woods and fields in the East End and with them being right out in the sticks they could run as wild as they liked and not get into any bother. May and Violet didn't take to it at all and missed the rest of the family, what with being so close before. What brought them back in the end was that old Charlie started to turn up there and getting up to his usual with the drink. Might have made things a bit embarrassing where they were billeted – I don't know. In the end Johnny drove down in his lorry and brought them all back, and that was the end of that.

About the same time it was my turn to take off because I'd volunteered to join the navy. Both Charlie and me signed on at the same time because when you're that age it all seems like a bit of a lark. We did our basic training together and all that, but by the time I was sent to Davenport in Plymouth I was on my own. All in all Charlie didn't spend too much time in the navy, and from what he told me when we caught up with each other, he didn't see any active service. The only fighting he got into was in the ring because he did a lot of boxing and tournaments and what have you. I thought that was a bit strange considering the medical board signed the papers saying he was unfit for duty and let him go. Seems like he had a dodgy ticker – murmur they called it – but as it kept banging away for the next fifty-seven years I've got a strong feeling he'd managed to pull a stroke somehow. Though when I found myself clinging on to a sinking ship I couldn't blame him one bit.

What it was, they'd stuck me in Combined Operations, and the idea was to invade France. We sailed across the channel and no sooner got in the landing craft to make for shore when a storm came up. Being well overloaded with blokes and laying low in the water, we got swamped out and it keeled over leaving half of us hanging on and the rest in the sea. There was men drowning and we couldn't do nothing to help them. Terrible thing to have to go through, and hard to come to terms with when you're only eighteen. Eventually, those that made it through were picked up and shipped straight back to a survivors' camp in Saint-Aubin-sur-Mer in France, which for anybody fit enough was in walking distance from the beach. Pretty soon them up top gave up on the French operation and us navy fellas weren't needed, so they decided to second us all into the army.

Now I'd enlisted in the navy in the first place because I knew if I didn't it wouldn't be too long before I got my papers and ended up with all that square bashing and what have you. So you can imagine I wasn't too best pleased when they told me I was going to end up as a squaddie anyway. We all kicked up a fuss but we might as well have saved our breath because once all the paperwork was sorted, me and loads of other blokes were given a train ticket and told to make our own way up to a camp near Liverpool.

I'll always remember jumping down on the platform at the other end with another fella I'd palled up with. It was freezing cold, we were pissed off and Liverpool was a bit of a hole back then. We looked at each other – both said, "Fuck this" at the same time, crossed the line and jumped on the first train back to London. They could stick the war up their arse – I was off home. I mean half a dozen lines here doesn't begin to explain what me and thousands like me went through – and for what?

Greasing over the side, or deserting if you want to put it like that, had nothing to do with cowardice. Blokes out of the East End just wasn't used to being pushed around by a load of jumped-up nothings. You'd get some geezer who couldn't find his own arse in the dark, suddenly made up into officer and giving us orders – and all our lives we'd been standing up for ourselves and fighting for everything we had. No, it wasn't for me, and as it turned out it wasn't for half the geezers I knew from around those parts.

I've just said I was making for home, but that wouldn't have been a very clever move because before the day was out the army would have notified the police and my name would be on a list with all the others, and they'd have been banging on my mother's door. So I hid out at my Aunt Rosie's and don't ask me why but really the law never came looking for me there at all.

Trouble was, my Uncle Charlie never even got as far as putting a pair of army boots on before he went on the run, and when he wasn't away he took turns at which house in Vallance Road he hid in. I think local coppers thought he was taking the piss and it became a challenge to get hold of him, so that made it difficult for me. A couple of times they nearly got me when they were looking for him.

I suppose the twins got mixed up trying to remember all those years ago, but a couple of incidents they put down to their father in their books actually happened to me.

I was in Aunt Violet's one day having a cup of tea in the kitchen when the law arrived. They didn't hang about waiting to be invited in – bang on the door and walk in. "Mrs Kray, I've had a report that your husband's in the house." Luckily she kept them talking long enough for me to squeeze under the sink and pull the curtain across – no fancy units then. They turned the place over and never thought of looking there. Another time they burst into Johnny's at 172 so fast the copper slipped on the mat and skidded across the floor, ending up on his arse.

It was down to my uncle that I didn't get lifted the second time. Him and Maude had opened a café on the corner opposite our houses and he was standing outside watching some coppers who'd just gone into Rosie's, where I was living. Then he clocked me coming under the arches so he's jumped in his motor, swung it round in the road, and managed to get to me before I got to the door. I didn't know what was going on but when he told me to jump in I did without even asking.

This wasn't happening every day, and if it wasn't for old Charlie I'd have been all right, but I got fed up living on my nerves and made up my mind to take the risk and move in with my mother for a bit. Some risk. I was arrested after two or three days, slung in detention for three months, then without even being allowed to come home, shipped straight overseas.

By the time the war was over and I'd managed to get back to the East End, Reg and Ron was getting themselves in the paper and making a name for themselves. But for a while the "write-ups" were praising them up and not knocking them back because they were following in the footsteps of all the other blokes in the family (except their old man) and had taken up serious boxing.

4.   The "two-ones"

Rita Smith

When I was born in 1936 the twins were about three years old, and Charlie would have been ten. Right from the start I was their little sister and that never changed for the rest of their lives.

I look back and can't help thinking that I grew up in the best environment anyone could have wished for. I had everything. My dad, Albert Filler, was the nicest man you could ever meet. He was quiet spoken, never raised his voice or hand to either Mum or me. He worked steadily all his life and loved us both to death, and I suppose what made him more special was when I compared him with the father the boys had.

Fortunately for all of us Uncle Charlie was away a lot, but when he was home and he'd been drinking I used to be a bit frightened of him because he was loud and violent.

My mother was what you'd expect a proper mum to be and her sisters were all the same. In fact because of the way we lived, all close together in Vallance Road, it was like having four mums. All the doors were open and I went in and out of each house as though they were my own. Whichever one was the nearest when anything happened to me – like falling over or knocking my head – that's the one I would go to for a plaster or a cuddle.

Nanny was on the corner and I spent hours and hours sitting by the fire with her, just listening to her talking about when she was a girl and stories about the family. I don't think I ever saw that fire go out. She had a large brown teapot that sat on a trivet next to the flames so there was always a cup of tea on the go. One day she asked me to put some water in this pot and when I took the lid off it was full to the brim with tea leaves – must have been there for weeks and weeks with her just topping it up without emptying it each time.

Then I had the boys to look after me or play with, and I looked upon them like real brothers. As soon as I got up in the morning, so Mum told me, I wanted to go and find the "two-ones" as I called them. They were so alike when they were young and most of the time I couldn't tell which was which, so in my mind they were one person.

Something else Mum told me that I would be too young to remember, was her, Violet and Rose were sitting in the kitchen when Reg came marching in from the yard, smacking his little fat hands together and saying proudly, "Done it. I've done it." When they asked him what he had done he took Mum by the hand, led her outside and showed her my pram that he'd tipped completely over, with me underneath. For him, getting on for four years old, it was a big achievement and he didn't see anything wrong in it at all.

Any other boys would've run a mile from a little girl following them everywhere they went, but if Reg and Ron did get fed up with me they never once showed it. Quite often they would come and find me and take me round the park to push me on the swings, or help me up the steps of the slide – always very protective, even at that age.

We all went to the same school up Dunbridge Road, called Wood Close. On the way there or back they would both hold my hand and make sure I looked right and left before crossing the road. If other boys were getting too rough kicking a ball around or tearing about, Ron would stand close behind me and Reg in front, making sure I didn't get knocked over. They didn't threaten any of the boys or become aggressive because they weren't like that then. In similar situations in later years, when the rough houses would be men, their protectiveness would be more intimidating.

With the three boys gone now, and in fact almost every one of the family I loved so much, I often sit and try to understand what went wrong with the twins. Every paper or book I have picked up over the last thirty years or so has branded them as evil monsters. Much of what they did I can't deny or defend – it never made me stop loving them, but often I thought the media were writing about two different people from the ones I knew.

It's difficult to come to terms with what was to happen when I compare it with the happy life we all shared in those early years. A time when they were more polite, more considerate and more caring than most other boys of the same age. I've seen them playing with dolls – not because they wanted to, but because they knew it would please me to join in. It makes me smile now to think how they both used to suffer in silence as I brushed and combed their hair, and stuck Kirby grips into their heads as I pretended to be a hairdresser.

Aunt Violet kept chickens at one time, and in the back yard was a disused run and little wooden coop. The three of us took this over as a den – put an old carpet inside and sat and read comics, and drank lemonade from my tea set. As we got older, but not too much, the twins would say to me, "You go and get some matches and we'll try and nick some fags". Then we'd sit there puffing away as though we were really grown up.

One day a voice came over the fence: "Before you lot go indoors you'd better chew on some of that mint, or your mothers will kill you." This was Aunt Rose and she didn't care about anything. As for the mint, that was growing all over the yard. I didn't just chew it, I swallowed a lot and was sick.

In the end my mum and Auntie Violet caught us when they spotted clouds of smoke coming out of the wire in the sides of the coop. No one worried about the dangers of smoking in those days so I think they were more concerned in case we burnt the shed down with us in it.

Reg and Ron were in their own house one afternoon. Violet was out shopping and they were sitting under the table on the cross pieces, with the table cloth right down to the floor, pretending it was a tent. My mum called in and with nobody being there, stood for a little while admiring how clean the place was. She was always talking to herself, so as she's looked round she's said, "Mm, very tasty – very sweet," then gone back home. Well, those boys couldn't wait until their mum came in so that they could tell her that Auntie May had come in and eaten a cake or something out of the kitchen because she kept saying it was very tasty. That gave them all a good laugh, but when I innocently told tales it caused a bit of trouble between the sisters.

I was in Aunt Violet's house and playing quietly on the floor while her and Rose were talking and taking no notice of me. Typical child, I was pretending to be engrossed in my dolls but really I was eavesdropping like mad to their adult talk. And were they giving this Dinah some stick. She was this; she was that – in all, a bit of a cow, and I was dying to know who she was. That evening I told my mother that my two aunts had been saying terrible things about a woman called Dinah – did she know her? I couldn't believe the way she reacted. "Know her? I effing well know her all right – that's me they were running down, and I'll effing well have them," and she stormed out. They came to blows over that and I felt really guilty. Later Mum told me that when she was a little girl cab drivers used to line up opposite her house. She was a pretty little thing and every time they saw her they'd sing that song "Dinah, is there anyone finer," and the name stuck.

Another time I was in Nanny Lee's with Uncle Joe when my mum came bursting in, hair all over the place and a swollen eye. Jokingly he said to her, "Who you been having six rounds with, sis?" She said, "You want to go and ask that effing cow next door [meaning Rose]. She did this." Next day it would all be forgotten and they'd be the best of friends.

When I think of the language I heard every day as a child it's a wonder my hair didn't turn curly. With a few exceptions everybody around me swore, but to be honest it was so much part of life I didn't take any notice. I somehow knew not to use the words myself, but accepted all the b—s and f—s that popped out in every conversation. My father didn't use it and I can't remember hearing Aunt Violet say as much as a "damn".

In that film, which we all find ourselves coming back to time and time again, they seemed to take the personalities of Rose and Violet and swap them over. There is a scene in the hospital where Violet gets aggressive and says, "You b—s are not keeping my Ronnie". And when we watched it we all said, "That's not Vi – that's Rose". I don't know why she was so different from all the rest, she just was.

This might be the same with most families, but the two people who seemed to keep us all together were Nanny and Grandad Lee.

At some point during the day every single member of the family would at some time call into their house, even if it was only for five minutes – and that includes those that didn't even live in that bit of road the locals called Lee Street. I think it gave us all a feeling of stability because where they were concerned, nothing changed. To open the front door if it wasn't already wide open, all you had to do was pull the key through the letterbox where it was hanging on a piece of string.

The dining room was very Victorian, which shouldn't be surprising, as that was the time they both grew up in. There were heavy maroon velvet curtains up at the window and matching velvet tacked round the mantelpiece with yellow tassels hanging down. Everywhere you looked were little china ornaments that would be called antiques today and be valuable, but then nobody thought of such things.

When she wasn't outside the street door saying hello to everyone that passed, Nanny would be beside the fire shelling peas or sewing. She always looked the same: pinafore dress on, dyed blond hair, with a bead necklace round her neck and big dangly earrings. Grandad would be opposite in his favourite armchair and sticking out of the fire between the two of them was always a big lump of wood. He said it wasn't worth the trouble of sawing up because it burnt just the same, but you always had to be careful in case you tripped over it. This firewood was often as much as four feet long and Grandad would just keep nudging it in with his foot as it burnt down.

Balanced on the arm of his chair he'd have his tin of Nosegay tobacco, and sticking up by the chair was a long thin gas pipe that was alight day and night. What he'd done was run this pipe from the gas stove and bent it to shape so that it was just at the right height for him to light his roll-ups. He was proud of that because he said it saved him a fortune in matches, but as it burnt twenty-four hours a day for years, the cost of gas must have outweighed the cost of matches at a penny a box. If the flame got blown out when somebody opened the door he'd eff and blind because he had to waste a match relighting it.

He was like that, always making or inventing something. It's only now that I think that none of us gave him the credit he was due. We just used to laugh behind his back and think he was a bit strange.

We all went to Margate one day in Uncle John's charabanc, and along the front outside the arcades were glass cases with mechanical dolls and clowns. Put a penny in and they danced to music. Every one we came to he'd stand sucking his one tooth and scratching his head. Days after we came back, he copied one of these things and it worked. No case or music, but the three little figures twirled round and lifted their arms up. I thought it was wonderful.

He could be so clever on one hand, then so silly on the other. Like the time he made up his mind to build himself a car in the upstairs bedroom – a full-sized open-topped metal car. He worked on this for months, clumping up and down the stairs with sheets of tin he'd cadged or found. As it took shape and he put seats in it everyone who called had to go up and sit in it. The twins and me spent hours taking turns at pretending to be driving it, or just watching him banging and snipping shapes out. We were too young to see the obvious, and he was so engrossed in seeing it finished that neither had he. But what the rest of the family thought and didn't want to ask him was how was he going to get it out of the room? Whether he thought they could lift it out through the window I don't know, but he got my cousins Joe, Billy and Charlie up there one Saturday to give him a hand, and it was only then that the penny dropped.

Wasn't his fault though, it was the "poxy hole he lived in – effing windows too small – effing door not big enough," and so on. The last we saw of it was on the back of the scrap man's cart, all broken up in pieces.

Something he did invent should have made him a lot of money, but such things as patents would never have entered his head. This was before I was born but Mum told me about it.

My Grandad Lee's sister, Aunt Poll had married Jim Jollie, who was the manager of a gum factory in Digby Road over at Homerton. I'm not sure what this gum or resin was but I know it came from abroad and they made glue and polish from it. My mum and Auntie

Rose worked there, but not Auntie Violet. What they did was sit in front of large trays and separate it into different sizes by hand. Grandad was often round there, so I suppose his brain started ticking over, and in no time at all he made a working model of a machine that would grade this gum automatically. Uncle Jim got to hear about this and brought his boss round to see it. Mum told me that they said it was very clever and praised him up for a well-thought-out piece of work but they couldn't see that it was possible for it to work on a larger scale.

In this factory there were obviously a lot of rooms but there was one that the girls were never allowed to go in. That was enough to make all of them desperate to get a peek in there, and one day when whoever was in charge left the door unlocked my mum managed to have a quick look. I can't imagine what they all thought was going to be behind this door, but whatever it was Mum certainly didn't expect to see a half-built, very much bigger version of the model gum grader that her dad had made.

She was really mad and when she saw her Uncle Jim she gave him what for, even though he was her boss, and told him she was going to tell her dad as soon as she got home. And she did. It caused no end of trouble. Grandad was angry and him being the way he was it's a wonder he didn't go round and "up" his brother-in-law, as he was so fond of saying. But for once he didn't and though he tried all ways he never received a penny from the firm and it must have earned them thousands.

Nanny's father, John Houghton, managed another gum factory in Kelday Road but this was a different firm entirely.

When I think of what Reg and Ron were to get up to in later years, hurting people and eventually killing a man each, I shouldn't really be surprised. One half of me can never accept everything that was said about them. I suppose I must be biased in their favour, but that's only because they kept that sort of thing away from me. My other half looks back at those early years, when they were children, at the violence and fighting that flared up in the family almost weekly. It seems to me that every argument within the family – no matter how trivial – was answered with fists.

I'm not making myself any better than the others, but when I think about it I was the only one who never did lift my hand to anyone. Perhaps I was shy or delicate, I don't know, but I was certainly the odd one out. Auntie Rose was the worst. There was some sort of upset with my cousin Joe – he hit Billy or threatened to – and Rose went for him. Uncle Joe stepped in and she grabbed a knife and tried to stab him. It was that sort of influence that didn't do the boys any favours because they idolized her, particularly Ron, so if she said this sort of thing was normal and acceptable, then they would follow it.

They weren't always the tough men they turned out to be, and if they got a punch or slap from some other boy while they were playing, Rose would egg them on to go out together and get stuck in. Even Auntie Violet, as kind and caring as she was, wouldn't allow herself to be put upon, and more than once ended up punching and pulling hair with my mum or Rose. I doubt the twins were even aware of what they were soaking up because it was just part of everyday life.

Rose got into an argument with old Charlie outside in the street. They were shouting and swearing at each other, and in the end Charlie took a swing at her – because that's the sort of man he was. He missed, but right at that moment cousin Billy came along, saw what was happening and punched him to the ground. As he went down his head hit the kerb, splitting it open and knocking him unconscious, though because of the blood they all thought he was dead. They carried him indoors and laid him on the floor, and all the while Rose was screaming, "Oh God, my Billy's going to hang because of that bastard". It didn't worry her that he was dead – only that her son would get into trouble.

For ten minutes he laid there without moving a muscle, then he sat up effing and blinding, went into the kitchen and put his head under the tap. He must have been concussed because for the rest of the day he just sat in the chair staring at the wall. That wasn't the end of it. His brothers Bert and Alfie got to hear about what had happened and told everyone they were going to do Billy over. Uncle Joe went after them and they swore they'd never said anything of the sort because they were frightened of him. Still word kept coming back that they were going to smash him up.

Billy was a right little tearaway but he was everyone's favourite. He got up to all sorts, but never in a nasty way. When Nanny Lee heard what they were saying she said, "I'll fucking well give them hurt my Billy". And she went down the market to sort them out. They had a stall down Brick Lane, and she caused a real scene. They told her the same story they'd told Uncle Joe, that people must have got it all wrong, but she said to them, "Listen, you gutless pair. If you so much as touch a hair on that boy's head I'll be back and turn this effing stall on top of you." One of our neighbours came in and told my mum that he'd been up the market and had seen what went on. He said, "I see Mother Lee up the Waste and cor blimey was she giving them Kray boys what for".

None of them seemed to have any time for the Krays, and Grandad often said, "They ain't worth two bob, not one of 'em". Although it was in the past and supposedly all forgotten, I don't think he ever came to terms with Violet going off with Charlie like she did.

I could never blame Ron, Reg or young Charlie for their loyalty toward their dad, at least publicly. Each one of them at some time or other wrote in their books that he never laid hands on them or their mother. Young Charlie was beaten unmercifully time and time again, yet he was the quietest, most gentle boy in the family, who only ever looked for his father's approval.

The twins, true enough, never took any real physical punishment from him, but the mental torment of things they were witness to must have gone a long way toward how they would eventually turn out.

When they were too young to understand why or be able to stop it in any way, they would have to watch as the mother they loved more than anything was slapped, punched and kicked by their father. But there was worse – much worse – and the shame for her and the horror it must have been for those boys doesn't bear thinking about.

But it wasn't just behind closed doors. When he was drunk Charlie didn't seem to care who saw him being a bully. I was in our yard before the fences were taken down, and Auntie Violet was standing on a box hanging washing out. I could see her head and shoulders and she was singing away to herself. I said "Hello, Auntie," and as she said, "Hello luv, are you all right?" an arm came up, punched her in the face and she disappeared. I looked through a knothole and Uncle Charlie was kicking her on the ground and shouting, "Where's my effing dinner?" I ran screaming in to my mum and she got Rose and they ran round and managed to stop him.

That wasn't a one-off. It happened over and over again. It really used to upset me, so what did it do to those little boys?

The strange thing was that he could be a nice man with a dry sense of humour, but inside he must have had something dark and nasty for it to come out when he'd had a drink.

My cousins never spoke of what went on and in later years buried it in their minds, but deep down they must have hated him. You might think that when they became "gangsters" as the papers called them, they might have sorted him out once and for all, but they didn't.

Ronnie walked into the kitchen one night just in time to see his mother taking a slap. He grabbed his father by the throat, threw him up against the wall and said to him, "It's because of you I hurt people. Because of you somebody else is going to get badly hurt." As though out of some misplaced respect he would do to others what he really wanted to do to his father.

Eventually he overcame whatever it was that held him back and beat Charlie up, telling him, "If you touch our mother once more we'll kill you". Whether or not his father thought he was capable of it, he never did hit Violet ever again – at least as far as we were all aware.

Toward the end of my aunt and uncle's life she hated him. She might have hated him since early in their marriage, but she kept it all inside and only shared what she felt in private with her sisters. But later on in life her dislike of him was open. He had a chest complaint that made breathing difficult and I've seen her deliberately shake a dusty cloth in his face to make him cough.

Almost sixty years too late, in his own way he tried to make up for what he'd done to Auntie Violet, but she would have none of it. She scorned and put down every little thing he tried to do, whether it was to buy a small bunch of flowers or maybe make a cup of tea. He brought everything on himself, but when I look at late photographs – and my aunt's body language says it all – in a strange way I feel sorry for him.

I often walk past where our little row of houses stood in Vallance Road, and it never fails to bring the memories flooding back. Grandad stuck up on the roof when the kids took his ladder away; coloured lights strung along the front of his house. With the fact that he painted it every few weeks, passengers passing on the trains that overlooked us must have thought it was a fairground. People would say to Nanny as she sat outside her front door, "Morning, Mother Lee. See the old man's been having a paint up again."

Everything's changed except the railway arches where we used to shelter from the bombs and laugh at Grandad as he sang and danced on a stage he'd made up, so we wouldn't be frightened.

In later years, Sunday afternoons were a time for being entertained by Grandad. Reg or Ron would give him some money and he'd be straight out of the door and up to Brick Lane to waste it on old and often broken musical instruments. An accordion with some of the keys missing, a violin with only two strings or a banjo that had seen better days. One afternoon he pushed a battered old piano all the way home then got it into the front room on his own. Then we'd all have to sit and listen to him sing and play for a couple of hours. He couldn't read music but it didn't matter what the instrument was, he could get a tune out of it.

If I've got time to dawdle I can stand on the corner looking and the "self-build" houses that are on the site now disappear and I can see our old places with the arched-top doorways as clear as anything. I can see all the posh cars lined up – Mercedes, Rolls-Royce, Jaguar – that the twins and their friends had. And I can see my mum, Rose, Violet and Nanny sitting side by side on chairs they've brought from indoors. Strangely enough the council pulled those old houses down and you'd never know they'd ever been there, yet they left the pavement just as it was. I played hopscotch on it and every one of my family walked on it. Almost all of them are gone now, so that gives me a little bit of comfort sometimes. Let in the paving slabs just up from the corner there's one of those metal water tap covers. It was right outside my mum's door so I'd always know exactly where she used to sit.

I know the new houses are only a few years old, but sometimes I wonder if the ghosts we had are still hanging around. They say we had gypsies in the family a long, long time ago, and most people know that they're supposed to have psychic powers. That's the only reason I can think of to explain why we used to see things and occasionally have premonitions – and I mean all of us.

I was in bed one night and in the light of the street lamp I saw an old man standing at the foot of my bed. He wasn't horrible or anything; in fact he was smiling. I pulled the covers over my head and told myself I was a silly cow and that I was imagining him, but when I looked again he was still there and we just looked at each other until he disappeared. You might say that it's quite normal for a young girl to dream something like that up, like conjuring up in my mind somebody I'd seen outside somewhere, but the next time it was someone who I could never have known. This time I was coming down the stairs and at the bottom stood a little old lady. She was wearing a black bustle skirt and a tight fitting jacket-like top with lots of buttons up the front. She had a cameo brooch at the neck and her hair was rolled up like they used to in the old days. I don't know why, because I'm not the bravest of people, but I wasn't frightened. Really it looked to me as if she wasn't aware I was looking at her. When I told my nan what I'd seen she wasn't a bit surprised. "Oh 'er," she said. "That's Mrs Doyle who lived in your place years ago. She's always turning up."

One early evening Auntie Violet wanted to get one of Reggie's shirts from upstairs but she heard noises and got a bit frightened. She went and got Auntie Rose and she came in full of her usual "I'll have them" sort of attitude, but for some reason she couldn't climb the stairs. Afterward she said it was like something was holding her back. In the end they asked a passing policeman to go up and have a look, which he did but he couldn't find anything out of place.

We lived with rats and mice all the time we were in those houses and we knew the difference between their scratching and scampering, so whatever it was it wasn't down to them.

Reg was haunted. Not by anything he saw in this case, but by the memory of the little boy that was killed by the van. A friend of ours called Alfie used to help the Wonderloaf man by doing little errands like running the loaves to the doors. He was only nine so it wasn't really a job – just something to earn a few pennies. I was playing round the side of an old shelter and Reg was talking to Alfie on the corner. The next thing I was aware of was the two boys running past me looking terrified and both crying. I thought some big boys had hit them, so I ran after Reg and followed him into his house. He was in a dreadful state and no one could understand what he was saying because he was hysterical. I still didn't know what was going on and eventually Auntie Violet and Rose took him outside. Mum made me stay indoors so I never did see what had upset him, but I was told about it later on.

It seems while the van driver was having a cup of tea in one of the houses the two boys had sat in the van and pretended to drive it. In those days you started motors with a button and when Alfie pressed it the van didn't start but it jerked back because it was in gear, and crushed a small boy against the shelter. He was killed outright. It went to court for an inquest and they ruled that it was an accident, which it was. To save his own neck or the firm's, the rounds man told Alfie never to tell anyone that he was working for him, so by that saved himself getting the sack and the firm from paying compensation to that poor boy's family. What seemed to make it worse for Reg was that the little boy was a twin, same as himself, though it was a boy and girl in that case. Not long after the mother moved away because she couldn't bear to walk past the shelter where it happened.

I don't think Reg ever got over that experience, and going back to talk of haunting and ghosts – for a long time he thought the boy might turn up in the house. More than once he'd ask me if it could happen, and I'd try and reassure him by saying that it hadn't been his fault in any way — he just happened to be there. Even the boy's mother didn't blame him but it never stopped him brooding about it.

Years later it would pop up in the newspaper saying "First killing at eight years old," as though this was the beginning of a career of violence. On the other hand over the years Reg and Ron didn't do themselves any favours with what they wrote about themselves. In a funny way they were like entertainers giving their public what they wanted to hear, whether it was the truth or not. How many times have I read lines like "We were right little sods," or "We were evil little bastards," and this referring to when they were little kids.

When they got older they became a lot of things. Selfish, manipulative, even arrogant, but always with one eye on the newspapers that loved to pick up stories of their violence and spreading the word that here were two men not to be messed around with. As far as the papers went, if it was one punch they'd turn it into a battle, or if it was to do with an empty gun they'd turn it into a war. But I'll never believe that the word evil could be applied to either of my cousins at any stage of their lives. Evil is Peter Sutcliffe or Brady and Hindley and people like that – not the twins, whatever they did.

So while they might have liked to put over that they were little tearaways as boys, to go with the later image, that's not what I or the rest of the family saw.

As I've said, fighting was actively encouraged. They saw it in the family and if it wasn't Rose telling them to "Go out and do the bleeders" if they'd been hit outside, it would be Grandad or Nan telling them that if they got punched once, then give the boy two or three back. At the end of the day it was only kids' stuff – a bloody nose or a red cheek.

I can't remember a time when they, or me for that matter, ever answered back to an adult or gave them cheek. It wasn't that we were frightened to, it just wasn't done. I don't remember respect being drummed into us; it just seemed the natural thing to do. Whatever might be said against the twins, no one could ever accuse them of being disrespectful to either the elderly or women – which is fortunate when you consider those boys were brought up in an atmosphere where their father actively demonstrated that if a woman stepped out of line she should be kicked or punched.

What wasn't encouraged in the Lee houses was stealing. Almost any book you pick up that deals with the East End gives the impression that everyone's "at it" as though we were all thieves. If any of us three swiped a bubble gum or a packet of Smarties and they were seen, indoors it was "Get that right back where you took it from – now". And that would be worse than anything to have to go into Mr Blewitt's shop under the arches and pretend we'd forgotten to pay for it. He knew – and of course we knew – but he never said anything because he was a nice man, and after that we didn't do it again, so it was a lesson. I'm not suggesting it didn't go on – I'm sure a little bit goes on in every family. What I'm saying is it was frowned upon most times.

I laugh when I think that the one you'd least suspect of being light-fingered did something right in front of me. I was out with my two aunties and we came past the furniture shop near our house. Rose said, "See that lovely plant stand – I reckon that would look smashing in my front room". We all looked at it then walked on. Auntie Vi said, "Hang on a minute," went back to the shop, picked up this stand and came back to us. "'Ere you are Rose – a little present." When Rose said, "You cow – you never paid for it," Violet said, "Well it was stood on the pavement – expect he was chucking it out anyway." And they both laughed. I didn't say anything; I just thought, "Ooer – she shouldn't have done that".

Billy though was an exception, and because of the way he was, everyone expected it of him. Because his dad had left home when he was only a baby his mum, Auntie Rose, had to go out to work, what with being a one-parent family, so he was virtually brought up by Nanny Lee. She loved him to death and he couldn't do wrong in her eyes.

We were all sitting in her front room one evening about half five, and we heard this banging and crashing coming down the road – sounded like old tin cans being thrown about. Then the door opened and in came young Billy with kettles and pans all tied on string and hanging from both shoulders. He'd nicked them from where he worked. The whole family had a share of this tinware and Nanny kept saying, "Oh, isn't he a good boy?" The next job he had was with Howard Ward Lighters, and everyone in the street ended up with two or three lighters from their stock. He used to stutter a lot and I'm not surprised – his nerves must have been in shreds with what he got up to.

Then there was the story of Grandad's weighing scales – the ones he never paid for, and we all knew it off by heart. He might be reading the *Gazette* and he'd comment on some local thieving or other and say, "Little bleeders – want their effing hands cut off". If Uncle Joe was there he'd wink at us and say to him, "What about them scales then?" Grandad would get all huffy and we'd burst out laughing because it happened time and time again.

Even those on the other side of the family, the Krays, weren't thieves or villains. Uncle Charlie's brothers were dealers the same as he was, and I suppose there was always the chance of something a bit iffy, but generally none of them were bad people. Yet because of that name (that most of them have now changed to Gray or something like) and our relationship as Lees, a lot of people assume we're all part of Reg and Ron's gang. Nothing could be further from the truth. Again with his writing Reg hasn't helped the way people think. He has said, "The only way out of the East End was either by sport or villainy," and he's not the only one to trot that out. Famous actors from around here often put in magazines or on the telly that if they hadn't taken up acting they would've ended up in prison because there was no other way. I suppose that makes them seem tough or colourful, but my blood boils when I hear this and I feel like shouting, "What's wrong with hard work?"

Grandad Lee came out of awful poverty, like it was in the old days, yet not only did he work from the age of thirteen, he was still working at the age of ninety. True, he might have been more of a hindrance than help at that age, particularly when he helped out a local builder. As Uncle Joe said, "You'd be better off paying him to keep away from your house". But whatever, he was prepared to roll his sleeves up because he just didn't know how to stop working.

Uncle Johnny, Uncle Joe, Cousin Joe and Cousin Billy – I can't list all the names of the family that worked hard and made something of themselves, and none of them ever in trouble with the police. My own two children, both born in Bethnal Green, have never caused me a day's worry, and I brought them up on my own. David works in the banking business and my Kimmy, who Reg loved to bits, used to be a children's nurse but now she's a housewife.

My own dad, Albert, should have been an example to Reg, Ron and Charlie, because unlike other men in the family who moved away, he was right under their noses proving that regular work pays the best dividends in the end. His life wasn't exciting or glamorous, but he loved my mum and me, gave us a good stable home and managed to put a bit by out of his wages. They say crime doesn't pay, which I don't think is strictly true, but in the times that it didn't, who did the boys turn to when they were short of a few bob? My dad, of course. It might only have been fives and tens, but he had to work hard for that money and most of the time he never saw it again. It wasn't that he was a soft touch; he just couldn't see anyone go short when he knew he had the cash to help them out. Not a lot of it, mind you, because his wages weren't all that, but they were regular and he didn't waste it on drink or going out.

Years after the twins and Charlie were sent to prison Auntie Violet came to him with an old cine camera she'd found in the boys' bedroom. Which one it belonged to I don't know, but she was very short of money and wanted to sell it. If she'd come to dad without this camera he would've given her money, but leaving her with self-respect he made out it was just what he wanted and would she take a hundred pounds for it? Realistically the camera must have been worth about twenty pounds, and Dad needed something like that as much as a kick up the behind, so he was doing Auntie a favour. Nothing was said but he knew she wanted the money so that she could pay her fare to three different prisons and take her boys tobacco and a few bits of toiletries.

As soon as she went out the of the door Dad put it into the back of a cupboard and it stayed there without seeing the light of day until after he died. It was only then that we discovered that there was a film inside it. When we had it carefully printed, because it was old and cracked, there was footage of my cousins, Nanny and Grandad and my Aunts. In fact it was the only piece of film with the twins on that was ever kept from the old days, apart from a few minutes they both did on a television programme.

Like it or not Reg and Ron were very famous by the time this film came to light. Famous for all the wrong reasons as far as I was concerned, but people out there couldn't get enough of them. So in a way these images from when they were young should have been worth a fortune, but Mum was no businesswoman and, same as my dad, if somebody asked for the coat off her back she'd give it without question – and throw in a pair of shoes as well.

Somehow word leaked out that this film existed and one of the television channels came knocking on our door very quickly, with the result that they got an exclusive and rare piece of history if you like – and Mum got a one pound coin for something that should have been worth thousands. A pound coin, when at that time a packet of soap powder would've cost more than that. She put it in the back of her purse and it was still there when she passed away.

Going back to hard work, the twins were willing and quite capable of getting their hands dirty on honest labour, at least when they were young, but their father discouraged it. In any other family it would be the complete opposite, with fathers insisting their kids get out there and do something – but not old Charlie. "You don't want to work for a guv'nor, they're taking the piss." Or, "You don't want to get out of bed for peanuts". That's what he drummed into the twins. They tried their hand at all kinds of work but in the end Charlie's sneering at their efforts made them think he was right, so they stopped trying.

The first work I can remember them doing was helping their other Grandad on the clothes stall he had. This was only at the weekends because we were all at Dane Street School by then. I was still following them about wherever they went and when my mum said it was OK, which was most of the time, I'd go with them. The twins must have been sensible in my mother's eyes because she never worried about me when she knew I was with them. Not when I was a little girl or when I was an adult. Yet with her granddaughter, my Kimmy, she worried every time she went out of the door because she didn't have the same protection.

Reg and Ron would call for me early on a Sunday morning and we'd walk up to Jimmy Kray's house in Gorsuch Street to sort out whatever he wanted taking to his stall. I thought the boys looked ever so much grown up in their working clothes, though looking back they must have looked like extras from the film *The Magic Box* – which I think everyone knows that Ron had a small part in when he was about eleven. Long trousers, cloth caps and scarves round their necks. They were trying to look like their grandfather and every other man in the market.

Up in the bedroom there'd be piles of clothes and shoes, and I loved the smell that hit us as we walked in – all musty, mothballs and lavender. I don't think I was much help because all I wanted to do was try on old skirts and high-heeled shoes, or wrap fox furs round my shoulders. It's a wonder I didn't catch something because who knows where all this stuff came from. The boys though would carry armfuls of clothes downstairs and heap them on a barrow. When it was full I'd climb in the middle and we'd set off for Brick Lane, which was only across Hackney Road and through a few back streets.

Other than Uncle Charlie I never really got to know the Kray family because with one thing or another the Lees had fallen out with them years before – or the other way round. But speak as you find, I thought that Jimmy Kray was quite a nice man. If he came across a fancy hat while he was sorting out his stock he'd stick it on my head saying, "Cor, don't you look a smasher". Or if a colourful child's dress or coat came out of the pile he'd give it to me (though whatever it was would mysteriously disappear five minutes after showing it to my mum).

Late in the afternoon when most of the clothes were sold old Jimmy would pay the boys from a biscuit tin of loose change. I don't know what he gave them but every time without fail he'd walk away then say, "'Ere, nearly forgot little blondie," and he'd come back and give me sixpence. Then it was a ride back to Gorsuch Street without any clothes under me to soften the bumps. Ron would be pulling the barrow at top speed and I'd be hanging on for dear life until Reg, who was always the more thoughtful, would shout "Oi, Ronnie, hang about, you'll have her in the road".

While then, and for a lot of years after, you could hardly tell them apart, their personalities were quite different. It is difficult not to colour the past with everything that's happened since, because as I've said, those boys were as normal as any of the others we mixed with. No worse, and often better behaved than most of our playmates. But when I think about it Ron was withdrawn some of the time, which makes me think that perhaps he was more affected by what went on behind closed doors than anyone realized. He wasn't in Reggie's pocket, nor Reg in his, and he liked to spend time on his own; though when he wanted company it was Rose he went to because I think she understood him. I know he liked me and he often said so, but he was never as close as he might have been, and I don't put that down to what he'd say later in life about girls being no good and a waste of time. If he did have something inside him then that would eventually turn him gay, I doubt if he was even aware of it, and none of the rest of the family were either.

Reg, on the other hand, spent a lot of time in my company as children and as teenagers. If I was in our yard he might call over the fence, "Is your mum and dad in tonight?" If I said no, he'd say, "I've bought a new record. I'll bring it round later." So round he'd come and we'd play records and dance to the big band sound that was all the rage, or we'd just sit and talk. He always spoke quietly and while he did he'd look straight into your eyes, and I've always thought that a sign of someone you can trust.

Something else: he was a good listener and showed interest in whatever it was. I mean a lot of the time I must have talked about fashion and about this boy or that boy, and he never seemed to get bored or try to cut me off. In a lot of ways I think he was a bit insecure – which sounds strange when I think of how many people only see him and Ron as tough men – but people who are confident in themselves don't need to prove anything. They just get on with their lives and are quite content.

Reg talked all the time about what he would do once he became a world champion boxer. He'd buy us all new houses. Fur coats for all the women, cars for all the men. He'd move into the country and keep animals, and so on. I know it was just a young man dreaming, but from what the family said and what was printed in the sports pages of the *Gazette* and *Advertiser*, I really do think he could have done it.

He loved me and he trusted me, but he never said anything about what he thought of his dad. He knew that I knew what Uncle Charlie got up to, and I always thought that one day he'd tell me how he felt – but he never did, which was a shame because sharing something like that with someone other than Ron, who was in the same boat, might have got a lot of anger out of his system while he was young. As it was he kept it all inside and I think it came out in a bad way when he was a man.

When Reg left school and started work with a local builder, he bought me a present out of his first week's wages. He came round on the Friday night before he even got changed because he was covered in this black tarry stuff, and stuck a bag in my hand, a little embarrassed. When I opened it there were four sets of doll's clothes. I was ever so pleased but I couldn't help laughing and said to him, "You never went in the shop and got these on your own?" He said, "Course I did, but I didn't know what ones to get so I got all they had". After that he was always buying me little things. So did Ron, but not so often.

Later on Reg used to wait outside where I worked to walk me home, and he'd always have some gift or other. One of these was a beautiful powder compact with a tiny watch set into the centre. Not expensive, but at that age you didn't consider price. I might still have had it forty-eight years on except when I was married to Ritchie Smith he thought nothing of selling my bits of jewellery when he needed money for drink.

Reg often met me when I came out of work and seeing him waiting for me those girls that didn't know he was my cousin would be saying, "Ooo, isn"t he lovely," or "I'll have him when you're finished with him". And sometimes worse things because I'm talking about East End girls now. He was handsome though, and I felt quite proud, even though he was just family.

When I went anywhere between the two of them I felt the same and I knew people, especially girls, were looking and thinking, "Look at her – lucky cow". They did look impressive even before they started wearing all those flash suits. Mind you, I think they both knew what impression they gave. One on his own was enough, but put two mirror images together and who could help but look.

With hindsight it's always easier to look back and put a finger on various reasons as to why the twins started to go wrong. Was it because of how their father acted? Or Grandad's endless stories of villains and fighters. There was a stream of these people in and out of the houses in Vallance Road, and to two young boys what these got up to must have seemed very glamorous and exciting. They were all big tough men who didn't care about anything – people like Wassle Newman and Dodger Mullins – but what they didn't tell those kids was that they had hardly spent one Christmas with their families until they were old men. No one made any allowances for a young girl who might be listening (pretending as usual not to), and their conversations would be peppered with "Effing cozzers" and "I upped this effing copper". And the twins must have thought that this sort of talk from grown-ups made going against the law almost acceptable.

Then there was Auntie Rose, who hated the police because of the way they treated her when they were raiding the houses looking for Uncle Charlie or cousin Joe when they were deserters. I've seen her in an upstairs room, with the twins giggling behind her, waiting for a policeman to walk by so that she could shake a dirty rug over him. I mean it was funny at the time, like a harmless joke, but it was only in later life that I thought this wasn't a message to give to impressionable boys.

So when they got into trouble at about twelve years of age, they must have thought their aunt and all the other men must have been right all along, especially when they didn't feel as though they'd done anything wrong. Reg and Ron and another boy named Ronnie had been camping out near Epping Forest, which was only a few stops on the train. On the way back, messing about like boys do, Reg fired an air pistol out of the window as they went through a station. Somebody saw him do it and when the train came to the next stop the railway police were waiting for them.

It was something and nothing. I'd seen this gun they had and it was just a cheap little toy that couldn't put a slug through a piece of paper. I know because they used to shoot things that were hanging on the washing line in the back yard. Anyway, the ones that caught them handed them over to the real police, and after taking them to the station brought them home. Then they had to wait weeks for it to come up in the juvenile court. Never mind sticking their noses up to the law in later years, right then the two of them were really frightened. Not outside with their friends, I don't suppose, but indoors they'd be saying "What if we go to prison?"

Auntie Rose had a right go at the coppers, telling them they should be out catching real criminals and not upsetting little kids; though she put it a lot stronger than that.

In the end our school priest spoke up for them and nothing came of it. Might have been a fine or something, I can't remember.

Another time the police gave them a really rough time over somebody they were supposed to have had a fight with. They swore they had nothing to do with it but still these two policemen took them down Leman Street and kept them there for hours before letting them out. I'm not just saying this in defence of my cousins, but I know they wasn't involved because I was with them in the café in Wentworth Street when it was supposed to have happened. As it turned out Reg and Ron knew the two boys who had done the beating up, but they never said a word – even to get themselves out of trouble. I think at that time they were more bothered by that sort of treatment than they let on because often they used to say, "Why do you think the police pick on us, Rita. Is it because we're twins?"

Somebody with a bit of respect for the law would've changed their minds very quickly after being pushed around for nothing, but the twins had very little to start with so you can imagine things could only get worse.

5. "They wouldn't do anything like that"

Rita Smith

I was always clever with a needle – most women were when I was a girl – so when I left school I applied for and got a job as a trainee to become a royal seamstress. I couldn't believe my luck because it sounded so posh and couldn't I hold my head up when I mentioned that "royal" bit. My dream of making something really special of myself only lasted until the week before I was supposed to start. The job was up west and having given it some thought my mother said, "No. I'm not having you travelling up there." I cried, I sulked and stamped about. I went to Nanny and my aunties and pleaded with them to put a word in for me but Mum still said, "No. It's not right a young girl rubbing shoulders, and whatever else, with all those men on the train every day. Tell them you can't do it."

I told some story about ill health and on the Monday, instead of sewing buttons on Queen Mary's best frock, I was pedalling like mad on an old sewing machine in Mr Gold's factory in Underwood Road.

After I got over my disappointment I was happy enough and well thought of, but after a while I moved on to work for another Jewish man, Mr Stirling and his wife, who had turned their big house into a sort of factory. They must have liked me as well because Mrs Stirling came up to me one day and gave me a lovely gold brooch, but told me not to tell the other girls. Somehow this escaped being sold off or pawned by Ritchie and I still have it somewhere around my flat.

We knew it was coming because all boys grew up either dreading the thought of being separated from their families, or looked forward to the experience as a bit of an adventure, yet when Reg and Ron's call-up papers arrived for National Service I can remember feeling quite upset. They had mixed feelings. On the one hand they didn't want to leave the comfortable security of Vallance Road, but at the same time, as they were at an age when they spent a lot of time out and about getting up to whatever young lads do, they didn't want this to end either. On the other hand they knew that everyone said that while you might go in as a boy, two years later you'd come out the other side as a man – and that was something they'd always aimed for.

Ronnie's only thought was that he'd be able to get his hands on the guns he'd always been fascinated with.

I didn't want them to go at all because we were close and they'd been a part of my life since day one. I looked on them as big brothers and I knew I'd miss them. I know I cried the night before they left, but they both kept saying two years was nothing and they'd get lots of leave and would be able to take me up west every time they came home. That helped a bit and we said our goodbyes that night because they had to be at the Tower of London for six in the morning. A lot of the girls at work had boyfriends in the army, with being the age they were, and they told me that after the first six weeks they came home almost every weekend, so that cheered me up as well.

I got home latish that night and Mum asked me to pop round Auntie Violet's before I took my coat off because she'd run out of sugar. I said we had a full bag that morning but when she said she'd been baking I didn't give it another thought and went out of the door. Imagine my face when I walked into Auntie's and there were the twins sitting at the table with big grins on their faces – Mum had set me up. I didn't know what to say first – what; where; why, and they couldn't stop laughing. When they eventually told me that they'd got fed up and walked out I said, "I thought you had to wait six weeks. Didn't they mind?" and that made them laugh even more. Auntie Violet looked like she'd just won a prize and kept looking at them as much as to say, "Aren't they lovely, my boys".

I started to get worried when they told me the police would be looking for them because I knew what it was like when cousin Joe hid out in Auntie Rosie's house, so when a neighbour from down the road knocked on the door my heart nearly stopped. I couldn't believe how those two treated the whole thing like a joke, and it was a long time before I realized that as far as they were concerned that's exactly what it was.

From the moment they both walked out of the Tower they knew they would be back in a very short time. They knew it wouldn't be long before the police or MPs arrived, and that's why they were sitting with their mother instead of hiding out somewhere. It was showing the authorities that these two East End boys couldn't be pushed around, and it was like I was seeing a side of them that I'd never seen before. Why it took so long I don't know, but it wasn't until seven the next morning that the police came and arrested them and took them away in a Black Maria.

That was March 1952 and they didn't come home properly until March again in 1954. I say properly because unlike most of the young lads who went in the army and accepted whatever it was they had to do and got normal leave and all that, Reg and Ron spent almost all their time fighting the system and either being locked up or on the run.

Different from the first night when it was just a bit of fun, every other time they showed up in Vallance Road they didn't want to be captured, so only came in the early hours when it was dark. Even then they didn't stay very long. A few good meals, hello to all of us, then they'd be off again without telling any of us where they were going. Half the time I don't think they knew themselves. What those two years was all about and what they got up to, I don't really know.

Being their little sister in a way, they knew they didn't have to impress me with stories of how tough they were. The men in the family got all the details but when it came to me they spoke as though it was one big laugh, and with always being a bit innocent, I believed them.

At home it really was strange with them not being around, but as they say, "Life goes on," so we carried on the same as we always did.

I haven't said much about my cousin Charlie, but with him being ten years older than me he always seemed so grown up, so obviously I hardly spent any time with him at all. Later in life that gap in years closes up to nothing and then I got to know him much better, though I was never quite as close to him as I was with the twins. He was so unlike his brothers that if you didn't know better you'd think he was from a different family.

While there was a spare room going at Auntie Violet's, Charlie had moved in with his wife, Dolly, and their little boy, Gary. Apart from that there were very little changes in our daily lives.

I only saw Ron once in the last ten months of his service and that was when my boyfriend Harry Skinner took me to see them in the army prison at Shepton Mallet. I didn't see Reg at all, not even on that visit, because then I think he was in solitary or something, though why the two of them weren't locked up together I don't know. Harry and me were taken in to see Ron and he was sitting with his friend Dickie Morgan and behind them all up the wall was brown stuff that I hoped wasn't what it looked like. When Ron saw me looking at it he laughed and said, "Don't look so disgusted, Rita, it's only cocoa. I slung it up there to piss them off." Something else he'd done to piddle them off from what I could see was that he'd only shaved one side of his face. He did look funny. He said that he was appearing in court first thing in the morning and that they'd get the message that they didn't worry him at all. It was a bit upsetting to see him locked up and in such a state, but at the same time he still had his sense of humour so things couldn't be that bad.

Cousin Joe took Auntie Violet and Uncle Charlie to see them a few times, but I never got the chance again because what with me working, my days off never seemed to coincide with the days they were going. The boys both wrote to me every week and I spoke to them on the phone three or four times I think, and every time, even after all they'd been through they still said, "Don't worry, everything is fine". So when they did finally come home I wasn't prepared for the change that had taken place in such a short time.

They seemed very confident; they'd filled out a lot, and they seemed much older than I expected after only two years. I suppose they were just as surprised to see that I had grown into a woman, but then from sixteen to eighteen dramatic changes happen to girls. So with them studying me and me doing the same to them, we were like strangers for a while. That soon passed and in no time at all we were having a laugh, the same as we always had.

Well, not quite the same, but almost as near as we would ever be to those younger days. Ronnie seemed much more dominant than he used to be. Before, one would suggest something and they'd do it – or it would be the other, and more often than not they'd have the same idea at the same time. Now it seemed it was always Ron that was saying, "We've got to do this, Reg," or "C'mon, Reg, we're going out". And Reg wouldn't argue or question whatever it was. I'm not saying he was being ordered about because nobody could do that – it just seemed he was quite content to go along with whatever his brother suggested.

I'd look at Ronnie with this new-found confidence and think to myself that it only seemed like days ago he was marching up and down outside the house with a wooden sword over his shoulder and a toy gun tucked in his belt, oblivious to everything. Billy would watch him out of the window and say to Nanny, "Look at him out there – he looks a right effing idiot". She'd get all upset and say "No, don't say that. He looks like a little soldier."

But those days were long gone and would never come back. I don't think they had any great plans for what they wanted to do with themselves. Reg had the idea that he should get back into boxing so he stopped smoking and started going out for early morning runs and down the gym with Charlie, but his heart wasn't in it and he gave it up after a few months and joined Ron, who'd been sitting around doing nothing since their release.

The only money they had was when they could borrow off anyone who had some to spare, my Dad usually. I was earning a wage but they would never take a penny off of me, even when I offered – male pride, I suppose.

It was about this time I started meeting men they had been mixing with for years – a lot of them not very nice people, though I wouldn't realize that until much later. I took people at face value without knowing anything about their background, so when I was older and might mention a name in conversation, whoever I was talking to might say "Ooh, wasn't you frightened?" Then they'd tell me that this one or that one was a terrible gangster or a murderer, but it wasn't like that.

One of these men I met was Jack Spot, who the twins called "Spotty" behind his back. I must have been very naïve because I'd never heard of him, even though at that time they say he was running all the criminal business in London. I was in the café in Wentworth Street where I'd gone to meet Reg and as I walked in the door and stood looking round, this man sitting with my cousin said, "Hello, green eyes. Come over here a minute." As I walked over I heard Reg say, "That's my cousin," and Spotty's manner changed because until then I think he had ideas of chatting me up. Mind you, he was good looking in a film tough guy sort of way, especially with the scar all down one cheek. On top of that he wore a grey trilby hat, which he took off when he spoke to me (I thought that was very polite) and in his hand a very long cigar. He was interesting to talk to and we chatted for a while, and that was that really. Rita Filler meets Gangland Legend, but I never thought of it like that, to me he was just another friend of Reggie's.

Another man who Reg and Ron introduced to me should really take some of the blame for the path those boys were heading down. Bobby Ramsey was about eleven or twelve years older than they were and they'd met him when they were sixteen. In a lot of ways he must have been everything they hoped they'd become. He'd made a good name for himself as a boxer, dressed really smart and drove around in a big red American car. What the boys must have known but I didn't was that he worked for the gang boss Alfred Dimes and was up to all kinds of things with London gangsters. He was a tough ex-boxer and I suppose he was just the man they needed when it came to a bit of violence or intimidation at the race tracks. Thankfully, he never involved the twins in anything bad; at least nothing that ever came to light. But he would eventually, and as far as I'm concerned that would be the beginning of the end for my cousins – particularly Ronnie. Before this though Bobby took a fancy to me.

Today I have to look at old photographs to remind myself just how nice looking I was back then. I always dressed well and with my green eyes and very long blond hair I shouldn't have been surprised that this much older man should pester and pester to take me out. I was flattered because he was very handsome – even that boxer's nose he had gave him that rugged look that women can't resist. Trouble was I knew my mother would kill me if she knew how old he was. Then, like Reg used to do, he waited outside my work and gave me a tortoiseshell handbag and a ring with a large pearl set in it, which wasn't really the way to my heart because I hated the look of both of these gifts. But he stood there looking so pleased that he'd pleased me that I gave in and said I'd go out with him. He took me to a show at the Hackney Empire and we had a lovely time. I must say, tearaway or not he treated me like a lady and behaved himself.

He told me later that he'd asked all different people where would be a nice place to take me because he'd never been out with a decent girl before, which I thought was very sweet. He took me to the races a few times, dancing up the West End, and was always buying me bits and pieces. And I have to say, whatever reputation he had or was going to get he never did anything out of place with me and was always a gentleman.

But I never did intend our relationship to go anywhere, especially what with Mum keep asking who this boy was who wouldn't pick me up from the house. Then one day when I was passing our local tailors the Jewish man who ran the shop came out and told me that he'd seen me a few times with Bobby Ramsey, and as a friend was warning me that going out with a man like that could only end in trouble for me. I took his advice but only because I'd already made up my mind to finish it. Bobby didn't take it too well but I just made a point of keeping out of his way.

Some time later a couple of boys of our own age invited me and my friend to a party. As we walked into the flat, over the fireplace was a big photograph of a boxer. I said to somebody, "Who's flat is this?" and they pointed at the picture and said, "His – Bobby Ramsey. He's gone out for some beer." We took off as fast as we could.

I think the twins had a lot of respect for Ramsey, and were even in awe of him, otherwise they would not have let him approach me; which was something again I wasn't aware of at the time – just how protective if not possessive of me they were behind the scenes, particularly Reg. I say they were possessive, but I think mainly Ron went along with what Reg did. As far as he was concerned he was only ever possessive about his twin.

I'd go dancing with them both, not that I ever saw Ron take a girl on to the floor. He'd just sit there glaring. Reg was a good dancer and we'd have a good time doing the foxtrot or that Latin American dance. But if we spent too much time together, laughing and messing about, Ron would dodge through all the people and say to me, "You've got to go now, Rita. It's getting late." This might only be ten o'clock, but rather than let me argue he'd get me by the arm and walk me towards the cloakrooms. And Reg let him.

Ron butting in like that happened quite a few times, and naïve me again, never gave it too much thought at the time. I should've wondered why he didn't like us getting too close, but I didn't, and nor did I consider that he was seeing something that I'd missed completely.

I accepted that Reg loved me like he would a sister until one night we were sitting indoors. As he got older he got more serious and didn't go in for making silly remarks. He sat and looked at me for ages until I said, "What's the matter? Have I got a spot on my nose?" "No," he said, "no, I was just thinking that if you weren't my cousin I'd marry you." I can't remember what I said, probably "Thank you, sir," or something like that to turn it into a joke, but he didn't laugh. Just said, "Time I went home". He never said anything like it again, but it did make me think.

I didn't realize what a reputation they had by now nor, as I said earlier, how much they were looking out for me. If they didn't think someone was suitable to take me out, he'd get a warning to stay away, and in my ignorance I'd be left wondering why I was only asked out for one date.

I was at a dance one night and a man came up to me and started to make a nuisance of himself; nothing too serious and I wasn't particularly worried, but he kept touching a necklace I was wearing, which I thought was getting too personal. Reg had seen what was going on and came over. And this is how he fooled people, because he never raised his voice and was polite. He asked the man to go away, but because he wasn't shouting or angry the other man didn't take him seriously and told him to piss off. Still very calm Reg led me away, called a cab and I went home. Somebody told me that as soon as I'd left Reg walked straight over and knocked him unconscious. The following week this man was made to stand in the middle of the dance floor and publicly apologize to me. I felt really sorry for him.

When the twins had their clubs I often overheard different things because not everyone knew who I was. Men might say to each other – quietly I have to say – "I could do them two midgets any day," or "Don't those c—s fancy themselves," and I'd be thinking, "Ooh, please don't hear this, Reg and Ron," because though they shouldn't have been saying things, they were somebody's sons and I knew what could happen to them.

I went out with one young man two or three times. He was quite an ordinary sort of person and not involved with gangs or tearaways or anything like that. One night after he'd taken me home he set off walking home because he didn't have a car or nothing. As he went up Eric Street and was just going to go past the billiard hall, a big hand came out of the darkness, grabbed him by the throat and dragged him inside. I won't say what he told me that he nearly did, but I gathered he was a big frightened. He was taken into a back room, sat in a chair surrounded by all these fellas, then Reg and Ron came in demanding to know what his intentions were toward their cousin. Whatever answer he came up with must have satisfied the boys because I went out with him for quite a while. Though why he didn't run a mile after an experience like that I'll never know.

When I said to the twins, "What did you have to go and do a thing like that for?" they just said, "We're looking after you. There's a lot of nasty people walking the streets."

Another time I was walking down Wentworth Street with a young chap and he said to me, "What would your cousins do to me if they saw me out with you?" I said, "What do you mean? What are you saying?" He said, "Oh, I was just a bit worried they might do me over". I couldn't believe it. I told him, "Reg and Ron are nice – they wouldn't do anything like that". And I'll always remember he gave me a funny look that didn't mean a thing at the time, but would later on.

People might think it's a bit strange when I say that I didn't really have any idea of how they were thought of then. What do people imagine they were like indoors and to the family? "Hello Mum, I cut a man's face last night!" "All right, Rita? Just smashed a fella's jaw in the club!" It never happened, and no one could expect it to. We knew they were tough and knew they got respect because of this, but don't forget all our lives we'd known men that got the same. Only now do I know that a lot of the men that sat in our house drinking tea were really terrible villains, but growing up with them being friends or at least acquaintances of the family, I looked on a lot of them as almost uncles.

The first time I saw Reg strike someone in anger as an adult just reinforced the fact that there was a side to these boys I didn't really know. I was looking out of my bedroom window one night, just as it was starting to get dark. I saw a man bending down and doing something round the bottom of my dad's car. I ran downstairs and asked dad if someone was mending the car and when he said no, I told him what I'd seen. He said, "You stay here," and rushed outside to confront this man who was still there. Dad wasn't that big and as far as I knew not a fighter, but he did have "bottle", as they say. It turned out this big man was trying to steal the hubcaps, and then put them on his own car that was parked just up the road. There was a scuffle as the man ran off and tried to get in his car, but Dad pushed him away, leaned in and grabbed the keys – so there was going to be a fight. Mum wasn't in and I was leaning out of the front door shouting, "Come indoors, Dad, quick".

Then Reg came walking down the road, hands in his pockets – really casual. I couldn't hear but Dad told me after that Reg never got wild or nothing. He just asked what was going on and when he was told, said to the man, "Right, first I want you to apologize to my uncle, then I want you to get in your car and never show yourself round here again". By this time the man must have realized who he was dealing with, and though he was much bigger than Reg he could hardly speak to Dad because he was so worried and relieved that it wasn't worse. He put the hubcaps back on, said sorry to my dad, then as he turned to go Reg said, "Just one more thing," and hit him full in the face and knocked him over the bonnet of the car. He was still lying there even after they both came indoors.

Then the twins and a few others got into some serious trouble. And this is what I meant when I said Ramsey was no good for them, because what happened was all down to him.

It seems that a gang of men who were called the Watney Street Mob had beaten up Bobby Ramsey. When he wanted to get his own back he came looking for Reg and Ron to help him out. I remember him coming that evening because I saw his car pull up from our window, and I thought I'm not opening the door because I thought he was looking for me. He wasn't, and he went next door. The next thing he drove off with Ron and Billy Jones, who I knew vaguely. I had no reason to think that this was anything other than a boys' night out. I was just a little bit surprised that Reg wasn't with them – until he came knocking on our door in the early hours to tell us that Ron and the others had been arrested.

He didn't know all the details, but he kept walking up and down the room saying, "Those effing guns. I've told him they'd be trouble." And that wasn't like Reg at all because he never used words like that in front of me or any of the women in the family. I didn't know Ron had guns but he did have lots of knives and a couple of old swords in their bedroom. I didn't like them much but a lot of people collect that sort of thing so I never thought there was anything sinister about it.

I got a shock the next day and Reg got a bigger one when about ten policemen came and arrested him as well. Afterward they came back and searched Auntie Violet's house and Nanny's but didn't come into Rosie's or ours. One of them went to open a cupboard door and Nanny said, "You don't want to go in there, it's full of mices". And he shut it quickly and went downstairs. Could've been full of guns for all he knew, but he wasn't going to look.

Auntie Violet was quite upset by the whole thing and cried after they took Reg away. She kept saying, "The police must have made a mistake. You read about that sort of thing, don't you?"

Once they were bailed and back home I learned what had happened. The three of them – not Reg – had gone after two men to have a fight. They couldn't find them so attacked the brother of one of them, Terry Martin. Bobby Ramsey had stuck a knife into him, and that really shook me when I thought I'd gone out with someone who could do such a thing. Ron hadn't really done anything, but when they were stopped by the police they found a gun in his pocket and that was taken very seriously even back then.

Over two months they had to wait before it went to court, and I'm sure I worried about it more than they did. Reg and Ron had a lot of arguments about what had happened, and nearly came to blows one time. But it seemed that the arguments were not so much about Reg being dragged in by the police when he was innocent, but more about why Ron had got involved without him. Perhaps if he had, the gun might not have been taken because Reg was never into using weapons. He often said, "If someone can't look after themselves with just their fists, then they should stay at home and keep out of trouble".

The day they went to the Old Bailey I was at work, though I might as well not have been because I kept making mistakes with my machine because I felt sick. I went straight to Auntie Violet's when I finished work, and as I walked in the door I knew the worst had happened. Uncle Charlie wasn't there but my aunt had the front of her pinafore pulled over her face and was rocking backward and forward, while Reg sat at the table as white as a sheet. He tried to say something and it wouldn't come out, then he managed, "Three years, Rita. He's got three years." Well, I just burst into tears. I walked round the table, put my hand on Violet's shoulders and my arm round Reg, and we all cried. I wouldn't look at his face though, not even when he let go and went into the kitchen and splashed around under the tap. That way we could pretend that he hadn't let his guard down and shown what men think of as weakness.

As Reg hadn't been involved in the affair at all, it was obvious he had to be acquitted. Well, you would think it would be obvious, but he said it had been touch and go; what with lies and false statements being put forward by the prosecution. Yet instead of being pleased that he was free he seemed to feel guilty that he hadn't been sent away with his brother.

In twenty-three years the only time they had been separated was when they were in hospital as babies, and neither of them could remember that anyway. So we all wondered how they were going to get through the next three years. They were so close, they really were "two-ones" as I used to call them. They even had the same dreams.

In that film about them the producers made out that these dreams were all fanciful, with birds flying high above clouds, or something that was obviously out of their imagination rather than that of the twins. But unless they had something like that and never mentioned it, from what I remember they were very ordinary. Even so it always made the hair on my neck prickle as first Reg would tell us about his dream, and then ten minutes later Ron would repeat it word for word. At first I told them they weren't kidding me with their little joke, but when they both swore on their mother's life they were telling the truth, I had to believe them, because like the rest of the family they were too superstitious to lie with that at stake. Those dreams, and lots of other little things, became part of our lives where the twins were concerned.

Like when they were small, Ron might graze his knee out in the yard and Reg would start crying indoors for no reason at all. Or Reg might be limping after being kicked playing football, and in no time Ron would be unconsciously doing the same. It never went away, even when they grew up. One of them would walk in the room and say something, and five minutes later the other would come in and say exactly the same thing and then wonder why we all laughed.

I suppose this has all been explained away by psychologists, but when you live with it year after year, it's certainly strange.

It's often said they even had their own language, but the truth is it was a way of speaking that was quite common in the East End. I think it was known as back-slang and really when you understood it, it was so simple you wouldn't think it would fool a child. Yet when it was spoken fast as the twins did you'd be surprised how effective it could be. What you did was take off the first letter of a word, put it on the end and add ay. So Rita would be Itaray, gun would be Ungay or punch, Unchpay. Usually this language was used in front of children who couldn't keep up with it, though I've heard Reg and

Ron talking to each other in a club and the puzzled looks on the faces of the other people was hilarious.

I really did think that Reg might have a breakdown when Ron was sent to gaol, because in those first weeks he wasn't himself at all. When he wasn't visiting the prison he'd just sit around smoking. He was scruffy and unshaven, and seemed to lose interest in the billiard hall, no matter what any of us said to try and get him out of himself.

Ron was in Wandsworth so it was no hardship to visit him whenever we could. I think I cried every time I went because I hated seeing him caged up like an animal, especially when he hadn't really done anything to deserve such a long sentence – unlike Ramsey. But he was always cheerful and seemed to be coping well, so that helped us all, particularly Reg, who started to come out of his depression and get closer to cousin Charlie. Apart from their shared interest in boxing, the twins didn't normally have a lot do to with him, but that's probably quite normal in any family when there's a seven-year age difference.

Now they started spending a lot of time together and whether it was a deliberate plan to take Reg's mind off of Ron or just one of those things that happen, Charlie found an old house in Poplar and suggested they both turn it into a club. Charlie put the money up, which might sound as though he was well off, but in the late fifties a run down place in east London could be bought for a few hundred pounds. They couldn't afford to get builders in, so at some point over the next six months every one of us in the family got roped in to clean and paint the place up. Eventually it opened and I can remember feeling really proud that my two cousins were proper businessmen. I never counted the Regal because that struck me as just a place for men to hang around in, but this was different and seemed to be earning them a lot of money.

I don't mean it in a nasty way, but being separated from Ron seemed to do Reg the world of good. He was different somehow – relaxed and friendly and without that scowl on his face that we'd seen too much of over the past few years. He hadn't forgotten Ron though. Not only was he very much part of this club, even though he'd never seen it, Reg named it the Double R and I know that really pleased Ron.

They had two men on the front doors to keep any troublemakers out. One of these was Tommy Brown, and he was a lovely man. He must have been about six feet six, very broad and he had a boxer's face, so of course no one would ever argue with him. Yet he was one of the most gentle men you could meet. The other one was big Pat Connolly, and he stayed overnight in our house once.

I was getting ready for bed and I had a funny feeling that I was being watched. Mum was already in bed and Dad was at work. Anyway, I had a quick wash at the sink, put on my pyjamas and ran upstairs and got in with Mum, as I always did when we were on our own. I'd forgotten my glasses but no way was I going back down to get them. Mum said, "What's up? Is Mrs Doyle about again?" I said, "No, I've got a feeling someone's down there". Then we heard a window open and our little Jack Russell ran to the top of the stairs and barked its head off.

We just clung to each other really terrified. There was a bit of banging then footsteps running up the passage and out of the back door. I think we sat up in bed for about two hours until we thought it was safe, then I ran down the road to get Grandad.

It was funny when the police came after he phoned them, because this young constable looked at a photo of the twins on the wall and said, "Who'd be silly enough to break in with them two about?" He must have known who they were but didn't mention Ron being in prison. Whoever had broken in stole my handbag, took out my purse then threw the bag away. But what he didn't get was the takings from the Double R. I don't know why but Reg used to give my mum bundles of cash to look after for him until he needed it. She kept it in a biscuit tin, and luckily the person hadn't opened it because it was only on the sideboard. Reg was really angry and he told Mum he was putting one of his men in to look after us because he knew burglars often came back after a few days.

That night Pat Connolly turned up with the idea that he would sit by the door until Dad came home. What a night we had. He gave up on the chair, stretched out on the settee and for the rest of the night he snored, he shouted and he yelled out in his sleep. In the morning Mum said to him, "You was supposed to be protecting us and you was asleep". He said, "No, May. It might have looked like I was asleep just because I closed my eyes but I was ready for anything." Mum told Reg to take him away, saying she'd rather have the burglar than that bleeding racket all night.

But then we had something more to worry about other than Ronnie being locked away. Auntie Rose came to my mum one day to ask her advice about a rash on her arms that she couldn't seem to get rid of. Why she asked her was because Mum always had a nice skin and people often commented on it. Even Nanny had said to her one time, "'Ere May, what do you put on your face 'cos it's always nice and smooth". So Mum said, "I rub in a bit of zinc and borax cream every night". Nanny's given her a strange look and said "Ooer, that's a funny name for a cream innit?" Mum said, "No, not really; you can get some at Boots the Chemist. So during the week Nanny's gone to the chemist and asked for some of that there "zinc and bollocks" cream. Imagine what she said to Mum when she came home?

As far as the rash on Rose's arm was concerned, Mum told her that it was probably caused by nerves because she had been really upset about Ron.

Apart from his mother first and Reg second, Aunt Rose was closer to him than anyone else could ever be. She seemed to understand his need to be different and encouraged him when he wanted to talk about his heroes like Lawrence of Arabia or Gordon of Khartoum, without laughing at him like Reg or Billy did. And I don't know, but it wouldn't surprise me if she knew about his sexuality years before any of us others even suspected it.

When Nanny insisted that she went to the doctors to get something for the rash that hadn't cleared up, he sent her to the London Hospital. A week later she was diagnosed with leukaemia. Today this illness is serious, but in most cases curable. Then it was just a question of how long you had left. I can't begin to say how we all felt – devastated sums it up in one word. Rose, so full of life; so fiery and so generous. If she had half a crown, two shillings was for anyone who needed it, and often they didn't even have to ask. Remember, she'd been a single mother since Billy was a baby but every Friday when she got her wages, she'd buy something for the twins and she did that right up until they were teenagers.

We daren't tell Ron because he couldn't have taken it in his situation, and when he questioned why she wasn't visiting we told him she had a bad hip and couldn't travel. We thought that with time off for good behaviour, and he was a model prisoner, he would be out long before the end, and being with her he might come to terms with it. She went in and out of hospital, each time getting weaker and weaker. They couldn't do much for her anyway, so Nanny and her sisters decided they would nurse her at home. They set up a bed in the sitting room at Nan's, but apart from at night it was a job to keep her in it as weak as she was. She never gave up though, and on good days would do housework or go round the shops.

I'll give you an example of the spirit she had and of how tough she was. For some time she had been going out with a local villain by the name of Jimmy Stannard. In fact he'd moved in with her for a while, though that didn't last. None of us thought much of him, although he wasn't half as bad as his brother Ted, who the twins looked on as some sort of hero because he'd served seven years in Dartmoor for slashing a man's face. Auntie Rosie's brother Joe was always telling her to get rid of this Jimmy, but being the way she was she did just what she wanted to do.

She must have fallen out with him because when he called in to see her one Sunday morning with his sister, she told them both to "eff off", with the result they both set about her – though the sister had more to do with that than her brother. When Uncle Joe heard about this he went after him. And although this man might have thought he was as tough as his brother, when Joe got hold of him he couldn't apologize enough.

In fact afterward he went to Rose and said how sorry he was, that they'd both been drunk and it would never happen again, and so on. What makes me think that he hadn't been too much out of order that morning was that Rose let it go as far as he was concerned, but told us that she was going after the sister.

With the influence she'd had over Ronnie for years and years, it's no wonder that he picked up the attitude that even the smallest slight had to be punished. No matter how many times we told her that she was ill and shouldn't be thinking about such things, her answer was always the same. "I'm going to bleedin' well 'ave 'er for what she done." It had to happen.

She was out with Auntie Violet and Mum and she did look awful. As they got to Bethnal Green Road by the butcher's on the corner of Maker Street, Stannard's sister and another woman came out of the shop. Rose saw her and said to her sisters, "Right, she's for it now". They tried to stop her but she ran at this woman shouting, "Come in my house and start punching away, you cow? Now it's your turn," and hit her full in the face. All along the front of the shop were egg boxes laid out on the slant, and she fell backward into the lot of them. Rose jumped on top of her and punched her again and again – about half a dozen times. The man from the greengrocer's a few shops down came out and said to Violet, "Make her pack it in; she's ruining that man's stock." And though he was very big and used to be a boxer, Auntie Violet of all people told him to mind his own business or she'd put him in the eggs as well. He went back to his shop.

When Rose had finished the Stannard woman's face was all bloody and she was crying, but Rose just dusted her hands off and told her that next time she'd get even worse.

There was never a next time though, because she died about three weeks later. A fighter all her life and right up to the end.

As I said, we'd all hoped that Ron would've been out by the time this happened and we could all have supported him. It didn't work out and Reg had the terrible job of breaking the news to him. We were surprised that he took it as well as he did. Being the man he was there was no way he was going to break down and cry in front of the prison officers, though that's what he must have felt like doing. Instead him and Reg calmly discussed the funeral and what suit Ron wanted bringing in to wear on the day.

If Rose had been his mother or sister, there wouldn't have been a problem. As it was aunts didn't come into the category that would have allowed him escorted leave for the day, and they turned down his request.

REGGIE –
He had the skill and
temperament to have
been a champion boxer,
but chose another path.

RONNIE –
He was a slugger who
wore down his opponents
with brute force. Note
the different ways they
tied their laces.

REG AND RON – Already beginning to look different.

ROYAL ALBERT HALL

Manager - - - C. S. TAYLOR

JACK CAPPELL PRESENTS AN INTERNATIONAL BOXING TOURNAMENT

TUESDAY, DECEMBER 11th 1951

Doors open 6.45. Commence 7.30. Matchmaker: JOHN S. SHARPE

10 (3-min.) Rounds International Lightweight Contest at 9.11

TOMMY **McGOVERN**
Lightweight Champion of Great Britain. versus
ALLAN **TANNER**
(British Guiana). Sensationally defeated Ellis Ask, Tony Lombard

8 3-min. Rds. Welterweight at 10.10 | 8 3-min. Rds. Bantamweight at 8.9

JACKIE	CHRISTIAN	RON	JIMMY
BRADDOCK v **CHRISTENSEN**	**JOHNSON** v **CARDEW**
(Manchester)	(Denmark)	(Bethnal Green)	(Holloway)

8 3-min. Rds. Middleweight at 11.9 | 6 3-min. Rds. Welterweight at 10.9

JIMMY	JIMMY	LEW	CHARLIE
DAVIS v **JAMES**	**LAZAR** v **KRAY**
(Bethnal Green)	(Trinidad)	(Aldgate)	(Bethnal Green)

8 3-min. Rds. International Cruiserweight Contest at 12.10

JOHNNY **McGOWAN** v ERIC **JENSEN**
Central Area Champion Light-heavyweight Champion of Denmark

6 3-min. Rds. Lightweight Contest | 6 3-min. Rds. Lightweight Contest

REG	BOB	RON	BILL
KRAY v **MANITO**	**KRAY** v **SLINEY**
(Bethnal Green)	(Clapham)	(Bethnal Green)	(Kings Cross)

PRICES: 42/- 30/- 21/- 15/- 10/6 5/- 2/6 Special Ringside 63/-

Betting Strictly Prohibited Rights of admission reserved

Tickets from: PHIL COREN (Box Office Manager) GER 1742
Jack Cappell Promotions (GER 1742-3-4) Royal Albert Hall. (Ken 8212)

BOXING PROGRAMME AT THE ALBERT HALL –
The last time the three brothers would fight on the same card together.

BILLY WILTSHIRE (*third row*) AND GEORGE CORNELL (*bottom*) in Malta doing their National Service. When this picture was taken, George Cornell could not have possibly imagined that over twenty years later he would be one of the most famous murder victims in British criminal history.

BILLY WILTSHIRE, RITA AND MAY

A YOUNG CHARLIE KRAY (14th September 1942).

MAY, RITA AND VIOLET

RITA, RON AND REG – In Nanny Lee's back yard. Reg is holding his brother Charlie's son Gary, then aged two.

RITA SMITH – aged 18

ALBERT FILLER –
Although only related by marriage, he willingly took on the problems of his wife May's sisters and their boys. Although only earning a working-man's wage he never refused any request for financial help from any of them.

VIOLET, REG AND RITA – In the Double R. They made a nice couple. Hardly surprising that Reg told Rita that he would have married her if they had not been cousins.

MR AND MRS RITCHIE SMITH —
When Rita married Ritchie he was an honest,
hardworking man. Unfortunately this was not to last
after he started mixing with the wrong crowd.

VIOLET AND MAY – On a day out in Southend.

CHARLIE AND VIOLET – Her smile for the outside world
hid her true feelings about her marriage.

RONNIE – catching the sun with a friend

RONNIE – With some of "the firm" outside the club.
Unlike Reg and Charlie, Ronnie had little interest in
making a business of club life.

GRANDAD LEE – Whenever the twins gave him some money he'd take off to Brick Lane market and waste it, invariably on broken and tatty musical instruments, which he still managed to get a tune out of.

VIOLET, A YOUNG FRANCES AND GARY –
Frances looking very much the teenager she was.

CHARLIE AND VIOLET KRAY – Must have been a good night, he's smiling for a change.

CHARLIE –
Enjoying himself – honestly.

RONNIE WITH CHARLIE'S SON GARY

CHARLIE, SON GARY AND REG

How he felt inside himself, or in his cell at night, we don't know, but on the surface he accepted the decision. Then a tiny incident tipped him over the edge. As a mark of respect, and the only way he could see to mark the passing of his beloved Rose, he asked to be allowed to wear a black armband. This was refused as well, and he went completely berserk. He smashed up his cell and attacked officers, and from what we were told it took five men to hold him down while a doctor injected him with Stematol.

Weeks later I went to see him with my auntie and Reg, and I wished I hadn't. He was unshaven and puffy faced, and his eyes were vacant. When we spoke to him the only answer we got was either a nod or a shake of his head.

On the way home Auntie Violet said, "I thought he looked a bit rundown," as though she was blanking out that he looked close to death's door.

I blamed the prison authorities for the state he was in. If only they had shown a little bit of compassion – bent the rules and allowed him out, or simplest of all had let him wear that armband – the rest of his life might have been changed.

As it was, an example of how callous they could be came in a brief official letter not too long after. Auntie Violet and Uncle Charlie both came round to my mum clutching this letter and not really understanding what it meant, though it was plain enough. As cold as you like it said, "Mr and Mrs Kray, I regret to inform you that your son Ronald Kray has been certified insane". No explanation, nothing, apart from telling them that he was being transferred to Long Grove Hospital. Violet's answer, as always, was to keep saying, "There must be some mistake," while Charlie tried to laugh it off by saying, "Ronnie knows what he's doing. Loads of blokes did it to get out of the army."

Nanny and Grandad weren't even told – they wouldn't have understood either, and if they did it would only have upset them.

As for Reg, he wouldn't accept what they said at all and like his dad put it down to Ron playing games with the authorities like when they were in the army prison. At least that's what he said to us all. But Nanny told me that he'd asked more than once what exactly had been wrong with his great grandfather, almost as if he was worried that there was something in the family that might come out in himself one day.

6.   The Double R

Rita Smith

I said before that life goes on, and in my case I got married to Ritchie Smith and we moved into the top two rooms at Mum's house, number 174. When I first met him you couldn't have found a more ordinary working man than he was. He knew the twins and a lot of the sort of people they mixed with, but that wasn't for him. All he wanted was to work hard at the timber yard and come home at night.

Years later friends of my cousins would say to me that while they were Jack the Lads, suited up and standing around on street corners, they'd see my Ritchie trudging home from work in heavy boots, with a lunch bag on his shoulder and wonder about his mentality. He'd have a word with them and all that, but they couldn't understand how anyone would rather get their hands dirty working for a boss, when they could be like them – up to all kinds to raise money, and hanging about with their friends.

I suppose it was too good to last and what changed him into someone I didn't know was when he got a job in the docks and started mixing with what you could only call real villains. When he was eventually made redundant and given a lump sum of money, the combination of this, those men and a liking for too much drink changed his life and mine because then I found myself in a similar position to my Auntie Violet.

Isn't it strange how things repeat themselves in families? After what I'd seen I always vowed that no man would ever treat me badly, and there I was putting up with abuse after drunken abuse and accepting it for the sake of my two children. They say, "Don't judge a man (or woman) unless you've walked in their shoes". It was only then I understood why my aunt had been so protective of Uncle Charlie, even after he did the most horrible things to her. A lot of people wanted to give him a really good hiding but she wouldn't let them. And here was me, the favourite little sister of two of the most powerful men in London (not that I knew it then), and I couldn't tell them – daren't tell them because of what I knew they would do to Ritchie.

The final straw came when he made me sit in a chair while he held a loaded shotgun to my head from midnight until he fell asleep at six o'clock in the morning, allowing me to grab the gun and throw it down the rubbish chute. Afterward he was sorry as usual, but I was worn out with it all and wanted him out. Even sober he could be nasty, because before he left he said to our son, David, after he'd had another last go at me, "Don't look at me wishing you were bigger and could have a go, 'cos you'll never be that big".

The only way I managed to get through those bad days was with the help of my friend Jenny Crossley. I know I had my family to turn to, but sometimes I needed someone my own age to talk things through with and she was always there for me. Some time later, when the situation was reversed and she was having problems, I was only too pleased to be able to do the same for her. She's died since and I still miss her, but I would just like her two daughters, Julie and Daryl, to know what a nice person I thought their mother was.

A long while after he showed how different he'd become from the hard working young man I'd fallen in love with – he did an armed robbery and went on the run.

By this time Reg and Ron were in prison for life, and suddenly I got a small taste of what they'd been up against since they first got into trouble as boys. I was arrested, along with my Kimmy and David. I had nothing to do with Ritchie nor the kids with their father, but that didn't stop the police from taking us all to Leman Street and treating us like criminals. Kimmy, taking after my Aunt Rose, had a little bit too much to say for herself, which was understandable as she hadn't done anything, but even so a policewoman gave her a hard slap round the face and told her she was just like her father.

You wouldn't think innocent people could be treated in this way, especially in Britain, but it happened and made me understand why so many people I knew had no respect for the law.

But back then as we worried about Ron, all that was a long time in the future.

A few months went by and Reg called in late one night. He'd been to the hospital that day but instead of being down like he usually was, he had a big smile on his face. I said, "You look happy. Ron must be doing well." He laughed and said, "Couldn't be better. He's out." I couldn't believe it. "That's a bit short notice. Why didn't they let us know? Is he with your mum?" He just laughed again and said, "They couldn't tell us he was coming out because they didn't know themselves until a few hours ago, and now he's somewhere they'll never find him". Then he explained how he'd changed places with him and Ron had walked out. He went on to say that he wouldn't tell me where he was hiding in case the police forced it out of me when they turned up, which they did early next morning.

So once again all of us had to suffer policemen tramping through the house and looking in cupboards that a cat couldn't hide in. We should have been used to it because this sort of thing had been going on since Uncle Charlie first deserted – but we never came to terms with having our private things being pulled out and tossed around.

Later Reg told me that Ron was safe in a caravan at Sudbury with Teddy Smith, and was loving every minute of it. I knew he loved the countryside and I was happy for him, but worried that the police might hurt him when they caught him, because in the papers they were saying he was a violent madman.

We all wanted to go and see him but Reg said the police were probably watching us, though if he could he'd try and bring him up for a quick visit. So you can imagine how we felt when they both turned up at a party we were all at in Tottenham. I didn't know what an insane person was supposed to be like, but as far as I could see it was the same old Ronnie. A bit fatter but apart from that he seemed really well, and obviously had got over his little breakdown.

What I couldn't have known was this was the last time I'd ever see the Ron that I'd grown up with.

Reggie's idea in the first place was to keep Ron out long enough so that when he went back in he'd no longer be classed as insane. Charlie had found out that anyone who'd been certified had, by law, to be re-assessed if they could live normally outside for over six weeks. It must have looked very simple because they never believed he was mad in the first place. But as time went on I think they both realized they'd made a mistake.

From making a big joke over having pulled a fast one on the law, or laughing about this and that Ron might have said or done on a visit to the caravan, Reg seemed to go quiet over the whole business.

Everything was going well with the Double R, and him and Charlie were getting on better than they ever had. But every time he came back from Sudbury, which was about twice a week, he looked more and more worried. Until one day he said to me he thought he'd have to bring Ron home, whatever the risks, because he was acting very strangely. I knew that Reg had been getting different kinds of pills to take down to Ron, but as these weren't prescribed who knows what they were doing to him.

A few days later Reg came upstairs and told me that he'd brought Ron home in the small hours, and would I go and sit with him. He was in my mum's house with the idea that being there would allow a small breathing space should the police turn up at Auntie Violet's.

For his sake I didn't cry when I walked in the door and saw him huddled on the settee. I'd been warned that he probably wouldn't know who I was, but he said "Hello Rita. You all right?" In a few months he'd gone from being Reggie's double to someone I'd never seen before. He wasn't fat; he was bloated and his eyes bulged out of his head. I didn't know what to say or what to do, so I sat beside him patting his hand, and every few minutes he'd say, "You all right?" as though it was the first time he'd seen me. Mum just sat there with tears in her eyes, and Reg looked green, as though what we were looking at was his fault – which in a roundabout sort of way it was, though I'd never have said so. Reg stayed for an hour, then had to go back to the club, but when he said ta-ra to Ron he was told to "eff off out of it", and that must have hurt him.

For days and days we all took turns at sitting with him because he couldn't be left on his own, but if Reg thought being with his mum and family was going to make him better, it wasn't working.

Mum lit one of those radiant paraffin heaters one morning. Ron was watching her with those blank eyes he had at the time, and as it popped and the red glow flared up, he jumped up screaming and ran out of the front door. When we found him he was hiding behind the counter in the sweet shop, with his arms over his head and crying uncontrollably.

Mr Blewitt, the owner, was crying as well because he'd known the boys all their lives and thought a lot of them. His daughter had been coming home late one night when a man started following her making rude remarks. Ron happened to come along and escorted her until she was indoors, then went after the man. I don't know what happened but I'm sure he didn't accost ladies ever again. Mr Blewitt never forgot that and the twins could do no wrong in his eyes after that.

When Ron wasn't following us around the house asking if we were all right, he was crying or mumbling to himself that he was going to kill someone. These ranged from the local vicar (who he thought the world of) to some boy who'd hit him when he was at school. It couldn't go on. He was getting worse and it was tearing the family's heart out.

In the end we all got together when he was knocked out with sleeping pills, and so that the decision wasn't only Reggie's or Charlie's, we all decided that he had to go back to hospital. In one way it seemed like we were betraying Ron, but on the other we could see it wouldn't do him any favours to keep him out.

The next day he was picked up and taken back to Long Grove. It was heartbreaking to see him being led out of the house with a look on his face like a lost boy, but it could only be for the best. In hindsight Reg agreed Ron should never have been taken out in the first place, but he didn't learn a lesson from it because later on him and Ron would both do the same with Frank Mitchell, and everyone knows how that ended up.

Within weeks of getting proper medical care Ron was stabilized and sent to Wandsworth as an ordinary prisoner, and less than a year later was back home. But we could never turn the clock back and he'd never be our Ronnie again up to the day he died.

I couldn't believe the famous people we were rubbing shoulders with at the club. There was us, the most ordinary people you could find, brought up in falling down old terraces, chatting to celebrities like we'd always known them. Judy Garland, for instance, even then was a super superstar, and I found myself sitting next to her. The first thing she said to me was, "I just love your jacket. I noticed it the minute I walked in the door." Her outfit must have cost more than my year's wages, and she was admiring my jacket that was less than twelve pounds in Marks and Sparks. She also said, "Y'know, I wish my daughter was here. I think you two would get along fine."

I won't mention all the names but because of what I thought of as "those two shy cousins of mine", we felt we were celebrities as well.

Looking back, though, they must have been like Jekyll and Hyde, because I honestly never knew they were anything else but how I saw them. At least up until the papers started to print stories about them, and even then I thought what they said was exaggerated.

Then it was Reggie's turn to be sent to prison, and though it never made any difference to how I felt about him or Ron, I have to say it opened my eyes to the fact that perhaps I'd been missing something over the past few years. Somehow the shock of him getting eighteen months for demanding money with menaces didn't seem as great as it was when Ron was sent down. I shouldn't say it but really there was no shame when one of the family was. None of us were criminals but a lot of people we knew were, whether petty or otherwise, and there was always someone going in or coming out all our lives. Also Reg seemed to make light of it, saying he'd be out in less than twelve months and he could do that standing on his head.

What he hadn't allowed for was while he was out on bail he'd fall properly in love for the first time in his life.

He came to my flat one evening and quite honestly he was hyperactive. I was trying to make a cup of tea and he was up and down and in and out of the kitchen. The kettle wasn't boiling quick enough for him because he wanted me to finish and sit down, so it was obvious he wanted to talk. I'd hardly sat down before he said, "Rita, you won't believe this, but I've just met the loveliest girl you've ever seen". I asked him who she was and he said, "Frank Shea's sister". I went, "You're not serious, Reg, she's only a baby". Because the last time I'd seen her she was wearing a gymslip and white socks. But he got all defensive saying, "No she's not, she's nearly sixteen," so I didn't say any more because he wouldn't have listened anyway. I'd never seen him like that before. He'd been out with lots of girls and was always the centre of attraction when there were women about, but none of them ever put him in that state before.

He took her out a few times then he had to go back to prison, and from what he wrote to me it was painful for him because he desperately wanted to be with Frances.

When he was released in the summer of 1961 he made straight for her parents' house in Ormsby Street before going home to see his mother, and that was really out of character for him.

We had a small family party the following night to celebrate his coming home, and I was introduced to her properly. I had to admit it to Reg that no, she wasn't such a baby as I remembered, but a very pretty young woman. She struck me as being painfully shy, but then meeting all of us at once must have been a bit daunting – bearing in mind that while she looked like a woman she was only a child.

In some ways Reg and Frances were very much alike, and I'm saying that from the point of view of the Reg I knew and not the public face he showed everywhere in London – but not at home. When he was relaxed and felt he could let his guard down among family and behind closed doors, he could be very vulnerable. He was also insecure, and I often think his tough-guy front was a way of hiding this. Quiet in his manner and in the way he spoke, he often gave the impression that while he was talking to you on one level, his mind was somewhere else altogether.

Frances shared all these things. What made them different was while Reg could put on a front that hid the real him from the type of people he mixed with, she couldn't. What you saw was what she was.

I don't think Ron liked her from the beginning. He was always polite to her, but that's not the same as being friendly and it seemed as though at every opportunity he was looking for ways to spoil things between them. And it didn't take long before him and Reg were having blazing rows about her. I think if Reg was having one-night stands, or a girlfriend for a week or two, Ron wouldn't have bothered in the slightest, but he saw what they had together and knew it was going to become permanent. Quite simply he was jealous that anyone could become closer to his brother than he was, though I'm not sure it was as clear as that in his own head.

We were all aware by now that Ron had no time for women because he said it often enough, yet for some reason he separated us in the family from those outside. He'd say to me, "Girls are no good. All they want is your money," completely unaware that he was talking to one. So while it was no secret that he had a down on females, we didn't think of him as gay. Queers, as everyone called them then, were not as common as they are today, and the ones we were aware of (and I had a good friend that was gay) were effeminate and "limp wristed", you know, like Kenneth Williams in the *Carry On...* films. Our Ronnie was nothing like that at all. Even the pretty-looking boys that he always had hanging around him in the club didn't make us think. Again, a strange thing to say about someone as supposedly frightening as they say he was, he never really grew up and could be quite childlike sometimes, so we just assumed he got something from their youth.

His humour, when he cared to show any, was very simple. His favourite joke was to stand talking to Grandad Lee and either jingle the loose change in his pocket or carefully count the notes in his wallet. Grandad would sit there like a dog waiting for crumbs to drop from a biscuit, and then Ron would say "Gotta go, see you," and walk out of the door. Grandad would say to anyone with him, "That Ronnie is the greediest bastard I've ever come across," and then Ron would come back in. "Sorry, Grandad, nearly forgot," and he'd give him some money. Then it changed: "God bless you, son. Ronnie's all right, he is." Time after time he did this and never tired of the joke.

Most of the time, and especially since he'd been ill, humour wasn't his strong point, so when one of the young vicars from the Red Church asked me to help him wind Ron up one day, I had my doubts if it was a good idea.

David and John were different from any vicars I'd ever known. They were both good looking, trendy and always out for a laugh. If we had parties they'd come along and dance all night long and drink as much as anyone else. Years later when people said to me, "Have you seen that young vicar in *EastEnders*? Not real to life is he?" I'd say, "He's just like those two I used to know".

Anyway David came over one day and just as I was leaving Mum's to go home he stopped me and asked if the twins were indoors. When I said they were, he laughed and said, "Right, you go in and tell them somebody's just driven off in their Mercedes". Knowing how Ron could be if you caught him on a wrong day I told him I'd better not, but he coaxed me along until I thought, "Oh, why not?" I walked into Auntie Violet's and Ron was dozing in the armchair and Reg was on the phone. I said to them what David had told me to and they knocked me over in their rush to get out. Ron was shouting he'd kill the bastard before he got out of the door. Reg saw the funny side of it when he saw the vicar leaning against the car, but Ron looked as though he was going to hit him and I'm sure it was only respect for his collar that stopped him.

Not too many years ago I bumped into one of my old Sunday-school teachers in Bethnal Green Road, and she told me that she'd just had a letter from this David, who was now working in Zambia. He'd said in his letter, "Say hello to Rita Lee when you see her. She was my pin-up when we were younger." I'm sure I must have blushed when I said to her, "I didn't think that was allowed". She laughed and said, "No, they couldn't get married but they're still men all the same, and that doesn't stop them thinking".

For the first year they were together Reg and Frances were inseparable, but what was bothering him was Frances kept putting him off whenever he mentioned getting married, and that must have taken some doing because he could be very persuasive when he wanted something.

My Kimmy was just a baby and I used to watch him play with her and think he'd make a really good father one day. If she was awake the first thing he'd do when he came in was pick her up and cuddle her. If she was asleep he'd hover around waiting for her eyes to open. I used to dread his knock on the door because I knew he'd walk in with the biggest teddy bear he could find, or a swing – and one time a full-size rocking horse, and my room couldn't fit anything else in.

I was so tight for space I put the horse in the only clear space I could find and that was right in front of the window. I mean it was perfectly safe otherwise I'd have moved it myself, but as Kimmy threw herself backward and forward on it, Reg would get all worried and stand by her in case she rocked straight out of the window. Most of the time he acted like he was a father himself. He loved feeding her with a bottle and making all kinds of soppy noises while he was giving her a cuddle. When she gurgled at him his face lit up, but if she cried he'd ask me quite seriously if I was sure she liked him.

I'm sure that was one of the reasons he wanted to get married, and he often said that one day he'd have two or three babies just like Kimmy. The other reason was less romantic. He loved Frances to the point of obsession but he was very possessive and jealous, and in his mind he thought the quicker she was legally tied to him the better. When she wasn't there he'd say to me, "She keeps saying she's too young to settle down – I don't understand". I'd say things like, "Well, she is a little bit," or "Give it time, Reg," to stop him brooding on it. What I didn't say was that she'd already spoken to me about his proposals, and she really wasn't sure if that's what she wanted. Being "inseparable" meant that she had to be at his side wherever he wanted to go.

How jealous he could be showed up early one evening when the three of us were at Vallance Road. We were outside my Auntie's house and Frances went over to the sweet shop to get some cigarettes or something. As she came out of the shop two men said something to her and they all laughed. When she got over the road Reg wanted to know what they had said that was so funny and her without thinking said, "Nothing really, I just think they were trying to chat me up".

He went white, ran over the road and punched both of them to the ground, and carried on punching them as they lay there trying to cover their faces. Once we were back indoors he took his bloodstained shirt off, gave it to me and asked me if I'd wash it in cold water before the blood dried. Frances said, "No don't you, you're not his mother". So soft touch me said I'd do it, but even then she said to me, "Don't you. Make him do it himself – he was the one who got it messed up." This showed he was jealous but it also shows that she wasn't as under his thumb as a lot of people seem to think.

No matter how much Charlie tried to prop it up, the Double R had closed after Ronnie let the place go while Reg was in prison. They had taken over Esmerelda's Barn, so Frances would have spent night after night in its smoky atmosphere with nothing else to do but look pretty. Days would be spent in the company of lots of men, and if they went to Vallance Road there was always Ron and she said he made her feel uncomfortable. She got herself a job after Reg went back to prison, but as soon as he came out he made her give it up, so more and more she was finding excuses to stay at home. But as I've said, Reg could be persuasive and in the end she said she'd marry him.

Because he'd been a good family friend all our lives and helped the twins out of trouble more times than they'd like to remember, Father Hetherington was Reggie's only choice for someone to perform the ceremony. Hindsight is unfair because it allows you to read all kinds of things into the past, but what did the Father see in the future when he said he wouldn't do it? He wasn't our local priest any more because he'd moved to another parish, but Reg was quite happy to get married outside Bethnal Green – that wasn't a problem. Reg told me that he'd said he didn't approve of this marriage and left it at that. But I can't believe Reg would've accepted that without there being a good reason, so I feel that something was said that he kept to himself.

Either way, our local man said he would do it and the wedding took place in the spring of 1965 at St James's in Bethnal Green Road. Whenever I look at the photos from the day I'm always struck by the body language. Charlie in the background as usual, but Ron and Frances turning their bodies away from each other.

Whether it was "typical man" or just Reg, once the honeymoon was over things changed for the worse and not many months later

Frances left the flat they had in Sussex Gardens, not far from Hyde Park. Every time Reg sat in my flat with tears in his eyes, asking why she didn't love him, I'd try and tell him a girl needed more out of life than gold rings and chains. Then he'd start talking of the big house he would buy in the country with ponies for the kids and everything, as soon as this was sorted or that was cleared up. I'm sure he meant it at the time, but by the time he did it would be too late for Frances.

When I think how stubborn, obstinate, strong-willed or just pig-headed Reg could be, I was amazed at the patience he took to win Frances back. Night after night he'd stand outside her window telling her how much he loved her and pleading for a second chance to make things right. He could make the toughest men shake with fear and this little girl with the big eyes had him at her feet. Mind you, I know from experience that a man will say anything when he wants to get his own way, but I'd learned this the hard way. Frances would have to find out for herself when she finally gave in.

Reg rented a flat right next door to Ron in Cedra Court, and her life went right back to where it was before she left. More and more, Reg started asking me to spend time with her as though he didn't want her to be left on her own. Their flat was beautiful with rugs and furniture of quality I'd never seen in my life. I used to take Kimmy and David with me when I visited her, and being the age they were they climbed on chairs and spilt food and drink occasionally. Frances never turned a hair. "Don't worry – it doesn't matter," she'd say after some little accident. She just didn't care. What's that song? "A Beautiful Bird In A Gilded Cage". That could have been written with her in mind, and I didn't envy her one bit.

She had a maid to do all the cleaning so it's not surprising a bit of mess didn't upset her. All she had to do all day was buff her incredibly long fingernails. I'm not saying she was lazy or wouldn't do anything – it was that Reg wouldn't hear of her lifting a finger.

Outside of that posh sort of environment she was a much happier person and what she really liked was to come and see us all at Vallance Road. For a while she could relax in ordinary homely surroundings, and then for a time we'd see little flashes of how she used to be.

Just the other day a man named Johnny Squibbs said on national television that our family didn't treat Frances very nice. I shouldn't really answer such a stupid remark from someone I don't remember being around Frances very much or from someone who was too cowardly to attack us while Reg was alive. But I will anyway. If we weren't nice to her, why did she want to spend so much time with us? The truth is none of us knew how to be nasty to anyone. Even people who deserved to be disliked got treated with politeness, it's just the way we were. But in Frances' case, because she was always so vulnerable we went out of our way to let her know that we all loved her, hoping that by making her feel wanted it might help to throw off the terrible depressions she was going into more and more.

I know that my conscience is clearer than most of the people who seem to be crawling out of the woodwork and trying to make a name for themselves with malicious accusations now the twins are gone.

It would be easy to blame Reg and his lifestyle for the way she was, but she'd had problems with her nerves long before she met him. Her own mother admitted that on two occasions she had tried to kill herself in her very early teens. These may have been just cries for help, but still it goes to show something was wrong. I can only think that it wouldn't have mattered who Frances had married – the end result would've been the same. It didn't help that she didn't like most of his friends, and that there were all kinds of things going on with the twins. Like them who saw all kinds of bad things between their mum and dad but kept it locked in their heads, I wonder if she was in the same position.

She'd never talk about it, but she must have overheard many conversations between Reg and Ron that for a young highly strung girl would've been quite frightening, because by now it was an open secret that Ronnie had killed George Cornell in the Blind Beggar. The police might not have had any proof that Ron was involved, but Mrs Cornell came to Vallance Road one night and smashed Auntie Violet's windows, then stood in the road screaming that she was the mother of a murderer. My mum went flying out and told her to clear off and when she wouldn't, Mum gave her a couple of punches. I think she felt sorry for the woman afterward, but there was no way she could stand by and see her sister abused like that.

As it turned out Cornell's wife was right about what she had been shouting, but at the time my auntie didn't believe a word of it so couldn't understand why she was being attacked. The twins were away on holiday but when they came back they were really furious with what Mrs Cornell had done to their mother so they had the caravan she lived in burnt to the ground.

About this time we all got letters from the council informing us that the whole area was under a compulsory purchase order and that we were to be rehoused. None of us owned the properties so from the point of view of renting, all it would mean to us would be that we'd be paying our rent to a different landlord. But from an emotional view it was going to be a terrible wrench for all of us.

Each house was small, decaying, damp and overrun with rats and mice, but every brick held a memory. I'd lived there for twenty-seven years. I couldn't remember ever living anywhere else, although Mum and Dad didn't actually move in until I was three years old. My little Kimmy was exactly the same age at that time as I had been when we arrived and now we were going to have to move out.

Auntie Violet was the first to go, and if you'd seen our tears you'd have thought she was emigrating instead of going a short bus ride to a flat in Bunhill Row. Until it was our time to go I think my eyes filled up every time I passed the front door of 178.

Next were Nanny and Grandad and they were virtually carried kicking and screaming to a lovely little maisonette in Cheshire Street.

Mum went to Charles Dickens House in Mansford Street, and I got the upper part of a maisonette in Blythendale House in Hackney Road. Below me was Jenny Crossley, and eventually I would bless the day we became neighbours.

In a matter of months we were all settled in these clean modern homes with inside toilets, modern bathrooms and kitchens – and not a mouse in sight – but life wasn't the same.

We had become a small example of what was happening right through the East End. Families the same as ours were separated from friends and neighbours they'd lived and shared their lives with for, in some cases, seventy or eighty years. It tore the heart out of the part I knew – Bethnal Green – and it was the end of an era.

Eventually I got myself an exchange and moved into the flat under my mum's because I missed her so much. But before that whenever I visited her we'd sit and look out of the window down to the empty site that used to be our homes, and say to each other "D'you remember this? D'you remember that?" and it was quite sad. Mum was always waiting for a letter from the council that would tell her that when they'd finished building whatever was to go up on the site, she could move back over there – but it never came.

When the fuss over that murder had died down the twins helped Frank Mitchell escape from Dartmoor and, as they've admitted since, eventually had him killed. But for years, even indoors with us family they could trust, they always said Frank had gone abroad and would turn up one day – but I can't blame them for that.

So with all these things going on in the background I suppose it made Frances' nerves even worse than they were normally. And something she had confided to me in the strictest confidence would have made my nerves bad as well in the same circumstances.

She said to me one day, "I know you'll give me an honest answer, Rita, do you think I'm attractive to men?" It was a silly question really but I could see she was deadly serious, so the only obvious thing I could say was, "You've seen the way they look at you and every one of them is thinking you're beautiful – but why are you asking me?" She said, "Reggie doesn't come near me". Naïvety again! I said, "Well, you know how busy he is with the clubs and everything else, but that'll change when things slow down". Her eyes filled up with tears and she almost whispered, "I don't mean that, I mean he's ... we've never actually done ... you know what married people do." Then she started crying, asking me, "What's wrong with me? Why doesn't he want to touch me?" I could see she was really upset so I said the first thing I could think of: "That sort of thing can affect any man if he's worried or under stress. They can't help it but it certainly doesn't mean he doesn't want to make love to you." I'd obviously got it wrong because she said, " Oh Rita, you don't understand. I'm saying that he doesn't touch me in any way, not just that."

I couldn't get my head around what she was telling me. They'd been together for years and she was telling me that they'd never shared any intimacy whatsoever. Seeing her so heartbroken at what she saw as her failure as a woman, I couldn't doubt what she said was the truth. But when I thought about it afterward I wondered if she was lying to me for the drama of it all, or that in her troubled mind she was somehow mentally rejecting herself.

Ronnie's sexuality had been out in the open for a long time and in different circumstances I might have considered that being twins Reg had the same tendencies. But I could think of a number of girls that he'd gone out with for a long time and the majority of them had been round the block more than once. In fact they were of a type that would have chucked him on the second date if he hadn't performed his duty, so I'm sure there was never any question about his virility. He had loads of one-night stands and what he'd do was pick some girl up in the club, spend the night with her then walk out in the morning leaving us to make small talk with this person we'd never seen before. This would go on and on until Auntie Violet would say, "I think it's time you went home now, dear. Reggie must have got tied up somewhere." This wasn't just once – it happened time and time again.

I'm not a psychiatrist so I can only guess what was going on in Reg's mind. But judging it from things they both said it strikes me that the only answer is that he put her so high on a pedestal that something as basic as the sex act would somehow spoil what he felt for her.

At the inquest after her death the coroner broadcast to everyone in the court that he had discovered during the autopsy that she was still a virgin. The shock for me was that what she had said had been true all along. Now it was too late to give her a hug and tell her I was sorry that I hadn't believed her when she was crying out for help and advice.

She'd been under a Harley Street specialist for years and was always taking pills, but half the time I don't think they did much for her. It only took the slightest upset to have her crying, then she'd reach for the pills, and I'm sure she didn't keep count of what she was taking. Poor Reg didn't know what to do for the best. They used to have blazing rows and most of the time she started them over something silly, but I've got to say that no matter what Reg did to other men, he never raised his hand to her once. I knew he wasn't like that with women anyway, but I did ask her more than once if he hit her and she always swore that he never had, and she'd no reason to lie to me because we were very close.

She'd been in hospital to try and get her medication sorted out once and for all, and when she came out she went to stay with her brother Frank for a little while. Her and Reg hadn't broken up or nothing, but he was giving her a bit of space. Well, it goes to show that they hadn't split up because they had arranged to go away for a couple of weeks' holiday on the 8th June. He called into my flat quite early in the morning on the day they were supposed to be setting off and he wasn't too happy.

When I asked how Frances was he said, "Rita, I don't even know if we're going away today". I asked him why not and he said, "Frankie was doing her nut yesterday because her hair's gone all wrong and she said she's not going out of the door looking like that." Whether it was lacquer or dye Reg didn't know, but her hair had gone all stiff or something, and that's all it took for her to go into despair. Reg had told her it was no problem because it wouldn't take a proper hairdresser twenty minutes to sort it out first thing in the morning. But nothing he seemed to say had any effect in calming her down so he left and went home.

We had a cup of tea and he sat looking out of the window and didn't speak for ages. Then he suddenly said, "There's something wrong with Frankie". I said, "We all know that but a nice holiday will make all the difference". He stood up and paced around the room. "No, I mean now. Something's not right." Then he pulled his sleeve up and said, "Look, my arms have gone all goose bumps". He sat down again staring at his arm for a couple of minutes, then jumped up shouting, "I've got to go," and with that he practically ran out of the flat without even saying goodbye.

He'd got me worried because though these flashes of telepathy, if that's the word, were rare, they weren't that unusual in our family and often came when something serious was happening. But as I couldn't do anything else I put that out of my mind and started to give the kids their breakfast.

The next time I saw Reg he was so grief stricken I thought he'd go out of his mind. He'd left my flat and raced over to Ormsby Street in his car and banged on the door. When he got no answer he broke a small window at the back, climbed in and found Frances dead in her bed. At the inquest they said it was suicide, but even after all these years I'm still personally convinced that it was as simple as taking one pill too many, especially with the drama she went through over her hair only hours before.

They had only been married two short years. She was twenty-four years old with her whole life in front of her. Mixed up, confused, sometimes out of her depth in the world Reg had introduced her to and often frightened by emotions she felt but couldn't control. Nevertheless, Reg loved her more than she could ever know. We all did. She was a lovely innocent girl who always looked on me as a friend and I missed her terribly.

Some people have said that Reg turned her into a drug addict. She might have been as far as her medication went, but in no way was it down to him because he hated all drugs. When I was having awful problems with Ritchie and my marriage, the doctor had prescribed Valium to help me get through it. On a visit to Reg, who was serving his life sentence then, he studied my eyes for a while then said, "Are you taking something, Rita?" When I told him it was Valium 10, he took me by the hand and made me promise I'd throw them away as soon as I got home.

Others have written that Frances was escaping from a violent and abusive marriage. But the worst, and something that hurt me very much, was the person that wrote a second hand story in our local paper claiming that Reg had sex with another woman while Frances lay beside them unconscious with drugs. This man knows who he is and he also must have known that this cheap publicity was a cowardly attack on a man who had been dead for less than a week and an insult to us family left behind. Time has passed since then, but I'm still so angry if I ever meet him in the street I'll slap him.

No one who knew them both could ever suggest any of these things. And knowing what Frances told me, made such a suggestion completely ludicrous.

Perhaps he was too busy to give her the attention she needed. Perhaps he was unthinking or wrapped up in his work, but that goes for most men anyway. It doesn't mean that they don't love or care. If it was any other way I would say so for the sake of truth. After all, it can't hurt either of them any more, but if he's guilty of anything at all as far as Frances goes, it's that he loved her too much. She was his very first love, and believe me, the very last. I know that for the next thirty-three years, right up until he died he would use women to carry out the things he couldn't do for himself while he was in prison. As outside messengers, as a means to earn him and others money or as fundraisers for the hundred and one schemes he had on the boil. He might pretend all kinds of emotions to get his own way, but real honest love or affection never came into it.

Apart from when he lost his mother, nothing, or any day, could be worse than when he dropped a single red rose into the grave of Frances. I'm sure something died inside him the moment she did, because after that he didn't seem to care about anything. He drank too much, then when he was drunk he got either tearful or angry. Then he'd blame himself for her death and other times the doctors who should have looked after her, or her parents for the same reason.

Her parents blamed him for losing their daughter and as a final act of defiance against Reg, they instructed the undertaker to put an underslip against her skin so that the wedding dress she was buried in wouldn't touch her body.

At times he got like Ron had been at the height of his mental illness and threatened to kill anyone who came to mind. So no one should have been too surprised when he carried out his threat five months later and murdered Jack McVitie.

When you suffer shock after shock your mind goes numb, and when Charlie told us to expect a visit from the police, and why they might be coming to our homes yet again, I barely reacted. My mind refused to believe that Reggie was capable of something so violent, and it was like we were talking about some stranger. The way Ron had changed over the years I wouldn't have been surprised to hear that he'd killed again – but not Reg. He'd always been the gentler of the two.

More than once when we were small Ron tried to get me to put on the boxing gloves against him, but I never wanted to and Reg would tell him to pack it in. Or his horseplay as little kids got too rough for my liking, and it was always Reg who slipped in and calmed things down. I thought of all the nice things he used to do, like buying me presents and playing for hours with little Kimmy. I really didn't think it was possible, but when I finally had to accept that he was guilty, I thought it was tragic for him and even more tragic that a man had to die indirectly because of Frances.

For the month or so after it happened we expected every knock on the door to be the police, but as time went on and nothing happened we thought less and less of them coming. I certainly didn't know any of the details, and what I thought had happened was that there had been a fight and a man had been stabbed. I know that's bad enough but at least I could tell myself that accidents happen and perhaps it wasn't as bad as it seemed.

It was five months before the police got round to arresting my three cousins but soon after they had, they turned their attention to the family, who weren't involved in any way. As if we hadn't suffered enough seeing them all dragged off to prison, yet again they put us all through the indignity of having our homes searched. If they were looking for Jack McVitie in our tiny flats and maisonettes they were in for a disappointment. In the end all they took away with them were Nanny and Grandad's pension books, and what earthly connection they had to do with the case only the police could tell you.

It was almost two months before their trial was to start, and considering they might be facing life sentences the three of them were quite confident. Well, the twins were confident that as before there wouldn't be enough evidence to convict them. While Charlie was confident that once his story was told the case against him would be dismissed straight away. I couldn't understand why he was locked up anyway because he'd already told us that he was in bed when the murder took place, so obviously he had to be found not guilty.

I was surprised how well Auntie Violet and Uncle Charlie accepted that all their boys were in prison. There were always tears on the way home from Brixton, but from what the boys said they believed it wouldn't be many months before they were all out. We all believed it because it was like we were letting them down if we thought anything else. Though as time went on the twins at least began to have doubts that they'd get a not guilty. Even then Ron would say to me, "Don't worry about us, Rita. The most we can get is fifteen years, and we'll be out in less than eight."

During the trial that went on for months and months, the only bit that has stayed in my mind is of my mum on the stand as a character witness. There were so many people and so many words that I didn't understand. The occasional days I did go to the Old Bailey went by in a blur.

Mum must have been all of sixty then but she never seemed the slightest bit nervous. She'd done herself up like she was going to make a stage appearance instead of court, though in a way it's much the same. It's not what she said that I remember but just a picture of that little blond-haired figure saying what she had to say to all these posh bigwigs. I didn't notice but she told me afterward that when she looked up to the dock with all these men in it, Ron had his head in his hands and his shoulders were going like he was crying. Mum thought, "That poor boy's suffering up there," but when she looked the next time, his head was up and he'd been laughing. I don't know if he found the whole thing funny or was laughing at something Mum said.

A while later she got a letter from one of the young men that was on trial, and he said that she really did look nice that day and reminded him of Mae West. Mum said to me "Ooh Rita, I wish I'd known. I'd have said, 'Come up and see me some time'."

Auntie Violet was in a daze as well and on one of the days she went on her own, for some reason she turned up with only one eye made up. Dot Walsh, a good friend of the twins and a clairvoyant, who was meeting her at the court, spotted this and told her she looked like a panda. She got her own make-up out and put it right, though I doubt whether Auntie even took it in.

On the day of the verdict she said to Mum that she didn't feel well so would stay at home and listen to whatever was going to be said on the wireless. Mum stayed with her and they both sat drinking tea and not saying very much. Just before the news came on Mum lifted her hand up to her face and the green stone in a ring that Ron had bought her, and that she'd worn for years, fell out and rolled across the floor. She was always superstitious and took that as an omen that meant something bad might happen. And that's exactly what it did when the verdict was eventually read out on the news.

Right at the crucial moment one of them must have rattled a cup or scraped a chair on the floor because Auntie Violet said, "D'you know what I thought he said? Thirty years, and that can't be right." Mum wasn't sure either and they guessed the news reader had said three, so they settled back to wait for the next bulletin but before that someone turned up at the door and my aunt found out she'd never see her "lovely twins" outside prison walls again.

Poor Charlie never wanted to be anything else but a successful businessman and now he had to face ten years away from his family for doing something he'd had to do all his life – looking out for his brothers.

If we'd all known then that the twins would spend the rest of their lives in prison I don't think we could have coped, but we lived in hope that things would change. If not this month, perhaps next and if not then, some time in the next – and that's how time passed.

No one had ever been given such a long sentence so we expected it to be reduced on one appeal or another, however long this might be. Never did we expect the authorities to stick to the judge's recommendation of no less than thirty years. Most of us had enough years on our side to look forward to the twins walking out of the gates, at worst in twelve to fifteen years. But Nanny and Grandad, already in their nineties, would never see or speak to the three boys ever again. "Cannonball" Lee, frightened of no man and as hard as nails all his life, sat and cried many times. I'd hold his hand and he'd say "That's it, gel. They might as well be dead 'cos I'll never see them again."

And in a way his pain summed up what all of us felt.

7.   "Them Kray brothers"

Joe Lee

I don't think our Rita ever really understood what the twins were capable of. They kept it all away from her and the other women in the family – even Grandad Lee, but the rest of us blokes couldn't avoid it.

I can't say I was surprised about the road they went down in the end because most of their lives their heroes were tough guys and people who was prepared to stick two fingers up to the law. The more slippery these blokes were the more the twins idolized them. And we had more than our fair share of these types coming through the house or living close by in Bethnal Green.

I could think about it until I went dizzy and I still couldn't come up with any single reason as to why they should turn out different from the rest of the family. Me and Charlie had all the same influences when we was growing up, and pretty much the same background, give or take a few bits and pieces.

Speaking for myself, I've always stuck reasonably close to the straight and narrow – no better and no worse than the average bloke getting through life. As for Charlie, all the aggravation he's had to suffer all his life came down to one thing – well two things really, those brothers of his. He was no gangster. All he ever wanted was a quiet life where he could nick a few quid for himself out of some legitimate business. But every time he thought he was getting somewhere he let himself get sucked into some scheme or other by Reg and Ron – and they could be a bit persuasive when they wanted to be.

It was like he always felt that because he was a lot older than them he had a responsibility to get involved in looking out for them, and that's what brought all kinds of trouble down on his head.

I mean it's not like you can blame upbringing or environment for shaping those boys because I can't think that anyone could have had a more secure and loving home life than they did. All right, leave their old man Charlie out of the picture because I don't think he done them a lot of favours when they was kids, but for the rest they grew up surrounded by close family who thought the sun shone out of them. Right from the days when my Aunt Violet used to push them up Bethnal Green Road in one of them double prams, with all the women stopping to have a look, they was always the flavour of the month. Didn't matter what they got up to one or the other of the family would jump in with excuses for them. Nanny Lee, Rose, May – they all thought the world of them and you daren't say a word against them twins if they was in earshot.

As for their mother – well, they were her life. They never went without decent grub and always had shoes on their feet and, down to her, so did other kids in the neighbourhood. Not too long ago I was talking to James Aish, an old friend of the twins, and he was going on about how lovely my Aunt Violet was. He said all the kids used to hang about the front door because they knew that eventually she'd bring them out a sugar sandwich or a piece of cake. One time she called him over and asked him why he didn't have no shoes on. When he said he didn't have any, she went indoors and brought out a pair of Reg's white plimsolls and gave them to him. I didn't know about shoes, but more times than I can remember I've seen her give different kids a jersey, a shirt or a pair of shorts. I mean, she didn't have much herself, but she could always find something for them that had even less.

Every morning those twins went out with clean clothes that had been washed and ironed the night before, and not too many kids around there at the time could say the same thing. They had decent men in the family to look up to – my dad, Uncle Johnny, Uncle Albert and Grandad – all straight and all good grafters, so why didn't they think it was worth following their example?

I suppose when they compared them with some of the other flash geezers they came across, and I'm talking about when they were kids, they was a bit ordinary, and that didn't fit in with their ideas of being something.

I think Rita hit it on the head when she reckoned they were insecure, and nine times out of ten that's the reason people push themselves forward to get in the limelight. Then there's the twin thing. None of us, unless they're in that position themselves, could ever understand in a million years what it's like to share your identity. Everything you do is shared, and twins or not it's only human nature to be on top so you're always looking for ways to be that bit more noticed than the other one. And those two certainly did that all right.

If one of them kissed their mum the other would have to give her two. If one of them climbed on a wall the other would have to climb up a lamppost and sit on the crossbar, just to be that bit higher. So the twins weren't just competing against the world, or the little bit of it they knew – but against each other day and night.

But this limelight thing; if you could have seen their faces when Grandad turned to the back of the *East London Advertiser* and they had a mention about their boxing, well, they was like a dog with two tails.

This was about the time I finished with the services and got my demob papers. Strange how a place looks so different after you've been half-way round the world for a couple of years. The East End was still a right mess after all the bombing, and when I went down Vallance Road to see Nanny and Grandad and all the rest, I couldn't believe how scruffy and old those houses were. I suppose I'd never really noticed it before, but then it wasn't so much that the area had changed because it hadn't. It was me, after having my eyes opened with things I'd seen.

Still it was home and I was pleased to be back. I couldn't believe those boys. I'd been away for a few years and when I saw them it was like it had only been yesterday, because straight off they're going, "Shall we get the gloves out, Joe? Are you coming out to the yard?" And I was thinking, "Fuck me, here we go again". What with Charlie keeping them at it and Grandad showing them all his tricky moves, I had to admit they were both coming along as a right pair of tasty little boxers. They told me about some fights they'd had with each other in a booth over the local fair, and how they'd got a couple of bob for doing it in front of the crowd.

When I mentioned it to my old man he told me that it was in a booth over Bruce Castle Park run by a fella called Stewart. This was where his regular fighters would take on all comers who fancied getting knocked about to earn themselves a fiver. And he told me they were still up to their old tricks. He had fighters like Buster Osbourne, his brother Stevie, Slasher Warner and Les Haycox on his bill, and when it was all over this Stewart would come out front and say to the crowd, "Ladies and gentlemen, I have some bad news for you. Les Haycox has had his purse stolen and after a great performance tonight I think we should all dig deep and help him out." Then a hat was sent round and all these mugs, full of sympathy, would chuck coins in it. Well, if you had half a brain you'd realize this was a scam, but it never failed and they all shared out the takings afterwards. Because they were always on the move from one patch to another they could pull this stunt at least once wherever they went, so it was a regular earner.

From what my aunt said the twins really went to town on each other that night and she wasn't too happy about it, but from what I'd seen them get up to out in the back yard it didn't seem as though it was anything out of the ordinary.

Give them their due they threw themselves into training like it was going out of fashion. If they weren't knocking the stuffing out of an old mattress that Grandad had slung over the washing line, they was punching the daylights out of an old kitbag stuffed with rags that my cousin Charlie had fixed up for them in a back bedroom. They was out on the road by six every morning and the same at night. Overdid it, I thought; got a bit obsessed, but that's often the way with young kids when they get into something. I've got to say in those three or four years they worked harder and sweated more than they ever would the rest of their lives. Still, it did pay off for them in the end because they both ended up as Junior Champions.

Talk about twins and doing everything the same, at different times they both got Hackney Schoolboy titles, and both took the London Junior Championship. Three years running they ended up fighting each other because they'd seen off the opposition. And I'll tell you what; when them two squared up you got your money's worth because, same as when they worried about the other one getting more peas or an extra half-inch of sausage, no way were they going to be beaten. Reg always had the edge because he was a thinker and it took a lot to get him rattled – and that's the worst thing a boxer can do. He went on to be a finalist in the Great Britain Championship, but didn't quite make it.

When it all came to an end them two and cousin Charlie was all on the same card at the Albert Hall. Charlie was fighting Lew Lazar as a welterweight and he took a bit of a hammering. Nothing against him, he put on a great show right to the end, but Lazar had a wicked left and the simple fact is he was a better boxer at the end of the day.

Ronnie had a bit of bad luck against Bill Sliney; and it was bad luck, because in the second he put Sliney down for a count of eight and we thought it was only a matter of time before he finished him off. Then Ron took a bang in the eye from the other bloke's head – nothing dirty, just one of those things and after that Sliney kept blind-siding him and after six rounds took the decision on points.

But the way Reg fought showed everybody that he really did have what it took to become a big name in the sport. It was like an exhibition match. We could see he was full of confidence and thought about every move he made. Bob Manito was a bit tasty and knew what he was doing, but it wasn't enough and he didn't have a chance. He was out-pointed in every one of those six rounds. I've still got the poster from that night and whenever I glance at it I can't help thinking that if those boys hadn't taken a left turn instead of a right, things could've been so different and their lives not wasted like they were.

When they left school they did have the idea that they could make a good living in the building trade. Uncle Charlie used to say, "Fuck that for a lark," to them, but they didn't take any notice and got themselves fixed up with a local bloke who done roofing and other bits and pieces. I think they were bucket boys, carrying hot asphalt up ladders so the other blokes could spread it on flat roofs. Talk about black-and-white minstrels, I'd see them coming home and they'd be as black as Newgate's Knocker. They'd have little burns on their necks, ear'oles and up the arms, so you can imagine what their mother made of that.

Reminds me of Grandad one time. He'd been up the market and bought himself a brand new pair of white plimsolls; cost him five bob I should think and he was as proud of them as if they'd been hand-made Italian leather. This was in the middle of summer and it was blazing hot. I was outside the house talking to Nanny when we heard this effing and blinding coming from half a mile away. It was Grandad coming along pulling his barrow. When he got to the door he was so wild he couldn't speak. He could swear though, and I thought he'd do himself an injury if he didn't shut up. What it was, the council had retarred the road and as he walked along he sunk into it. With this black stuff being soft in the sun his shoes were covered and there was enough sticking on the soles to redo another road. Did he go on? "Them fucking bastards, they want to be fucking prosecuted." He meant the council and he was going to sue them for every penny they had, but like everything else he forgot about it a few days later.

Before he gave up on the idea of taking them to court he wrote to them a couple of times and that was something considering he'd never had a day's schooling in his life. But that never held him back – he'd taught himself to read out of the newspapers, and he could write a lovely letter when he wanted.

Anyway, the twins got fed up scrubbing themselves raw every night and knocked the asphalt job on the head after about six weeks, and that's when my old man said he'd get them fixed up in Billingsgate Market if they was interested. They jumped at it because they didn't only like their Uncle Joe; they had a lot of respect for him as well. He never pampered them like a lot of the others, and he never took any nonsense either. All their lives they were the same, if you gave them an inch they took a mile, because they were crafty little bastards and if ever they saw an opening they was in there. But with my old man they knew how far they could go and thought a lot of him for it.

When they were little nippers they used to get up early and sit at the window hoping he was going to pull up in his cart and two pair horses. He usually did because most days he'd bring in a bit of fish for his mother and father and always kept an eye on them. Soon as he pulled up they'd rush out and jump in the back among all the fish boxes and ride with him to market. You never had to ask where they'd been – the fish scales all over their clothes and the stink soon told you that.

The guv'nor or foreman down at Billingsgate had asked my dad if he knew of a young strong lad who could do with a bit of work as an "empty boy". The old man's said, "As a matter of fact I do – my nephew. Well, actually there's two of them, can you take them both?" The bloke's agreed and fixed Reg up in the haddock market and Ron in the shop over Thames Street. Now they think they're fish porters but all they was doing really was running round picking up the empty crates and what have you. One day a buyer stopped Reg and asked him if he'd carry a few parcels of fish to his motor, and there'd be a drink in it for him. Flash a coin and either of them two would've stood on their heads – so that was sorted. The bloke did tell Reg that he had a bit of other business to do so he'd square up with him a bit later on.

That came and went and it wasn't until days later the geezer turned up, called Reg and pointing at some more parcels said, "Do us a favour again – same motor, same drink". Well Reg looked at him and said "Same deal? You can fuck off – you never paid me last time." The bloke must have thought Reg was a bit of a pie-can or something because he said, "You've got a short memory. I gave you ten bob the morning after you helped me out." Course it didn't take Reg more than a few seconds to work out what had happened and that he'd been stitched up by his own brother, so he went after him. They came to blows over that and had a right old barney, but at the end of the day Ron's excuse was, "Ain't my fucking fault if somebody wants to stick half a note in my pocket," and he never did hand it over.

I don't think it was many weeks humping boxes before they gave in to their old man telling them they were mugs getting up at four in the morning, and they jacked it in. And to be truthful I don't think they did an honest day's work from then until the day they died.

They did a spell on the knocker with their old man, but I can't see either of them thought it was much of a career move. Old Charlie had the gift of the gab and he'd been at the game all his life. I reckon he could've talked the queen into selling the crown jewels, and then get away with only giving her a couple of quid, but the boys never had the old chat you need in the pestering lark. If they could get away with one word instead of two, that's what you got and they were never any different. So when they put all that behind them, same as all the other bits of work they tried, they started hanging around. And when young fellas get into that lark trouble isn't very far away.

Our Uncle Johnny had opened up a transport café on the corner of Vallance Road and Cheshire Street, and it was a right little goldmine. Him and Aunt Maude couldn't go wrong because there was Ind Coope and Trumans and all the breweries close by, so all the workers went there for their breakfasts. Well, this was nice and handy for the twins and they'd get in there with Bobby Ramsey and Venables, a right pair and a lot older than Reg and Ron. Course, they'd sit there and soak up all their stories about crime and violence, and I suppose they soon got the impression that the law was for mugs.

Those boys had minds like sponges when it came to anything to do with fighting or somebody getting done over, and they was always pumping all of us about the past and what have you. They didn't get a lot of that out of me but I'd been in the war so they wanted all the ins and outs of had I killed anyone; had I used a bayonet; what was it like to fire a gun. I don't think I ever fired a gun in anger, but I'd spin them a tale and they lapped it up.

Same with my old man. Like I said he'd hung around with some tasty villains and he'd be saying to them, "I see this bloke put a chain in a sock and get stuck in," or "These fellas used to put a rusty razor blade in a potato – that way they get a terrible infected cut, but there ain't no danger of killing them". Their mouths would be hanging open. "Cor, Uncle Joe, did they use guns? Did you see anybody get shot?" This was Ronnie. Guns? It was like he was heading toward Cornell right from being a little kid. He had this fascination with them. Mind you, for years after the war guns were ten a penny. So many blokes hung on to them as souvenirs. If you really wanted one a word here and there would get you a dozen in half an hour.

It was inevitable with the way their minds were working that the twins would start collecting a bit of hardware to make them feel tough guys, the same as the blokes they were mixing with. I'd call in to see my aunt and the two of them would drag me upstairs to look at their little armoury. If they thought I was going to be impressed they had another thought coming, and in fact I told them more than once having this box of gear under the bed could get them into serious trouble. To be fair it was more Ronnie than Reggie. At least in his younger days Reg was more of the old school where he'd get stuck in with just his fists. But Ron loved all them films with a bit of swordplay and chucking knives around, so it was natural he thought they were the answer in a bit of bother.

The stuff he had – bayonets, Ghurkha knives, a sword that must have been three foot long, and then there was the guns: an old army Colt (bit like a cowboy gun), a silver pistol and an old Mauser that was so bunged up it would've taken your hand off if you fired it.

What with being about eight years older than they were, most of the time I must have seemed more like an uncle than a cousin, and they usually listened to what I had to say. But not over that lot, so what else could I say? Things might have been a bit slack during the war and just after when it came to firearms, but since then and the time I'm talking about, there'd been too many shootings involving coppers and the law tightened up. It had got that just being in possession meant you were guaranteed being banged up, no questions asked, and these two idiots had a few years apiece tucked under the bed.

I read in a book only recently that the fella who wrote it reckoned that he'd been in number 178 and seen guns all over the table. My mum used to say, "Anything sticks to paper," but what are these people on? Never in a million years would my aunt have stood for that. She turned a blind eye to a lot of what they got up to, and I think she knew a lot more than she made out, but she wasn't a silly woman by any means and those boys would've got their marching orders pretty sharpish if she came across something like that.

Nanny found a gun wrapped up and hidden in her wash basket one day, but they blagged their way out of that somehow, and with her thinking they was both angels anyway I suppose that wasn't too difficult.

This same geezer with the book printed that they had a minah bird that used to say "Ronnie's a gangster – Ronnie's a gangster". Leave it out. Grandad would've wrung its fucking neck. They did have a minah bird, one they bought up Petticoat Lane or Gamages, depending on which one was telling you. Anybody else bought a bird it would do nothing but look at you all day – but things always seemed to go their way and because it was theirs it used to talk like a good 'un. It would take the piss out of old Charlie, well it didn't really, but he seemed to think it did. He had a habit of clearing his throat – drove you mad sometimes, and the bird picked up on this and you'd hear "hrrrrm, hrrrrm" and you wouldn't know which one of them it was coming out of.

We used to have a couple of vicars from the Red Church in and out of our houses. They was good friends with the twins, and I think one of them had a bit of a fancy for our Rita but I never said nothing. When they'd be having a cup of tea Ronnie would say to this bird, "What's your name then?" And he knew what it would say, else he wouldn't have asked. "Bollocks," it came out with. Then he'd ask again and get the same answer: "Bollocks, bollocks." His game was to shock the pair of them but it was a waste of time really because these vicars didn't turn a hair. They were young and thought it was hilarious.

Then there was that dog. An aunt on my mother's side had a German Shepherd and she wanted to get rid of it because it was biting everybody. I gave her half a crown for it and she was pleased to take it just to get rid of the nuisance. I thought she must have been handling it wrong and with a little bit of training it would be as right as rain. My Aunt May loved it from the minute she saw him, and when she asked me if it was quiet like, I told her you couldn't find a better dog. That bastard bit everyone. The postman, the milkman, and when the doctor came we had to hold its mouth shut. Well that was right up Ronnie's street.

I happened to be walking past the house one day and I see him standing by the door with this Rex on a lead. I said "What are you up to, Ron, taking the dog for a walk?" And he said "No, I'm waiting here until that copper comes along, then I'm going to set this dog on to his police dog". I said, "Leave it out, Ron. It ain't got nothing to do with the dogs. Get inside and don't do it." He just stood there grinning at me, so whether he did after I was gone I don't know. But the intention was there. He always did have a cruel streak in him right from a nipper, and if he had his way he would've turned that dog real nasty.

With May and Rita it was nothing but a kitten. I've seen Rita dress it up in kiddies' clothes and walk it along the street, her holding his front legs up and him walking upright on his back legs. He was clever – no doubt about it. Don't ask me how, but they'd even trained it to bring a cup and saucer from beside the bed upstairs all the way down to the kitchen and it never broke one. Rita got a red face over this one day. They had some blokes in, decorators or gasmen or something, and while they're all standing in the sitting room, down the stairs came Rex and he's carefully carrying in his mouth the china potty from under her bed. Must have thought it was a giant cup. Course there was nothing in it because she never did use it, but May always put it there "just in case".

Ronnie turned up at Nanny's one day with a donkey on a bit of string. He's got this thing half-way up the passage and he's shouting for Nanny to bring him a piece of that shiny tassel you put on Christmas trees – tinsel. Don't ask. She didn't have none and he was a bit disappointed so he said, "Tell you what, Nan, you can keep it if you want". She said, "Keep it? What would I do with a fucking donkey? Take it back where you got it." Where it ended up I don't know.

Then there was a Rottweiler – then a racehorse – then a couple of snakes, but I'd given up keeping track by then.

Going back to that mob hanging about in Uncle Johnny's café reminds me of the first serious bit of bother they got themselves into.

I think Johnny was the only one in the family to have a motor then. In fact he was the only one for streets around. He got a phone call in the early hours from the twins saying they were in a spot of trouble. Would he come and pick them up from the nick? What with cars being few and far between then, when the law saw one driving around in the middle of the night they'd be thinking, "Hello, what's he up to?" and give them a pull. So Johnny's told the boys no, he's not going to suffer aggravation just so they could get a free ride home. Get a taxi. They were a bit brassic so in the end he gave in and went and got them. When he got them in the motor and asked them what it was all about Ronnie told him that he'd chinned a copper. Well, nobody in their right mind does that without a very good reason, so what does that suggest when Ron said he had to do it because this young copper had pushed him and told him to move along when he was stood outside Pellici's Café?

You can imagine how their uncle took that. "So you'll probably go down because he gave you a little shove?" Ronnie just said, "Well he was fucking asking for it". Johnny said to Reg, "An' how come they pulled you in as well? Did you join in?" Reg said. "No. I wasn't even there, but when I heard Ron had been lifted I went and found the same copper and gave him another one – then I was nicked."

I mean I wasn't there but I can only imagine Johnny must have shook his head and wondered where these two's brains were. They was lucky really. They should've got prison time and it might have been better for them if they had – short, sharp shock, if you know what I mean. OK, you could say Ron's reaction was a spur of the moment flare-up, but you couldn't say the same for Reg. He'd deliberately gone out of his way to find this copper and give him a spank. What do they call it? Premeditation or something?

As it was the old priest from up the road got up in the box and told the judge they was good boys at heart and all that cobblers, and they got away with a spot of probation. Which was the worst thing that could've happened because having got away with it the pair of them thought they was in Ramsey's league and never looked back after that.

I can remember thinking they might as well chuck the gloves out the window because once you get a conviction for violence outside the ring, nobody wants to touch you. But they had the arse'ole with all the early morning training anyway, so it didn't worry them too much.

About the same time Uncle Johnny got caught by a scam, that if he hadn't been blinded by pound notes he should've seen coming a mile off. I walked into the café one day and I see this geezer talking to him a bit deedy [suspicious] like. It was none of my business so I left them and walked out.

What it was, Johnny was being offered a load of tea and sugar over the side and at the right money. A few hundred quid's worth, but he could have it for a hundred notes – cash. Aunt Maude's brother Vic was stood there so this geezer said, "Give your mate here the money to hold, just in case we have trouble with Old Bill when we're doing the swap over".

Johnny had an old army truck then and the idea was he would drive to a quiet back street, the other bloke would meet him and they'd off-load the gear from one motor to another. Vic would stay in the café with the money, then hand it over when the deal was done. Simple enough. Johnny drives away to some place in Barking, parks up and waits – and waits. In the meantime this slippery bastard's gone back to the café, collared Vic and told him it was all squared away and that Johnny had said to hand over the cash, and he'd be along in a bit.

Course, Vic didn't know any different, paid up and thought he'd helped out on a sweet little deal – until his brother-in-law came steaming back effing and blinding because the geezer hadn't turned up. When he found out that he'd been done up like a Christmas turkey he went absolutely fucking mad.

I was walking down Kingsland Road with Stan, a pal of mine, and my uncle screamed up beside me in his motor and he's shouting, "You know a lot of fellas. I want something done 'cos I've been turned over." Then he gave me the story. It turned out that the bloke who nicked his dough had been put up to it by Venables, a right villain. Not Shaun, who the twins knocked about with, and was involved in doing that copper, but his old man, Tommy, who made a living in the con-game. One side of his face was like a road map, what with seeing the sharp edge of a razor more than once, and he was bad news. In later years Shaun took up driving those big juggernaught lorries and when he was on a ferry he left the engine running to warm the cab up, fell asleep and was suffocated by the fumes from a dodgy exhaust.

Anyway, Johnny left Tommy out of the picture because there are certain limits as to how far an ordinary bloke will go, but a long time after my uncle and a pal of his came across the geezer who'd ripped him off and beat him senseless. Reckons it was worth the hundred for the satisfaction it gave him.

Apart from the twins I don't think any of us in the family went out looking for trouble, but if it came or somebody took the piss, there was plenty of bottle in all the Lees and whoever put themselves up got well paid for their trouble.

Like the time somebody had a go at my old man. He was working at Billingsgate and some other fella, an ex-boxer and a bit saucy with it, said something or other out of order to Dad. Being a bit quick tempered he didn't need a lot of pulling so he's said something back and the next thing is they're both at it hammer and tongs. He was pushing on a bit then, but being like his own father, age never stopped him having a go, and he was sorting this ex-boxer out good and proper until the bloke's brother jumped on his back and brought him down to his knees.

This brother had a few things to say about the twins; that they was fuck-all without Ramsey behind them, that they were nothing, and of course the old man's mentioned what he'd been up against when he saw his nephews next time. A week or so later this geezer's training over Victoria Park and along comes Reg with Big Tommy Brown. Reg has got him by the throat and said, "Think you're a bit tasty knocking about an elderly man do you? Well have some of this." And he beat the shit out of him. And did he.

What with Aunt Rose and Grandad pumping into him over the years that one punch against you meant ten back, he always went the extra mile, and with one thing and another I don't think that fella walked again for a long time.

Really that's the only sort of justice people like that respected. If the old man had called the coppers what would have happened?

Nothing. Wouldn't have even gone to court. And the bloke that was nicking Uncle Albert's hubcaps? Two pound fine – don't do it again. As it was they got their desserts and probably thought twice about getting leery again.

Talking of Tommy Brown, now there was a bloke who was more than handy to have in your corner. I grew up with him being around because he was a good friend of my father's, and I often went with Dad to either Devonshire Hall or Jack Straw's Castle to watch him boxing or sparring. I'd get the gloves on against him when I was a nipper, same as we all did with the fighters that came through our door, and he'd be up there, six and a half feet tall and I'd be about two foot high, giving his knees what for. He was a giant when I was a kid and the same when I grew up.

Somebody told me that he was giving his missus Dot a driving lesson in a Mini when she did something wrong and some geezer behind got a bit upset, so he's overtaken them, cut in and forced them to pull over – road rage they call it now. Well he's jumped out of his motor swearing and ready for a go until Tommy unfolds himself out of this little motor and stood up. The geezer's gone "Oh", jumped back in his car and took off at a hundred miles an hour.

He thought the world of the twins and later on wherever they were, he was. Whenever Reg disappeared overnight you could always bet your life he was over Tommy's caravan. They were like travelling people – went all over the place, but when they were around London they always parked up on a bit of waste ground in Devons Road, Bow.

Dot told me that Reg would call in latish in the evening and sit fidgeting until she told him to take his shoes off and relax. Then he'd start yawning and she'd ask him if he wanted to stay the night – *bosh* – he's got himself tucked up behind the screens at one end in two minutes flat. That's what Reg had been after all the time. His excuse was he could never get a good night's sleep in Vallance Road because of the trains, but as she said, unless you parked on the railway line you couldn't get nearer to them than her trailer was.

Shame about Tommy. He kept an eye on those boys right up until they went into prison for the big one. With them being Category A the law wouldn't let Tommy visit them, and on top of that every letter he wrote came straight back from the prison with "Not to be passed on" stamped all over it. So it broke his heart that they might think he'd forgotten about them. As it was, he died without ever seeing them again once that door had slammed behind them.

At his funeral, when this much-bigger-than-usual coffin was sat there with hundreds of mourners filling the church up, the vicar said to Dot, "Mrs Walsh, he must really have been somebody," and she said, "No, just an ordinary man".

In the papers after the boys were sent away, and in lots of books, it's been said that a gypsy friend of the Kray twins put a curse on Judge Milford Stevenson, causing him to go blind, then die. I said to her, "What's all that about?" and she said, "Complete nonsense. I've never cursed anyone in my life – but . . . without my help things happen to people who hurt my friends." Makes you think.

Whatever the rest of the family thought, by the time the twins ended up at the Old Bailey on a charge of "Grievous Bodily Harm", or GBH, they was already well apprenticed into street fighting and well-over-the-top violence. I knew people and I heard things, and they were already picking up a name as a pair to keep away from.

At work I'd hear fellas saying, "Cor, I seen a fight up Tottenham last night and these two blokes was getting stuck in with chains round their hands – blood everywhere – two against five – dead spit of each other they were". And I'd think, "I don't have to ask who they were". This wasn't just once, it was regular. Or I might say I was going to this pub or that pub and somebody would say, "Keep your eyes open – them Kray brothers hang about over there". And I'd say, "Oh right, I'll keep my head down". They never knew who I was. No connection you see – I was Joey Lee and that was the end of it, and I never said nothing. I never have.

I wasn't ashamed to be connected, why should I be, and it wouldn't change the way things were even if I was. But I've always thought the least said the better, so it wasn't so much they were up in front of a judge, but more why hadn't they been up much earlier and more often.

What they were both nicked for was no better and no worse than a dozen other fights they'd got themselves involved in. OK, it was bad news that some young kid got badly done over, and I don't condone it, but they was all at it. These fellas were going out on the town and they're all carrying coshes and chains and razors. I mean, what reason could any of these boys have for going round tooled up if they weren't looking for trouble. And when trouble came they was going to use these weapons, so it was no good squealing when it went the other way.

It was just bad news for Reg and Ron that a couple of witnesses came forward and the lad that got badly hurt decided to talk to the law. Usually if you come off worse in these fights, you swallowed it and put it down to experience – but it didn't happen in this case, so what can you say? Still, on the day, the twins got an acquittal.

There was talk of a girl witness being threatened with having her face slashed if she didn't retract her statement, but I can't believe that. A bloke perhaps, but not a girl. I can't remember ever hearing the slightest rumour that the twins would raise a hand against a woman. They'd been brought up surrounded by them. Whichever way they turned there was their Nanny, their mum, their aunts and young Rita. They loved them all and they respected them, so it's hard to imagine that they didn't view all women the same outside the door.

They couldn't even stand anyone swearing in front of the ladies, and more than one fella got a warning then a punch in the jaw if they didn't take notice. One bloke called our Rita a Charlie Hunt, if you know what I'm saying – right to her face, and there's not a woman in the country who likes the sound of that swearword, let alone when she's called one. She's never been one for running to the boys with tales, but somehow Reg got to hear about it and the next thing this geezer's disappeared – never seen around Bethnal Green again. I'm not saying he's propping a bridge up somewhere, but the least he would've got was a stiff talking to, and after that thought it healthier to move somewhere else. So no, I don't really think there was any intimidation; just that some of the people involved had second thoughts about talking out of turn when they had to carry on living in the East End when it was all over.

A major plus on the boys' side was that Father Hetherington stood up in court again and gave them a bit of reference. I can only think he was out of touch with how they'd changed from when they were youngsters. And they weren't bad kids until they started mixing with the wrong crowd and older fellas. This vicar or priest, I can't remember exactly what he was, was a well-built bloke and handy with the gloves on. He wasn't one of them preaching down your ear'ole all the time kind, and the boys looked up to him. If he ever wanted help setting up stalls for charity things, or chairs stacking up after meetings, the twins were there without being asked. So when he spoke up for them he was speaking as he found and honestly believed that when they got into trouble, like this time and the time before, it was a bit out of the ordinary and they would soon straighten out. I'm afraid he made a bit of a misjudgement but that wasn't his fault, and his heart was always in the right place. So whether it was his little speech that done it or as they say lack of evidence, I don't know, but the twins walked out of the Old Bailey like they was "Lords of the Manor", and at that age they were nothing near.

When they got their call-up papers we all thought a bit of army training would straighten them out, same as it had with Billy Wiltshire, not that he got into anything like the trouble they did. And what happened? They turned out to be the two worst squaddies that ever put on a uniform. And what for? Because at the end of the day they still did their two years, same as they would've done if they'd knuckled down. But in their case they did it very hard.

OK, half the time they were knocking about the East End with all the tearaways when they should've been in camp, but being on the run is no life at all, and I should know. You can't relax and get on with things because you're looking over your shoulder every five minutes waiting to be collared.

They kept away from Vallance Road because the law had an eye open for them, but every now and then I'd bump into them in Wally's Café by the bus garage in Hackney, or another little place off the market. It's no wonder they went wrong when I think of the geezers they were spending their days with in these places. Tommy Smithson, Ron Diamond, Alfie Melvin – all right villains. And there was Rolfie, a friend of old Charlie's, who they was living with while they were on the trot. He must have taught them a thing or two, same as the others, because they'd all done plenty of time for thieving and violence.

I've only ever done prison time overnight if you like and never wanted any more than that, but to listen to these fellas talk you'd think they was swapping stories about holidays they'd been on. "Done five in Durham, seven in Dartmoor, ten on the island. Piece of piss." I bet they counted every day while they was doing their time and swore that would be the last. But sitting in the café with all the fellas, it's all behind them and they've got to make out they did it standing on their heads. Well, of course the twins soaked all this up; believed every word of it and went along with their way of thinking that working blokes like myself were mugs. I'm not saying the twins looked at me personally and thought I was an idiot for being straight. They were always pleased to see me and I'd have a crack with the blokes they were with.

Away from that lot I knew a lot of fellas that were a bit tasty and well over the side where the law was concerned, but speaking for myself, once I grew up I put all that old nonsense behind me and never had any inclination to get mixed up in all that again. I was married to Ann Curtis by then and all I wanted was to make a good living and enjoy my life with her.

Don't get me wrong, I was no angel when I was a younger man and I had my fair share of run-ins with the Old Bill because you couldn't avoid it where I grew up. No, that's not strictly true. You could avoid it but if you had bottle and a bit of a spark, well, stands to reason you're going to have a piece of whatever's going down. But then like most of the fellas I knocked about with you reach a point in your life where you have to make a decision to either pull back or carry on and risk ending up behind the door. And that's what I did. Knocked all that lark on the head, straightened myself up and moved on. I think about my cousins and a few other blokes who've spent half their lives inside and looking back down the years and weighing it all up, who was the mug? You tell me.

Eventually the twins were slung out of the army they'd never really been in, with dishonourable discharge stamped on their papers, and by then they'd learned a lot and was up to putting it into practice.

When Charlie and me was a bit younger we used to go up to the billiard hall in Eric Street, off the Mile End Road; it was a right dump then. When the twins asked me and Charlie to slip up there one night, it turned out to be even worse than I remembered it. There were about a dozen billiard tables in there and when I had a quick look the baize seemed in good shape, but then that green cloth's always been a bit sacred even in the roughest place. The rest of the Regal, as they called it, was a mess.

What it was, Reg and Ron had the idea of taking over the lease and wanted to know what we thought. Charlie wasn't too keen on the idea because he could see any dough for rent and what have you was going to come out of his pocket. I said to them the geezer would probably want a tenner a week, and the takings couldn't be worth more than five. Well, half of that pleased them as they'd already bid the landlord a fiver and he'd taken their arm off. They didn't want advice of off us two because they'd already made their minds up, and I think they was just letting us know they was a bit sharp when it came to pulling off a deal.

Give them their due, after they got their coats off and got stuck in with a paintbrush, it was a different place altogether, and a matter of weeks after they were coining a nice few quid out of it.

It was never a place you'd want to take your missus, but the boys never intended it would be anyway. What it turned into was a meeting place for all the tearaways the boys had ever come across, and their mates and so on. Well, once you get a mob like that meeting regular they're going to use it as their office for a bit of business, and with one thing and another the twins made sure they got a back-hander from all the little deals.

Sometimes it was like a supermarket out the back, and off-licence. Booze, fags, electric goods, a bit of tom [jewellery] – you name it you could buy it in the Regal.

I turned down the offer of having a piece in the hall but Charlie got himself involved, and though he was getting a good pension never really liked the way it turned out. Underneath he was a straight bloke really, who would rather have made a living on the right side of the law than the wrong.

Like I've said before, the twins had a way about them that sucked you in, and even though he was seven years older it was a case of do it their way or fuck off.

Something else Charlie didn't like was, when it came to light about the same time, that Ronnie was playing at the other end of the field, if you know what I mean.

He came to me one night and asked me what I made of all these soft-looking youngsters his brother spent all his time with. Well, I'd cottoned on to this ages ago and what with Charlie being an ex-navy man who'd seen what goes on, I thought he would've himself. But what could I say? It wasn't for me to start chucking accusations around so I just said, "I dunno, Charlie. What d'you think it's all about?" He said, "I've got my suspicions. I'm going to ask him outright," which I thought was taking a bit of a chance if he was wrong, because even then you had to be careful around Ron. Say the wrong word and he's up in the air. He never worried me but it wouldn't be the first time he'd upped one of his brothers.

Later Charlie came back and he's shaking his head. "Can't believe it. Can't believe it. He's told me he's the other way and I think it's fucking disgusting." I've gone, "Nah, not Ronnie. He's making out he's different – same as always." I wasn't surprised but I was putting over that it was news to me because he was a bit upset. He said, "Straight up, Joe. He's admitted it and I'm so wild I want to knock it out of him." Personally, I didn't give a monkey's; it takes all sorts, but Charlie, well he never did accept that this tough geezer of a brother could, as he looked at it, let the family down. Mind you, there's worse things to worry about than being the other way, as he would find out in years to come.

8.   The Firm

Joe Lee

When you consider the clientele of the billiard hall, there was very little trouble. If there were any little flare-ups, whoever kicked it off got one of Reg's right-handers, and if they came out of that with a jaw in one piece they could count their blessings. With the place belonging to the twins, if there was any sign of bother, all eyes would swivel round to that pair to see what they'd do. After a while this mob would look to them to weigh up their reaction to whatever was going down. So they became leaders if you like.

I think that was when they really started to collect a "firm" around them. I don't think it was ever their intention to set up a gang like the Watney Streeters or the Hoxton Mob; it was other people who saw they could handle themselves and thought, "Hang on, I'm better off behind these Kray boys than not, so I'll stick a bit close".

Though the night a mob tied up with Bernie Silvers and Frank Mifsud turned up, the twins were on their own and they came out on top without any help. This was when Silver and Mifsud were taking pensions out of the East End clubs and some years before they took over the West End. I wouldn't have thought these two cousins of mine had as much bottle as they did. Remember I first saw them when they looked like a couple of little monkeys at twenty minutes old, so in a way I never really saw them with the same eyes as strangers did.

Whatever, they showed how much they'd grown up when half a dozen of these Maltese gangsters walked into the Regal looking to take a bit of protection money out the till. That's one scene they did get right in that Kray film. Reg told me after that Ronnie went absolutely mad. "You should've been there, Joe, you'd have pissed yourself." I thought, "He's a bit right there, but it wouldn't have been through laughing". "Yeah," he said, "Ron chased them out like a bunch of girls and he's swinging that big sword round his head like a fucking windmill." I could imagine. Ever since I'd seen that collection of blades in the bedroom I'd wondered how long it would be before Ron used some of it. As it was, he didn't actually cut anybody that night, but no question he would've done.

Stands to reason, pick up a knife or machete and what do you do? You have a few stabs or a swipe in mid-air and wonder how you'd hold up in a fight. Same with a gun, even if it's only a water pistol – straight-arm; bang; somebody's took one in the head. It's human nature for blokes. It's the way we were brought up with films and what have you, but usually it don't go no further. Ronnie was a different kettle of fish and that's why he shot that fella in the car lot up Bethnal Green Road. There was no need for it but one way or another Ronnie was going to use one of his guns against a real target instead of just looking at it in his bedroom and practising cowboy draws in front of the mirror – and I saw him do that more than once.

This bloke's bought a car off the dealer, and usual thing – he's parted with forty quid, driven it down the road and it was rubbish. Thick oil in the engine, sawdust in the gear box to stop it rattling. He's gone steaming back demanding a refund and was told to piss off. Any ordinary punter would've wiped his mouth and walked away – put it down to experience like. But this fella got a bit leery and threatened to bring a few of his mates back to do the dealer over.

Back then most firms selling second-hand motors were on the fringe of the underworld, if you want to call it that, or they were connected with villains who were taking a pension out of them every week for protection. If they said they didn't need protection then these same villains, to prove that they did, would turn up overnight and go to work with brake fluid and hammers on his stock.

I know the twins and their little mob was into this game because they told me, and as it happens this particular car lot was under their wing. One phone call to the boys suggesting they should do something about this bloke and his threats and earn the few quid they were taking had Ronnie flying upstairs to dig out a bit of his hardware.

In the meantime the fella with the dodgy motor must have had seconds. He was mixed up with the Watney Streeters, but even so somebody must have marked his card that somewhere along the line these Krays were involved, so he's weighed up the options and decided to go back to the dealer and strike a deal without any trouble. Swap the banger for something else or at least get half his money back.

The dealer's no mug and doesn't want to end up in the middle of a war, so at the end of the day him and this fella have just got it sorted and shook hands when Ronnie turns up. He's so wild that somebody's taking the piss, and so desperate to have a pop with his gun, he doesn't even stop to ask what's going on. Straight in – *BANG* – puts a bullet in this fella's leg.

It makes me wonder what was going on in his head at the time. A lot of people and some of the family even reckon he was good as gold until he did a bit of prison time in his early twenties, then took a bad turn when Aunt Rose died. But it speaks for itself that going round shooting a gun off in broad daylight is not what I call normal behaviour, even allowing for the way things were in the East End back then.

So Ronnie's walked away as calm as you like and gone back home to tell Reg what he's done. I don't know where Reg was when this went down, but I'm convinced Ron knew what he was doing when he went flying off on his own. He knew Reg would've put the block on taking a gun when a broken jaw was all that was needed. It was like Ron never looked any further than what he had in his mind. Never considered the consequences. A bit like Reg when he tipped our Rita out of her pram. "Done it, now what are you going to do about it?" OK, if you're four years old; not so good if you're an adult.

Reg went up the wall and the pair of them ended up having a right barney, but as usual Reg was thinking on his feet and drove him over to some friends in Tottenham before the law arrived.

Unless you had a bent doctor there was no way of keeping a gunshot wound quiet. Hospitals had to report anything like that to the law, and within an hour they've got the name off the bloke with a hole in his leg, and they came and picked Reg up. Talk about cool as cucumber – he went along with the whole business. Identity parade and all that, where he was picked out because they were like two peas then, so it's a mistake anyone could make. Trouble was when they came to charge him he was able to produce half a dozen kosher people who'd seen him somewhere else when the shooting took place, so they had to let him go.

Tommy Smithson was the guv'nor around those parts then and the twins were well in with him, so one way or another he straightened up everybody who was involved and they all lost their memory. I did hear that the bloke that got shot ended up getting a drink for keeping his mouth shut, but if he did it was very unusual among that crowd when the normal price of silence was being thankful that you was still breathing.

When it all blew over and Ronnie came home, people were looking at him with different eyes and he loved it. Most of the young fellas that were hanging around them were plastic gangsters. They could have a fight when they were ten strong, and they all did a fair bit of talking about shooting this geezer or shooting that one, but when it came down to it, it takes a lot more bottle than they had to actually pull a trigger, then face ending up on a rope. Yet here was Ronnie, one of their own, and he'd done what they all liked to think they would do in the same situation – but never would – and he'd got clean away with it. So his status has gone right up and Reg's with it.

I can see Ron now sitting in the corner of the billiard hall, always facing the door and with a stern face on him. I used to think he was play-acting some character he'd seen in one of his gangster films, but perhaps he wasn't. I dunno. He certainly had threat in his face. Even as a kid he had eyes that seemed to look right into you, almost as though he was reading what was going on in your head, so you can imagine what he was like when he got older.

With Reg, though, people would look at him and wonder what all the talk was about – you know, where was the threat, because he was more open and friendly and did most of the talking for both of them. If you lived near them or came in contact with them and you went to work from nine until five, they wouldn't bother you in the slightest. They had no interest in pushing around ordinary working people. In fact they went out of their way to do them favours. I'm not saying they were Robin Hoods or nothing, but if we're going to talk about the bad things they got up to, that's got to be balanced against the good.

Some old woman had her house broken into and had a bit of money, some jewellery and a radio nicked – didn't have tellies or videos then. When the twins heard about it they wasn't very pleased, what with it being on their manor, as they liked to call it. They made themselves busy, put the word out and collared the young fella who'd done it. Broke his jaw and both his arms. The old lady got her radio back and more besides out of the boy's own pockets. If it was today that thief would get a few month's community service or be sent off on a rock climbing holiday. As it was, he got what he understood.

Another time they happened to be driving along Kingsland Road when they spotted some woman being messed about by a crowd of drunks. They've backed up, got out of the motor and knocked the four of them out, then given the woman a lift home.

I could go on and on, but you get the picture.

Same with money, though more in their younger days than later on. If they knew of someone down on their luck – *bomp* – here's a few quid, don't pay us back. I know they were copying what the old guv'nors like Timmy Hayes and Jimmy Spinks used to do, but if it meant somebody could buy a pair of shoes or some old girl a coat, it didn't matter what their reasons were.

People say that if they'd never been put away the streets in the East End would've been a lot safer, even today. I think that's a bit fanciful. Back then life was completely different. It was closer knit and nothing much went on that wasn't known about by the guv'nors and all the people that worked for them. Somebody got out of line the finger was easily pointed at them, and then they'd get justice without involving the law. It sounds a bit funny but years ago villainy was a business. Like the docks or the printing game, it was a closed shop and everybody knew each other. To get involved you had to be introduced by someone already in, whichever firm it was. If you wanted to join that was up to you and your own responsibility. If you didn't you was left alone.

Nowadays anything goes with gangsters shooting it out over drugs, and never mind the public who get caught in the middle. Today, and no disrespect to my cousins who've all gone now, the twins wouldn't have lasted five minutes. They might have been pretty ruthless in their day, but nothing compared to what you read in the papers now every week.

In the early fifties your ordinary working man never went near the West End. What was the point? It was expensive and who needed it when there was a pub or club in every street in the East End. They were downmarket, but then so were the majority of people that used them. The twins felt the same and were quite happy running the Regal that was still bringing in a nice weekly wage.

My Aunt May used to look after the takings in an old biscuit tin and one Sunday night she said, "'Ere Joe, how would you like this every week in your pocket?" and she opened this tin. Don't ask me how much cash was in there, but if I remember right there must have been twenty bundles and each one was like a little mattress. So obviously things were going OK and no need for change.

Then Bobby Ramsey got the boys involved in a club up west called Stragglers, and that opened their eyes to the possibilities of getting somewhere like that themselves. They both liked the idea of fronting a place that had a lot more class than an ex-cinema. When I say they got involved, I mean as protection for the club, not on the business side. It always had a reputation of attracting a bit of trouble even in this better-class position, but once word got round that the Krays had an interest it all quietened down.

They kept on at Charlie to keep on looking out for somewhere to open a similar club for themselves and he always said he would. But away from them two he told me it would be a waste of time. He liked the idea in principle but reckoned all the tearaways would make it a base and it would end up as just another speiler.

Then the twins did Ramsey a favour and it all changed. He'd had a spot of bother that ended up with him getting a fractured skull from an iron bar. Well Reg and Ron took this as an insult against themselves, what with Ramsey being a friend and a bloke they looked up to, so when he was back on his feet they was only too pleased to go after the mob who'd done him over.

From what I heard, the one bloke they did come across was a brother who'd never been involved and to be honest Ramsey could've done him with both hands behind his back. But no – the three of them have got stuck in and given him a good hiding, then Bobby finished him off with a sword. Out of order really, and why the three of them didn't end up on a murder charge, god only knows. Lucky too that Ronnie didn't shoot him because, as usual, he was carrying a loaded gun in his jacket, and that's what done him even though he never even fired it. He still had it when the law picked him up and you didn't even have to think about it – he was going down whatever he said.

They tried pulling the "which one of us is which" stunt again and that did get Reg off the hook, but Ramsey got a seven and Ronnie three – so he was going to have plenty of time to think about where he was going after that.

He wasn't behind the door five minutes before Charlie found a place that fitted the bill for the kind of club he'd been dead against up until then. Whether he would've been as keen if Ron was still on the streets I couldn't say – perhaps it was just coincidence that the two things happened at the same time. Either way, Reg and him got stuck into this house down Bow Road, and before we knew where we were they was running a very nice little drinker that wasn't too different from some of the clubs up west. They both took to it a treat. Charlie was happy because him and his brother were hitting it off better than they had in years. At the same time what they were doing was respectable and more like a business than the Regal.

Reg had been right upset when Ron went away, and no doubt he missed him. Unless you're a twin yourself you can't know what it's like being separated from what's part of yourself. But once he saw Ron didn't find prison life a hardship he brightened up a lot and started to enjoy his life a bit more.

I could be wrong but I've always felt that it was Ronnie that pulled Reg in the wrong direction. I don't suppose he needed a lot of pulling, but on his own he was always a different bloke, and this was very obvious when he was walking round the tables in their Double R club chatting to people and checking they was comfortable. Ann and me used to go in there quite a lot and when I looked round at the type of people coming through the doors I really did think they'd turned a corner, and all that villain stuff was out the window.

Right at the beginning a lot of the tearaways from the Regal thought they'd found another nice little berth, but when they saw the way it was being run it didn't suit them and they started to drop off. I mean, you're always going to get a bit of aggravation when there's drink flying about, but Reg jumped on that in his usual way and the message got across.

I even saw Charlie have a go a few times, and you didn't see him flare up too often. He could have a fight when it came down to it, though he was never like the twins. I suppose he took after his old man in that respect and quietened down any trouble with his tongue instead of flying in heavy-handed like his brothers.

I had my own life to lead and I never did get myself involved in all their capers, though I got the offer often enough. Reg would say, "C'mon, Joey, forget that working for a guv'nor lark. Come in with us and make yourself a few quid." But I was never tempted. I'd like to say that I was clever enough to see where it would all end up, but who could have known that? It's easy looking back because thinking about it all the signs were there, especially with Ronnie. He wouldn't be happy until he killed somebody, and being so close with Reg he was going to take him down too. No, I'd seen too many fellas ending up inside and it didn't matter how many times they told me it was no different from being in the services, I got the impression they was trying to convince themselves. So I never fell for it and steered well clear of anything that was iffy enough to merit a bit of prison time.

So Reg and Charlie were doing well for themselves. They didn't forget Ron and were always sticking a few quid in his prison account, but more often palming tens and twenties to him on a visit.

With the money they were taking out of the club my cousins even branched out into gambling clubs. I thought that was a bit of a strange move considering none of the family had ever had any interest in chucking their money away on betting.

Well, up to that time they hadn't, and no connection with what his grandsons were doing, but Grandad Lee thought he'd have a go at backing horses. Why at that time in his life he wanted to take up that mug's game I don't know. He was well old then and knew as much about putting on a bet as he did about flying to the moon.

Any rate, he's gone down to Danny Levy's and after a lot of picking and choosing he's written out a slip putting two bob on some old nag to win at 15–1, so you can guess it wasn't the favourite in the race. He sat with his ear'ole stuck to the radio, and what he's tuned into I don't know. Next thing he's flying round the bookies to pick up his winnings.

He's said to Levy, "Ha-ha – caught yer for thirty bob 'aven't I?" Levy's gone, "No you haven't. Your horse was last – you lost." Course, Grandad wouldn't have that and he's kicking up. "I won. I fucking won." And like he'd settled all his arguments, he started throwing punches around. The bookie's having none of it, so he says "OK, Mr Lee, that's enough. I'm not going to pay you out because you picked a loser, and if you keep it up I'll give Jimmy Taylor a call and he'll soon stop you." Taylor was a local hard man they used to bring in bad debts and what have you.

That don't worry Grandad and he tells him, "Fuck you and fuck Taylor. I want my thirty bob – or else!" Or else what I can't imagine because he was well in his eighties then, but he went home anyway and waited for my father to call in. Then he started. "That fucking Jew bastard Levy – he's caught me and he says he's going to get Taylor to do me over." As it happens Levy was a Jewish man but it wouldn't have mattered if he was Chinese. Whenever Grandad got tucked up or thought he had, whoever had done it was a Jew. Never gave it a second's thought and most of the older blokes came out with the same thing.

Anyway, now my old man's involved. He's no youngster himself but he wasn't having his dad threatened by some tearaway, so he's gone after the bookie. Course, Levy's all apologetic but explains that the old fella was causing a terrible ruck in his shop and he had to quieten him down. He showed Dad the printed results of the race, and that spoke for itself. Levy said he'd forget all about it, but never mentioned he'd already spoken to Taylor.

The next day when my old man was up the road he bumps into this minder, but before he could say anything himself the other bloke says, "What's all this about your father?" The old man explained and this Taylor, who wasn't a bad bloke if you knew him, said, "I won't fall out with your family. Leave it with me and I'll get it squared off." What he did was go back to Levy and tell him to cough up the money for the sake of peace and quiet. As he put it, "You ain't hard up and a few shillings is fuck all to you".

Later on that evening this Jimmy Taylor brought the money round to Grandad and handed it over. Was he pleased that he got a result out of Levy's good heart after backing a loser? No he wasn't. He snatched the money and said, "So that fucking crooked thieving bastard thought better of it, did he? I knew I'd won." Jimmy Taylor just gave him a funny look and walked out the door.

He never did have another bet – gave it up while he was ahead I suppose.

Betting hadn't long been legal then, but as soon as it was, you had shops opening up everywhere. Before that if you wanted a flutter you laid it with the runners who hung about on street corners. They stuck out a mile and all looked the same. Pork-pie hat on the head, racing paper under the arm and eyes going round like wheels on a fruit machine, looking all ways for coppers because they was nicked regular every week and fined a pound or so.

An uncle on my mother's side was a bookie's runner and I saw him one day so went up and tapped him on the shoulder. He jumped two feet in the air, and that was the first time I ever heard him swear. Nerves like violin strings in that game.

We were all hit bad when Aunt Rose died. We knew it was going to come eventually because what she had was incurable at the time, but being prepared doesn't help when it happens.

Outwardly anyway, it affected Ronnie the worst and whatever it was that was wrong with him got worse and came right to the front, and as we all know they certified him. Whether the same would have happened without Rose dying and him being locked up, who knows? Though I have a feeling he'd been headed that way for more years than the family would admit. Still, he was in good hands and there was nothing we could do about it.

I drove his mum and dad down to the hospital a few times and really it was a bit of a waste of time because you couldn't get more than a few words out of him. I mean, you had to feel for him because he didn't even seem to know where he was. I'd always got on well with him and he'd never done me any harm, and I come out of that place thinking, "What's it all about?"

Then Reg come up with the idea of springing him because he reckoned they were pumping him full of all kinds and making him worse. I was there when he put it to Charlie and he was dead against it. So was I but I kept my mouth shut. One, because it wasn't for me to stick my bit between two brothers, and two, didn't matter what I said, Reg would do what he thought – no matter what.

He got Charlie round to his way of thinking in the end, but he drew the line when it came to going and bringing Ron out. And so did I when Reg asked me to drive him down to Long Grove. He went a bit quiet over that but I thought, "fuck it". I wasn't risking going down for something I thought was a stupid idea anyway.

He got Georgie Osbourne to take him in the end and that was that. Whatever my opinion was I've got to hand it to him because he pulled it off, cool as you like. Swapped coats and glasses and Ron walked out and Reg fronted up the law when they turned up at the hospital. Anybody else would've lost their bottle or given the game away. Not him. He was never intimidated by any form of authority or the police, unlike most of us. He could look ahead and think things out and that's why I've always thought that without Ronnie and his daft capers, he could've gone a long way.

A lot of career criminals that didn't have half the knack he did for pulling something off are millionaires today. Sitting on some island in the sun and you don't even know their names. That could've been Reg, but he always stuck by his brother and I don't hold that against him, but it would eventually bring him down.

I think I saw Ron twice when he was on the run and once at Vallance Road when they brought him home just before they turned him back in. The first time was at a bit of a do the family was having over Tottenham. He only stayed an hour and a half but he seemed fine. The second time was when I took Reg down to this caravan he was hiding up in, and again he seemed all right – which made me think Reg had been right all along. He only turned a bit funny when it was time for us to leave. Didn't understand why we couldn't stay for a few days or why he couldn't come home with us.

The third time I saw him was when I called in at Vallance Road for something or other and Reg had brought him home. He did look a state. Reg wanted to shoot out so he asked me to chat to Ron while he was gone, and off he went. Well I looked at him and he looked at me as though he'd never seen me before. He was so strange I couldn't think of anything to say, then after five minutes of this he said, "Who are you then?" I thought he was having a laugh except he was dead serious. I said, "I'm Joey – your cousin Joey." He screwed up his eyes and gave me one of his looks and said, "You in here as well?" but I could tell he didn't have a clue who I was. I tried all kinds to liven him up, but he wouldn't even look at me let alone answer. So much for Reggie's "Have a chat with him". Then suddenly he said, "I've had diphtheria but I'm getting over it now". And I thought to myself you should be – that was over twenty years ago and as far as I knew he'd never remembered it before, but all I said was, "That's good, Ron. You'll soon be out and about."

When Reg came back I told him how he'd been and suggested it was about time they got a proper doctor to have a look at him because he wasn't all there at all. Reg always seemed to have the answers but this time he looked like he didn't know which way to turn and he said, "D'you think it would be like grassing him up if we sent him back to Long Grove?". I said, "No mate, you'd be doing him a big favour". And whether that swung him I don't know but the next I heard Ron was back where he belonged and getting looked after properly.

He was lucky that they didn't reassess his mental state as soon as they got him in hospital. If you can get out of a mental home and keep your nose clean for six weeks they have to say, "Well, he must be all right, else he couldn't have managed all that time," so they scratch the certification. Cobblers really because if they'd seen the state he was in while he was on the run, they'd have banged him up for good.

As it was they gave him all the right pills and what have you, brought him back from the edge then gave him all the tests. Naturally with the right medication he was fine and passed with flying colours, so they'd no choice but to sign him out and put him in a mainstream prison.

Again he was under supervision so they made sure he took his pills every day, which kept him straight, and he sailed through the rest of his sentence. Trouble was, and would be, without those pills that he was going to have to take for the rest of his life, he'd slip back. And that's what happened every time he thought he could get away without taking them.

Once he got into the Double R he wanted to take it over, and as Charlie often said, he made a fucking nuisance of himself. He wanted money, and there was plenty of that flying about, but he didn't have any interest in it. He'd think nothing of dipping in the till for two or three hundred quid and giving it to the first person that gave him a hard-luck story. In the end they was queuing up to tap him because he was an easy touch.

The funniest thing I heard was when he thought he'd pull in a bit extra by putting the squeeze on a local pub – protection money if you like. He's slipped in there on his own and told the landlord that he wanted a tenner a week or else, and he'd be back every Friday to collect. Now the firm was well into this caper anyway and this particular pub was already on the list, so the geezer came flying round to Reg wanting to know what's going on and why he was expected to pay twice. Reg told him to say nothing and to give Ron the money when he asked, then take it out of what he was already paying the firm.

The truth is Ron never recovered from that big breakdown, and without mincing words he was a mental case then and would be the rest of his life. Only thing was none of us could see it.

He was different – there's no two ways about it. He was a lazy bastard, but then he'd never been too keen on doing over much all his life. Reg and Charlie were ducking and diving all over the place, and he was quite content either to sit around in the club or lay out on the settee at his mum's. Reg used to say, "Joey, Ron's going to put us out of business". But he never said what he could do about it because he didn't know what to do himself. Then he got into a bit of bother and you could tell that with him out of the picture things were going to get worse.

I don't doubt that what Reg told me happened over Hampstead that day was the truth. He'd got no reason to lie to me and it was obvious to anyone with half an eye that he was stitched up. This Danny Shay was more a mate of Ronnie's than Reggie's, but for some reason it was Reg he took with him when he had something to sort out. I think Shay knew exactly what he was doing when he turned up at some shop with one of the Kray brothers right behind him. The geezer owed him a hundred pounds, or something like, so he's gone storming in shouting his mouth off that he was going to do this and that if he didn't get it. As far as Reg knew he was just along for the ride and didn't even want to be there in the first place. He didn't do nothing and didn't get involved apart from standing there looking tough, which he was pretty good at doing. But I suppose the shop owner got the message that he was being threatened by one of the top gangsters around at the time, and when they left he's phoned the law.

Not long after Reg was picked up and charged with demanding money with menaces. When I took his mum up to see him in Wandsworth he was convinced it would be thrown out of court once he'd given his story. As he said, "Would I be mug enough to get involved for a poxy hundred notes? You've seen it, Joey. There's ten times that in the club's petty cash tin." He was right, there was, so I had to agree with him. I'm not making out he wasn't capable of demanding a few quid; it was no secret that a good lump of the firm's wages came from that sort of thing. It's only my opinion but what I'm saying is, in that particular instance, he just happened to be in the wrong place at the wrong time.

I should think the law knew the score as well, and they also knew about what the twins were getting up to elsewhere, so in their opinion they were getting a nicking against one of them for something he didn't do because they couldn't pin down a charge on things they had. Swings and roundabouts, but no consolation to Reg getting banged up for fifteen months. Well he did it in two lumps really. Nine months on remand, a bit of bail on appeal, which he lost, and six months after they pulled him back in again.

Mind you, he made himself busy in between. The three of them did because they took over Esmerelda's Barn in Wilton Place. On top of that Reg had met a girl by the name of Frances Shea, so he had a couple of good reasons for looking forward to being back on the street.

Funny that the girl he was desperate to get out and see had the same name as the bloke that got him put away – same sound, different spelling.

I never did understand all the ins and outs of how they got their hands on such a plush moneymaker as Esmerelda's. You can bet your life it wasn't legal, but what I don't know I can't talk about and that suits me.

Ann and me went up there a few times, but to be honest it wasn't our cup of tea at all, what with all the nobs and the gambling. We wasn't alone in thinking like that. You're average man who lived in Bethnal Green wouldn't want to put his head round the door of a place like that. He thought, and wasn't far wrong, that they were full of corruption – even if it was the top people in the land who were the customers. And I've got to say there was a few faces pointed out to me that were high up – judges, coppers and politicians. Still, you've got to hand it to the boys, they did well in getting their feet under the table.

With Reg being out of the way, Ron didn't do the place any favours. If he took a fancy to someone (and I mean like – not the other thing) he'd think nothing of scrapping a table debt that could be as much as a couple of grand. What hair Charlie wasn't pulling out was turning grey with the worry of it all, and I think he was well pleased when Reg came out to back him up.

Poor old Charlie had enough problems with his marriage without that aggravation on his plate as well. I don't want to say too much against his missus, Dolly, because there's always two sides to everything – especially with relationships. But she never really fitted into the family, and that must say something because all the women accepted anyone at face value. Didn't matter if they were a tramp or a lord, they all got the same welcome.

The twins were the same really. One minute you'd see them talking to some old geezer sweeping the road outside the club, the next a film star, and they never talked up or down to either one. So something about Dolly must have got up their noses. This was before she started knocking about with George Ince, so you can imagine what it was like once rumours started flying about.

Charlie was always too easy-going for his own good and didn't do too much about it. Perhaps he didn't care over much. But Reg as usual took anything against his family as personal and done Ince over on a couple of occasions. He must have been well in love or had plenty of bottle, because who in their right mind would've thought of having an affair with a woman married to a Kray? Their goings on only really went public when Charlie was doing his ten and the twins life, and by then she'd changed her name to Dolly Grey. That made me laugh. If you're going to change your name to hide your identity you'd think of a hundred names that didn't come near sounding like your old one.

How she came to tell the world that she was having it off with this bloke and showing up Charlie who couldn't do nothing about it, was when Ince was charged with murder at the Barn Restaurant – nothing to do with and miles away from Esmerelda's Barn. Dolly stood up in court and told them her and Ince had been in bed together that night – and it was all out in the open. As it turned out he really wasn't involved and was proved innocent.

I went to visit Charlie the week after she visited him, once it was in the open. He said, "Joe, you wouldn't have believed this room last week. They must have had every screw in the place round me when she came in. I think they thought I was going to try and kill her, but

I don't give a fuck." Still, it was bothering him back then and wouldn't change until they started up in the Kentucky Club.

I don't think Reg was out of prison more than a couple of months before the law nicked the twins and Charlie over something laughable because it was so ridiculous.

Ron and Charlie were out with a mate, who was doing the driving. He pulled up in Dalston and told them to wait while he ran some sort of errand. After a while my cousins got fed up sitting in the motor so got out to stretch their legs. They're walking up and down and leaning on the car every now and then, like you do, when a squad car pulled up and arrested them for loitering with intent. As an afterthought, they slung in the report that they'd been seen trying door handles. How was that going to look in the papers? I was going to put two respectable businessmen, but I'll stick to the truth and say businessmen, which they were, owning a couple of clubs and between them more money than they knew what to do with. Where was the logic in trying to fit them up on a charge that wouldn't get a result with a twelve year old?

A couple of days later it was Reggie's turn, and I was there when the Old Bill turned up. I happened to be talking a few things over with Reg when there's a bang on the door and it's a copper with some woman going, "That's him. That's him." According to her she'd seen him running out of her house with a bundle of jewellery that he'd nicked. She was making such a fuss my Aunt May came out of her house and said to the copper, "Can't you lot ever leave him alone? Why don't you piss off." You have to laugh – the copper gave her a look and said; "Why don't you piss off indoors, madam?"

End of the day this Italian woman had identified Reg, so he was arrested. But before that, and showing again he always thought on his feet, he saw some bloke walking along across the other side of the road. He's shouted over, "Oi mate, come over 'ere a minute". I'll bet the bloke's arse was making buttons because everyone knew the Krays, but when he got over the road, Reg said, "I want you to be a witness that I've got nothing on me," and he started to empty his pockets out. He couldn't ask us because we were family, so it was a good move. The copper's saying, "No need for that – that'll do," and

REGGIE AND FRANCES – An ill-fated romance.

FRANCES WITH RITA'S
BABY KIMMY –
Frances was never
happier than when
she could get away
from the firm and
the clubs and spend
time with the Lees
in a normal family
environment.

REGGIE AND FRANCES —
He placed her so high
on a pedestal that their
relationship was doomed
from the start.

In Loving Memory
of my dear wife
Frances
who passed away
7th June, 1967 aged 23 years

———————

If I could write the beauty
of your eyes,
And in fresh numbers
Number all your graces,
The Age to come would say:
' This poet lies;
Such heavenly touches
ne'er touched earthly faces'.

FRANCES KRAY
'IN MEMORIAM' —
While her death was
a tragedy for Reg, it
must be remembered
it was also a tragedy
for her family.

DAVID, KIMMY, ALBERT AND REG'S DOG, REX

RITA, VIOLET AND MAY – Three good-looking blondes.

REGGIE WITH HIS AUNT ROSE – He not only had her temperament,
but her looks as well. Of anyone in the family, Rose was the one
that encouraged the twins in their fighting and disregard for the law.

REG WITH TOMMY BROWN (known as "The Bear") – It is often said that he was a minder for the twins. In fact he idolized the boys and simply looked out for them.

VIOLET, NANNY LEE AND RONNNIE – Nanny's tongue could strip paint but she had a heart of gold.

RONNIE – at Lake Lucerne.

YOUNG JOE, JOHNNY AND THE KEMP BROTHERS –
At the studio while making *The Krays* movie.

YOUNG JOE, MAY, CHARLIE AND OLD JOE – At a wedding.

CHARLIE AND RITA – They became closer as adults. All Charlie ever wanted was to make a living. Instead he was drawn into the criminal world of his brothers.

OLD JOE LEE – In Rose's front room, flanked by a teddy, supposedly made by Reg and sold for £10 (no family discount). On the right is the flower stand 'nicked' by Violet for Rose.

GANGMASTER BILL SHIPPEY – For a number of years he employed the Kray family for fruit picking contracts in the Wisbech area of the fens. A prized possession was a jewellery box "made" and given as a gift from the twins soon after they were imprisoned for life. Fond of the boys he and his wife kept in contact with them both over the years.

GRANDAD LEE AGED OVER NINETY – This photograph says it all.
He was loyal and honest (apart from those scales) but upset
him and he'd "up you" in a second.

CARD MADE UP BY RONNIE –
This was given to Peter Gerrard as a token gift on a visit.

REGGIE WHILST IN MAIDSTONE PRISON –
This was given to Peter Gerrard, again as a gift.

A PAINTING BY RONNIE – These were invariably dark
and brooding, perhaps suggesting his personal feelings.

ONE OF REGGIE'S DRAWINGS – Reg always depicted a pyramid shape somewhere in his pictures. Exercise for a psychiatrist?

YOUNG JOE, OLD JOE AGED 97 AND PETER GERRARD –
At Old Joe's flat in Sussex.

RITA AT RONNIE'S FUNERAL – What might have been forgotten
in the media circus surrounding the event, was the fact that the
few remaining family were burying a much-loved relative.

Reg said, "Fucking right, no need for that. I wasn't born yesterday." He took the bloke's name and told him he owed him one, and coming from one of the Kray brothers that was like money in the bank for the fella.

After he was taken away my aunt and me just looked at each other, and we were both thinking the same. You could lay a lot of bad things against him, and in the end the law did, but break into somebody's house and nick their gear like some teenage scrote – never in your life. No, the law tried to pull one and came unstuck when all three of them were acquitted. It was all over the papers and the Old Bill got such a knock back from that, they left the twins alone for a long time.

9.   The Blind Beggar to Broadmoor

Joe Lee

I used to think it was comical when they had meetings upstairs at Vallance Road. If I was around I never sat in because I was never one of the firm, but I might be downstairs talking to my aunt, and you'd hear *crash* as the table's gone over in the bedroom – somebody's said the wrong thing. Violet never turned a hair. She'd just raise her eyebrows at me as much as to say, "Boys, what are they like?" Or a fella would come head over heels down the stairs, pick himself up and run out the door. She'd call up, "Now, now," like they were a bunch of little kids getting over excited. I'm sure she never had a clue what they were really like because she never saw the end result of how vicious they could be.

To be fair most of the damage they did to people was forced on them. I mean, if you fronted either one of them up then you had to be prepared to take the consequences.

Uncle Johnny told me that a friend of his was in a motor dealer's talking to the guv'nor when two big dockers came in looking for Ronnie. The firm had an interest in the place that probably amounted to nipping a bit of protection every week. Either way, these geezers knew that he turned up every Thursday to collect, so they told the guv'nor they'd wait until he showed, what with it being pension day. This mate of Johnny's was no mug and took a good guess that these dockers weren't there for a friendly chat, so doing himself a bit of good he's made some excuse and gone and phoned up the Double R.

Twenty minutes later a taxi pulled up, Ronnie's jumped out and burst into the office shouting, "Where's these fucking gangsters?" One of them was sitting with his feet up on the desk. Ronnie never even asked who he was or what he wanted, just kicked his legs down and smashed him full in the face with one of those big old staplers they used to have in offices. Split him wide open. The other geezer took off like a rabbit. Ronnie's said, "Do what you want with him," gone out, got in the taxi and gone back to the club. Vicious yes, but it wasn't him who went looking for trouble – those dockers brought it to him.

And that happened time and time again.

Same as in the Blind Beggar one night, and this was long before the shooting. Four fellas came to give the twins a good hiding, and I'm talking about four tough guys here who were well-known villains. Did Reg and Ron bottle out? No, they locked the door so these fellas couldn't get out, then got stuck into them. The damage they did to these four made them legends around Bethnal Green once it leaked out. Then when you've got a reputation like that going in front of you, you don't have to do much to keep it up.

You've only got to look at their photographs to see they weren't too big; five foot nine or thereabouts? Twelve stone? But as they proved time and time again you don't have to be big if you've got it inside you. There were fellas out there built like brick shithouses, but once word got around that the twins were unbeatable, well it was better to be on their side than to come up against them.

Something else from their photos – not a mark on them and I don't remember ever seeing them with as much as a bloody nose. And that's saying something when you think how many battles they got into.

This reputation thing – they used that in other ways and it never did them any harm. Once they got well known all over London, anything that went down that was a bit strong got hung on them. If a villain disappeared or got shot or slashed to pieces, the whisper would go round that those Kray brothers had a hand in it. Eight times out of ten it would be nothing to do with them, but a nod's as good as a wink to a blind horse and the twins never confirmed and, better still, never denied all the rumours. They knew that the sound of their name caused a lot of fear and as far as they were concerned it could only help their empire get bigger and bigger.

I've never understood the fascination people have of rubbing shoulders with villains. I suppose when you've been brought up among them like I was, you see them for what they really were without all the romance that gets written up in books. I'm not talking about the twins here, I'm referring to the fellas Grandad knew, and them my old man knocked about with, and of course a lot of fellas that lived local and chose a different path from me. Pick a book up today and they come over as Robin Hoods, but if you knew the truth most of them were nothing but robbing bastards who'd rip off their own granny for a couple of shillings. Not nice people at all. How nice is it to run a razor round someone's face? Or brain damage someone with an iron bar who's got a wife and kids to support, because they said a word out of place?

Some of the hard men were of the old school. They gave respect and they got a lot of respect back, but too many of them frightened even me, because you never knew which way they were going to turn next, so you was always on your guard. But like I say there's always been this fascination straight goers have with mixing with the underworld and the people in it, who are prepared to do things they couldn't even dream of doing.

Like with the Kentucky Club. You wouldn't believe the punters who came in and out, every one of them looking up to the twins like they was royalty. There must have been a thousand clubs they could have gone to and had a great night out, but no, the club in the Mile End Road had a bonus as far as they were all concerned because it was run by gangsters.

Years after, one of the firm told me that in those days they were earning good money out of Northern club-owners for nothing more than an introduction to the twins. What they'd do was make themselves busy on the phone to all these places in Liverpool or Manchester, anywhere they could get a result, and for cash up front ranging from five hundred to a couple of grand, these fellas in the firm would arrange for the owner to come to London and have a drink with the boys. Sometimes all they got for their money was a handshake from Reg and a glare out of Ron, but it didn't matter. After that they could go home and spraunce up the truth about the time they had spent with the Kray twins. Did wonders for their business. If they were lucky they'd get a signed photo, "To my friend Jack – God bless," and all that cobblers – stick it on the wall behind their bar and it would act as a pretty strong deterrent to local tearaways. That's how far the Kray name had spread. Mind you, if you weigh it up these people were getting protection at cut price really.

Anyway, this sort of excitement their name brought out in straight people must have been one of the reasons why Barbara Windsor took Joan Littlewood along to the Kentucky when she was working on the film *Sparrers Can't Sing*. Course it cut both ways and Reg and Ron loved getting involved with all these actors and celebrities, so when it was suggested the club be used for a couple of scenes they were all up for it.

When it was all wrapped up and premiered at the Empire, Reg said to me in the Kentucky, "You ain't gonna believe this, Joey. Princess Margaret and her old man's gonna show up at the party here afterwards." It was true enough but it took a lot of believing that these two tearaway cousins of mine would be entertaining members of the royal family. As it turned out, they did go to the opening of the film, but then had another engagement straight after. That was the message the boys got but in my opinion somebody high up whispered in the princess's ear and told her it would be a bad move to be seen with the Krays. Stands to reason.

The Old Bill didn't have nothing on the twins, or at least not enough to get them in court, but they were watching their every move and just waiting for a slip, and when it came they didn't want the queen's sister mixed up in it.

It shows they were keeping them under surveillance because we were all indoors one day when Reg said, "That's the law sitting in that motor on the corner". So Ron said, "Watch this, I'll have a laugh". He made a couple of cups of tea, dug out a silver-plated tray he'd won at boxing, and took them over to these coppers. He's tapped on the car window, give them the tea and said, "'Ere you are, boys. Warm you up a bit. And by the way, don't nick my tray. Bring it back when you're finished." They didn't know what to say. Ron's humour was never sophisticated but you couldn't help laughing.

Barbara Windsor was only well known locally when she first came to the club, and I've got to say she was a right little head-turner. Blond hair, tidy figure, and of course that famous chest. She sent blood racing as soon as she walked in the door, but none as fast as our Charlie's because he fell head over heels from the first minute he clapped eyes on her. He was still married to Dolly even though things weren't going too well, but that didn't stop him having an affair with Barbara. He thought the world of her and if he'd been free I'm sure he would have married her like a shot. But being the bloke he was, loyal and always trying to please everyone, he knocked it on the head because he didn't want a divorce to upset his boy Gary. Shame really, he should've grabbed the chance for a bit of happiness while it was offered, because he didn't have too much of that in his life.

Then there was Reg with the girl he'd met between prison time. She was very young but nice enough and a bit of a looker, but I often wondered what the pair of them had in common. Reg wasn't the most talkative bloke in the world, but at least you could have a conversation with him. Frances, well you could sit there all night and she wouldn't open her mouth unless she had to. So you got the impression she chose not to join in or else she had nothing she felt worth saying. I could be speaking well out of turn here because when her and Reg were on their own perhaps she was a live wire, but it's hard to imagine. It didn't help that Ron took an instant dislike to her and never missed an opportunity to make it plain. Must have terrified the life out of her, especially when the twins had a row with her sitting in the middle, and when they did kick off with each other it would've put the wind up a strong fella, let alone a slip of a girl like she was.

Then her and Reg started rowing and it was all on one minute then all off the next. She was taking all kinds of pills for her nerves and what have you, so with one thing and another I'm surprised Reg didn't see the writing on the wall. But he wouldn't have a word said about her no matter how many times she took off back to her mother's. When they was together they'd end up fighting, and when they weren't he couldn't get her back fast enough. Still, if he knew what love was that's what he felt for her, and when the end came it tore the heart out of him.

He blamed her parents and they blamed him, but who knows what lay behind it. If she'd never got mixed up with the Krays and had married some ordinary bloke, would she still be alive today? Or like Ron, did she have some sort of mental problem right from the start? You can only guess. Either way, it was a tragedy for Reg and, what people forget, just as much of one for her family.

Looking back, it seems like there was so much going on over a short period of years, it was like they knew everything was going to come to a full stop and wanted to get the most out of what they had left, or make some sort of mark. With all the interests they had in drinking clubs and gambling clubs, they were making money hand over fist. They had coppers in their pockets and a few politicians as well.

I was having a cup of tea with Ron at Vallance Road. The phone rang, and with him having a shave in the kitchen I picked it up, and a posh voice said, "Can I speak to Ronnie, please". When I asked the bloke who he was he said, "It's Robert. Robert Boothby, Lord Boothby." I put my hand over the mouthpiece and told Ron who it was and he said, "Tell the old poof to fuck off," which I thought was rich coming from him, though if it ever came up he always said he was "homosexual" like there was some distinction. Well, I wasn't passing that on to a lord, so I just said I was afraid he wasn't available, and put the phone down. Ronnie stuck his head out of the kitchen and said, "That ain't what I said, Joe". I said, "I know. If you want to tell him that, you phone him back, but what's a geezer like that doing ringing you up?" He just laughed and tapped his nose. "He has his uses, don't you worry." I didn't worry because it was none of my business, but I couldn't help thinking about that call when it was splashed all over the *Daily Mirror* that something was going on between a top gangster and a politician.

Like I say, the boys were making themselves busy and with money to burn they bought themselves a mansion at Bildestone in Suffolk – not far from where they'd been evacuated to when they were kids, The Brooks. Tidy old place and worth a few quid, but knowing the way they worked it probably came to them a bit the other way, if you know what I mean.

Ron used to walk around the grounds and the village like he was Lord of the Manor. Big old coat on, flat cap and silver-topped cane. People would say good morning to him like he was gentry, and I used to think if only you knew who this geezer is. He loved the life, and if things were different back in London I'm sure he could've settled down to living there permanent. I think that spell in the countryside during the war stuck in both their minds and never went away.

Then they had another taste of country living when their Mum and Dad took them up to Wisbech every summer when they were twelve to fourteen, for a bit of fruit picking. It was like a holiday and earned a few bob at the same time.

Years later Ann and me ended up living not far from where they used to go and I happened to meet the old farmer that they worked for and he asked me in for a cup of tea. Bill Shippey – nice old boy. Well it was only natural to ask him if those little bastards had terrorized the village and turned the farm upside down, but he looked at me like I was gone out and told me no, they was polite lads and better behaved than the average cockney tearaway he had to employ. I mean he was so impressed he took the pair of them into his own house so they didn't have to live with their parents and all the other families in the big old sheds that was the normal billet.

After dinner and that, these two used to argue over who would do the washing up, made their own beds and run up and down to the local shop for the farmer's missus. I thought fucking hell – we can't be talking about the same two kids who I knew. Back home their mother had to do everything for them, even clean their shoes, so there must have been something special in the air up in the Fens.

This Mr Shippey took to the twins so much he kept in touch with them all the years they were away until he died himself a few years ago. From what he told me, one of his proudest possessions was a jewel box the twins had sent to him and his wife when they were together in Parkhurst. He dug this box out from a cupboard and sat it on his knee while he told me the boys made it with their own hands. It was a beautiful thing and any cabinet maker would've been happy to put his name on it, and to be honest I looked to see if he had, because no way could my cousins have put together such a thing. I can't remember them even knocking a six-inch nail in, let alone have the patience or talent for anything better.

I wasn't going to spoil things for the old chap, but this sort of caper helps the wheels go round in the prison system. You want a present for your mum or missus, get yourself half-ounce of snout and put the word out you're looking for a jewel box, a cuddly toy or the Eiffel Tower made out of matchsticks, and in two minutes all those fellas with nimble fingers would be queuing up to flog you some of their stock. I'm not having a knock at the twins because it was a nice enough gesture to send out a present and a lot of people have proudly got these things up on the mantelpiece today. But by their own hands? No. Sorry.

Going back to that big old mansion, my aunt and uncle spent a good bit of time up there, and when they did they lived in what used to be the gatekeeper's cottage – right at the entrance of the gravel drive that went up to the house. Reg and Ron wanted them to give up Vallance Road and live there full time but they wouldn't have it so they suggested buying them a place a bit nearer to London. But no – all their mates and family were in the East End and they wouldn't budge, not even when the council decided to pull down all the houses my family had lived in for years and years.

All the others was pleased enough to go, even Grandad, but Nanny Lee kicked up hell. Like she said, "They can pull the place down on me 'ead but I ain't leaving". She was a tough old girl and we could see she had it in her mind to barricade herself in, as old as she was. So in the end me, the old man and Uncle Johnny got a trailer and turned up on the day. She's still giving it some, so my dad told her, "Mother, you either walk out or we carry you out and tie you on top of all the furniture. It's up to you," and she gave in. Lovely little ground-floor maisonette it was that they went to, but even when they was settled in she'd still rather have been in the other place with rats and mice flying about all over.

I've said before there was always something going on with my grandparents – never a dull moment as they say. In this new place they had a little brick cubby-hole sort of thing out the front, with a flap door for the coalman to stick the coal in. I went round there one day and she's got this flap open and she's waving a broom handle round her head and shouting after the coal lorry that was up the road a bit. "Oi, you bastard," she's hollering. "Fucking well come back 'ere and I'll up you with this stick." Ninety years old this is. I've said, "What's up, Nan?" And she said, "Effing so-and-so's short changed me on the coal and I'll 'ave 'im".

Another time my old man was going to look in on her and a mate of his gave him a lift in his car. On the way Dad's said to this fella, "Look, when we get down there don't take any notice of my mother's language 'cos it can be a bit strong". The other bloke's laughed and said, "Don't worry, my old girl's just the same". True to form, as they pull up outside the maisonette she's out there effing and blinding and carrying on. When Dad asked her, "What's up?" she said, "This fucking hole you've stuck me in, I can't get the door open." She'd pulled the door to and locked herself out. But it was everybody else's fault, including the house, and not down to her.

The old man caught her cursing and swearing at some suited bloke one day. As he got closer, Dad caught the tail-end and she was saying, "I'll give you, come 'ere threatening women". And the bloke's walked away a bit smartish. Now for all the old man knows, this geezer's one of them that tries to con old girls out of their money, so while he's asking Nanny what's going on, he's keeping an eye on this fella who's gone further up the road. "Right, Mother, what's his game? How come he threatened you?" She said, "That one-eyed bastard wants the rent money and I paid it last week". The old man laughed and said, "Knowing you, you ain't paid it since last year, so it ain't the bloke's fault".

This sort of caper wasn't once in a blue moon like most families, it was every week if not every day.

Sometimes I wonder if the twins knew exactly how they were going to end up, and with one thing and another slowly worked toward their own downfall. There they were getting along nicely, plenty of respect, plenty of dough and both living in luxury flats in Cedra Court.

OK, Reg was having a few problems with Frances, but apart from that things couldn't have been better all round. So what do they do? They decide to spring Frank Mitchell out of Dartmoor and get it spread all over the papers. Of course, the law didn't catch up with the twins over that for a long time, but it surprised me when they ended up in court charged with murdering him that one of the blokes who put half a dozen bullets into Mitchell never even got a mention. When things started to get a bit warm he took off to Australia, but distance doesn't usually let anybody off the hook when it involves murder. So either the law couldn't afford the fare to go and pick him up or else all they were interested in was getting the twins behind bars. I don't know, but it makes you think – justice is a funny thing.

Talking of funny things, Uncle Johnny was working in a lorry depot and while him and some other fellas were having a tea break the conversation came round to families, and it came out that my uncle was related to the twins. One of the fellas – a bit leery like – said, "Them Kray twins, they're fuck all – nothing but front". Now Johnny might have looked like his sister Rose, but he'd never taken up with fighting like she had, so instead of taking this comment as an insult against the family, he just shrugged his shoulders and told the other bloke that everyone's entitled to an opinion and if that was his, good luck to him. But the fella won't leave it. He says, "Now if you want to talk about a guv'nor, a right tough geezer, I know a bloke who could do the pair of them with one hand". "Oh yeah," says Johnny, "who's that then, you?" He goes, "Nah, a bloke called George Cornell." Johnny still don't rise. He says, "I'll be seeing my nephews a bit later on. I'll pass your message on. It's bound to put the wind up them." Next day Ronnie walked into the Blind Beggar and shot Cornell through the head.

As Uncle Johnny said to me, talk like that was all bollocks and he'd never repeat something like it to the twins. But with the whole of East London knowing that Ronnie Kray had pulled the trigger even before the police did, this geezer with the big mouth packed his job up and disappeared thinking he might be the next.

As far as Cornell went, he was in the wrong place at the wrong time, and if it hadn't been him it would've been someone else. There's a lot of people out there today who are only alive now because Ronnie didn't happen to have a gun in his pocket when he had a go at them. They might have had a slap or a bollocking, but because of Ron's mental state at the time, they could just as easily have got the same as Cornell.

If Reg had known what was going to happen and could've talked him out of flying off the handle, it would've been prevented. But in my opinion if a shooting of some sort hadn't happened that night, it would've been the next week or the next month because it was firmly in Ron's head that somebody was going to die.

There's been a lot of old nonsense written about Cornell, like he was asking to be done what with going round saying this and that, but I don't think he was any better or any worse than most of the blokes knocking around then. In fact my old man was friendly with some of the family, and he didn't see much wrong in him. Same with cousin Billy and he should know because he was stationed alongside him out in Malta. Perhaps if people paint him blacker than he was it sort of justifies Ronnie killing him.

Mind you, my Aunt Violet was getting quite a lot of funny phone calls in the run-up to him getting killed. Sometimes there was nobody at the other end, or at least nobody who said anything, and other times this person would say, "Are those two ponces there?" Or, "I wanna word with one of them arse'oles". She passed the phone over to Ronnie one day when he happened to be there and all he did was chuck it down without speaking. He never did say to me who he thought it was, but Reg told me that right or wrong, Ron had it down to Cornell. If it was him you can only think he was pushing his luck a bit and as it turned out pushed it too far in the end.

Same as McVitie, it depends on who you talk to as to whether he was the nasty geezer word has it, or just another villain. Like Uncle Charlie, Jack was OK when he was sober. Put a bit too much drink inside him and he was a different bloke altogether. The Kray film didn't do him no favours what with getting Tom Bell to play his part. Good actor and all that, and it wasn't down to him how they wanted him to put over the character, but watching the film gives the impression that Jack was this snivelling old git who didn't know his arse from his elbow. In fact he was something like the opposite and from what I know, as game as a bagel. Not too old, well built and not a bad-looking fella, and I can't help thinking what his family must have gone through at the time and year after year ever since. I mean that's some funny sort of epitaph for anybody, just to be known as a murder victim and nothing else.

I was going to say how could Reg get himself mixed up in something like that, something so bloody it makes your blood run cold to think about it. But thinking back to the way the pair of them beat that chicken to death and a few other instances, I've got to admit that this sort of behaviour was inside them from the start.

A lot of things came to a head that night. Losing Frances like he did tipped Reg over the edge – no doubt about it. Then there was the pressure from the law that was closing in over Mitchell and Cornell, so with one thing and another he was living on his nerves. I mean, Ronnie didn't give a fuck because half the time he was off in his own world, but Reg was wide awake, knew things were getting bad and couldn't do nothing about it.

People make a lot out of the fact that Ron was supposed to have said, "I've done mine, now you've got to do yours". Well, according to Reg he never said no such thing and I believe him because with something like that Ron wouldn't have to open his mouth. Reg knew he had to keep up with his brother. It goes all the way back to counting those peas on a plate – neither one of them was going to be bested by the other.

If Jack McVitie was the weak sort of fella people have the idea he was, he would've laid down when the twins went for him and told them to get on with it. But talking to Reg and Ron and some of the other blokes who was there, it seems that Jack could've walked away and that bit of crime history might not have happened. I'm not saying he brought it on himself, but the choice was his not to hang about. Never mind that he was supposedly invited to a party. When he walked into that room Ronnie told him to fuck off out of it because he didn't want him there. He must have had some bottle, because instead of making himself scarce, Jack walked up and down the room punching one fist into the palm of his hand saying, "You can't talk to me like that – I won't have it". He got himself so wound up he punched out one of the panes of glass in the window. So he wasn't screaming to get out until one of them pushed his head into the glass. He did it himself out of temper. Stands to reason Ron's not going to suffer somebody showing off like that so he's passed Reg a gun, and we all know what happened next.

The only bit that was romanced up was him being pinned to the floor with the knife through his throat. Good reading for them that like that sort of thing, but it never happened, though Reg carving him up did, and you can't make any excuses for that at all.

If the twins really felt that McVitie had to be taken out of the picture there must have been a hundred and one ways they could've done it all nice and quiet, and nobody else involved. But typical of them they were selfish, only thought of themselves and what they wanted, so in getting their satisfaction they took all the other fellas that just happened to be there down with them. Even brother Charlie, who was in bed at the time.

Funny – peculiar that is – Charlie got a ten and served seven for nothing more than being a Kray, while Ronnie Hart, supposedly one of the family and well involved, did a deal that got them sent down, and he walked away from it a free man. He wanted to be a gangster and should've paid the price.

To be honest, none of us knew who he was when he turned up out of the blue. "Hello Reg, hello Ron – I'm your cousin." Course they'd made a name for themselves then, otherwise he'd never have shown his face, but next thing he's taken into the firm and that was the worst thing they could've done. Uncle Johnny said this geezer was his mother's sister's boy's boy – work that one out. But as far as all the family was concerned this bloke was no more a cousin than fly in the air. Rita's mum, my Aunt May, couldn't stand the bloke. Albert asked her to make this Ronnie something to eat one time and she said no and that wasn't like her at all. When he asked her why she wouldn't she said, "I don't like him. I get a feeling he's not what he makes out to be." So what's that if it's not a premonition for the future?

On top of that, according to Johnny he was nothing but a little creep. He was supposed to have gone to his grandmother's, that would be my great aunt, and nicked some money off her that she'd given him to go and buy some shopping for her – so that's the sort of geezer he was.

Again Johnny reckons that he'd tried to shoot some bloke, and when Nipper Read got on to it he gave that Hart fella the choice: "You tell us what you know about the Krays or you go down, simple as that." So he chose the easy option and shopped them. The twins never sought him out in the first place because he was nothing. He sucked up to them, played the hard man in their shadow and then turned Judas when it all went wrong.

Compare that with people like Tony and Chrissie Lambrianou or Ronnie Bender – never laid a finger on McVitie, but kept their mouths shut out of loyalty and took fifteen years without complaint. Who says blood's thicker than water? Still, that loyalty was about as misplaced as it could get, because when it came to the crunch the twins didn't give a fuck about any of them. It might not have made the slightest difference but I thought they could've at least tried to put in a good word for their supposed mates – but no, they were going down and taking the rest for a bit of company. On the other hand those boys couldn't complain. Like I said before, if you wanted to get involved in the underworld it was your choice as long as you were prepared for the consequences.

When the dust had settled after the judge's hammer came down, Charlie was in Chelmsford, Reggie in Parkhurst and Ronnie the other end of the country in Durham. All of them were Category A, which meant their movements were restricted and they had to suffer a red light on in the cell day and night. Any of us who wanted to visit had our backgrounds checked out with a fine-tooth comb before we could go on the list, and that was including Uncle Charlie and Aunt Violet – and those two were just starting a sentence of their own.

They didn't want to know what their boys had done; never talked about the fact that the twins had taken somebody's life other than it was a fit-up, some sort of mistake. So they stood behind them and never missed a visit. It's no good me saying why don't the authorities consider the families of prisoners, because they never have, but imagine what it was like to drive north one day and south the next, rain or shine, just to keep in contact with your kids. I found it hard enough and I was only in my forties at first, but my aunt and uncle were in their sixties.

What broke my aunt up was the fact that the twins were separated. People write that she campaigned to have things changed, but that makes out she was flying around with a placard held up in the air. That wasn't her game because she was just an ordinary mum trying to help her boys, but what she did do was keep on and on at the Home Office for three years until they got fed up with her and put the twins together in Parkhurst.

I mean, we all did our bit when it came down to a bit of cash or a lift to the prison, but Uncle Albert copped for a lot of it because he was right on the doorstep. He was a night worker, and I've seen him come home in the morning after a shift, the phone would ring and it would be Violet looking for a lift. He was as good as gold; he'd tell her to hang on while he had a wash then he'd be straight round. Did it time and time again and never complained.

People thought she was probably delivered to the prison gates in a limo, what with what the boys had had at one time, but the truth is almost overnight any money or property they had disappeared. I can't say they didn't have a pot to piss in because that's all they did have, only it had HMP stamped on the side.

The big old mansion got sold off to pay the bills, and bits of cash they had hidden up got eaten away in no time. In fact they had to get legal aid to fight the case. They were brassic and so were their parents.

All the capers they ever got up to were never about money. On the surface that's what it looked like and they might have believed it themselves, but really all they aimed for was to be either famous or infamous.

Ronnie was the worst. He liked his bit of gold and flash suits, but money to him was for giving away. One day he'd have a Rolex on his wrist and he'd say, "Look at this, Joey. Beautiful, innit?" Next day it's gone. Somebody's admired it and he's taken it off and given it to them. Rings, cuff links – expensive gear. You name it – there you go, take it. I made some comment about hankies one day. Probably something like "You can never have too many" or "I'm always losing them" – doesn't matter. Next thing he's got me a dozen boxes of handkerchiefs. Been round the shop and stuck them on his account. Once he was away though, this generosity went more into the world he lived in than to his family, who needed it just as much.

It's been said, but Uncle Albert would give the shirt off his back. He was visiting Ron one time and Ron said, "Have you got any money on you?" Without thinking Albert said, "As it happens I've just been paid. I haven't even opened my wage packet yet." As he's spoke he's pulled this packet out of his jacket. Quick as a flash Ron's said, "That'll do," took it out of his hand, got up and walked over to some geezer that probably murdered his grandmother and gave him the lot. Albert swallowed it but afterward he was fuming and told me that was it – none of them would ever get another penny out of him. And they never did, though he still dropped Violet a bit every now and then.

What can I say about those visits? You could drive three hundred miles and get there with your eyes hanging out of your head. Two hours and you're back on the road again and when you fall into bed all you can see is cat's eyes flashing in front of you. And all you've done is talk about "How they treating you?" "Yes, the old man's keeping well, thanks," "They've put traffic lights up Kingsland Road," "Won't be long before you're out," and all that. The smallest amount of small talk, but you had to do it because they were family and you couldn't just forget about them.

It makes me laugh when you get people who've only known the twins for five minutes, writing books about all these secrets they've been told on visits. All the ins and outs of murder and rackets, and this one and that one. Well, I've got to say they've got rich imaginations, or Reg and Ron were acting out of character, because I visited my cousins from the day they were sent down to the day they died, and the past never came up in conversation. Not their criminal past anyway. There was always that "D'you remember?"

stuff about the old days and people who'd died, but that's as far as it went. Their world was inside those walls and they gave me the impression that the world they used to live in was all forgotten.

I'll tell you what is a great leveller – a prison waiting room. On one side you might have some worn-out woman wearing a coat that's seen better days, and on the other some posh geezer, expensive suit, plum in his mouth – and neither can look up or down at the other because, like it or not, they've both got a con in the family. Different story outside when nobody knows, but while you're all sitting around waiting for those gates to open, you can't pretend.

I was at Broadmoor one time with Ann, and as we came out this couple started to chat to us. I suppose seeing us with Ronnie they wondered what we were made of. They were proper upper crust, and on a normal day wouldn't have given us five minutes, but because they were visiting family in a place for the criminally insane, they didn't see the point of putting on airs and graces.

Ron never lasted long in the ordinary prison system before he took a turn – four or five years I think. Same old story – medication gets messed up then *bomp* – it's all over and he's in Broadmoor. I took Violet there one day and he must have been thinking because he said to us both, "Great Grandad died in one of these places didn't he? And I'm going to die in here." What can you say? "No, course you ain't, Ronnie. You got better last time didn't you? Give it time." But while the words are coming out you know he's talking sense, and of course he was proved right in the end.

That film *The Krays* – who came up with the idea I don't know, probably Reg because he was always looking for some money-making scheme or other. The Who singer Roger Daltrey was going to do it in the first place, but that all went pear-shaped like things do in the film game and it was no fault of his. But right or wrong his name ended up on Ron's "Death List". In one way it's laughable, but he was deadly serious, and as the years went on this list got longer and longer. Even a close family friend ended up on it, and he was a respectable businessman and had done no end of favours for Ron's mother – but wrong word and he had him marked down on that list.

Anyway, when the film got up and running again they got us family involved. Charlie rang me up and told me to collect my old man and Uncle Johnny and get ourselves over to Cable Street, because the film people wanted us on set. They were shooting in Wellclose Square inside the Wilton, which I think is the oldest theatre in Britain. Charlie Chaplin appeared there, and as far as I know it's got a preservation order on it and they're going to open it again – might have done it already. My dad's ninety years old and Johnny's well in his seventies, but they were up for it.

Some American tart cut our hair, then we had to suffer powder, eye shadow, lipstick – make-up like, and all that caper. You'd have thought we was the stars instead of just walk-ons. The old man said to me, "You look like Air Ball Hugget," so I said, "Well, you look like his mate," so that shut him up. That was OK until they took us down to wardrobe, as they call it. This was the tail-end of the day and there wasn't much to choose from. I was all right, Johnny didn't care, then the old man took one look and his and said, "Look at it. I wore a better suit when I was doing the fish markets." That was it then; he'd had enough. I tried to talk him round but he said, "No. Fuck it, Joe, let's go home." So we all scarpered.

Thinking about it now though, I wished I'd pushed him a bit harder to stay because now he's gone it would be nice to stick the video on and see the old fella again. On the other hand you couldn't step six inches without tripping over a cable, so I had to consider – one little tumble at his age and it's all over.

On the Monday Charlie rang me again wondering what was up and when I told him the old man had got the arse'ole with hanging about, he said, "Never mind. Get Johnny and come down to Reading because they're filming a boxing scene." I thought, "I don't mind that. Couple of days on location, couple in the studios; nice few quid – not too much work." Cor, don't they go on in that game. Five, ten, twenty takes; you think they're never going to get it right. Midnight every night before I got home to bed.

There was a few faces on the set, but they were just walk-ons same as us. There was old Jack Kid Berg, Alex Steene and the fella they called the Guv'nor, Lenny McLean. He didn't half cause a ruck one day when he had a row with the cameraman and threatened to punch his head in. Don't know what over but they was going to shut the set down if he didn't leave. He told them "Fuck off" and stayed where he was, and nobody had the bottle to say any more. Then I got a bollocking for taking Kid Berg to Westcliffe for the day when we should've been filming, but they couldn't go too strong with me being family, and we both got paid out even though we hadn't been there. Alex and Ted didn't give a monkey's about the film – all they wanted to know was did they get paid out every night or when it was all over.

I mean you could criticize all day long about "they got this wrong and they got that wrong" but it was only a film after all and you couldn't take it too serious. It made a few quid for the boys, but where it went with them stuck inside I've no idea.

Charlie blew his on different business ventures because he was out, but the twins, well they wasn't buying flash clothes and motors. But whatever, it wasn't long before they were looking round for a few quid again.

I remember Ronnie phoning me up one time for a favour. He wanted me to pick up a woman friend of his and take her to Broadmoor. No problem – then he tells me he's going to marry her. What can you say? He wouldn't have been where he was if he had all his marbles. I did what he asked and I met up with her. Plainish looker – nothing wrong with that. About thirty years old – nice enough girl and perfectly normal. Elaine her name was. On the way there she says to me, "What's Ronnie like?" How do you answer that? She's prepared to marry a bloke and she don't know him from Adam.

They did get married and got divorced just as quick, and whatever reasons she had for getting hitched up to Ron in the first place, that was it – finished. She didn't write books, she didn't sell her story to the papers and she never traded on the Kray name, as far as I know. So all I can think is that she was genuine enough in how she felt even though to me the whole business was a bit strange, what with him only fancying blokes since he was a youngster.

The years went on and he met up with this other one who I've never met and don't know much about. But you hear things, put two and two together and weigh it up for yourself.

I've always got on better with Ron than with Reg and that's probably because I've seen more of him over the years, but even so you always had to be careful what you said to him because he could turn in a second. So when he said that he was going to get married again, I had to say to him, "This marrying lark, Ron. What's that all about?" He laughed and said, "You know what it's like, Joey. We all need some woman to run about for us." Stands to reason he wouldn't want one for anything else because he'd said often enough that he didn't have time for them. I wasn't a bit surprised when it all took a tumble after a short while.

I saw this Kate woman fronting some programme on the telly the other night and they was calling her Ronnie Kray's widow. A bit odd considering he gave her the elbow quick as you like when he thought she was out of order, so somebody's got it all wrong.

With both of them stuck behind the door I think that out of the two of them Ron got the best deal. Apart from his freedom he had everything he wanted. A few friends round him, a comfortable berth, plenty of visitors and no worries. I don't know if he was being crafty or he thought he was back in the old days when dough was flying around, but he had four faces visit him one day. As they were going he's asked if they could do him a favour and settle up his bill at the hospital shop. "No problem, Ronnie. Leave it to us," and all that. When they went to the desk they got stuck with a bill for twelve hundred quid. They all had to dig a bit deep but they paid it.

Reg, on the other hand, once he came off A Cat, went straight into the mainstream prison system. And though the only bird I've ever done was overnight, I know enough about it to realize he couldn't drop his guard for a minute, so that's a strain in itself. You only had to look round to see he got plenty of respect from the other cons, but he didn't get no favours from the screws. To them he was no different from anyone else.

I've spoken to people who've got their ideas from American gangster films, where the top geezer has everybody waiting on him, so they'd say, "I bet Reg has got a plush cell," imagining that he was suited up and still running this empire from an office behind bars. Nothing was further from the truth. What you've got to give him credit for is that he did all them years before he cracked up. Up until then he was fit, sharp and generous. OK, he was generous with other people's money, but he did put his name behind a lot of charity stuff when he could just as easily not have bothered.

Some kid needed an operation – *bomp* – he's knocked out one of his drawings to be auctioned off. Personally, I didn't think they were all that, but never mind, they raised a good bit of cash.

Then he changed almost overnight, and he was nothing like the old Reggie. What was it? Ronnie dying, or did it suddenly hit him that they were never going to let him out? I knew he was going to do the full stretch and I've got letters here from the Home Office more or less saying that, in a roundabout way. Never told him that but he was no fool. It seemed like he shut off from anybody or anything outside the walls. He fell out with decent people that had supported him for years, and was only interested in the little mob of youngsters that hung around him in the prison.

When he died he left a letter for the newspapers saying he was gay. Well, I'm not going to judge him on that because who knows what thirty years does to your head. But it was never a secret anyway. Never talked about, but it stuck out a mile. Different prison, different young fella would be introduced as his "friend", and whoever it was would be showing off a gold chain or a watch that Reggie's bought them. I thought half of them were taking the piss but Reg never saw it.

Then all of a sudden he's getting married, and I could only think it was for the same reason as Ron. Still it was his life and none of my business. Though you can't help wondering why a comparatively young, middle-class woman with supposedly a bit of a head piece on her would want to marry an ageing, partially deaf and gay ex-gangster. It's anyone's guess.

I won't say too much about it now because it's all over, but this Roberta didn't do us family any favours when Reg was dying. When I found out he'd been moved out of prison and into hospital I made myself busy trying to find out what was going on. But it was an uphill struggle. Remember, I'd been involved with him since him and Ron popped out like two little monkeys – sixty-six years ago. Now all of a sudden the papers are getting the story before us, and to my way of thinking that's all arse about face.

I eventually got hold of Roberta by ringing her home and she told me that Reg had a kidney infection. Well, she was either kidding me or kidding herself, because either way, a day or so later it was all over the news that he was suffering from terminal cancer.

What can I say about Reg's end when it came? I'd known he hadn't been in the best of health for a long while, but it still throws you when one of your own is on their last knockings. Me and Ann got ourselves up to Norwich hospital and in to see him. He was still a prisoner then so of course there was a couple of screws in the room, plus some woman keeping an eye on him. Bit of a joke really, because the man couldn't turn himself over in bed let alone do a runner. He did look a state – tubes, bottles, wires, you name it. And whether he knew it or not, I could tell it was only a matter of weeks – if he was lucky.

Funny how your mind works at a time like that. He was more taken with this new shirt I had on than anything else. He said, "You don't half look smart, Joey". And I said, "Should hope so, this shirt cost me fifty nicker". And that gave him a bit of a laugh. We had a chat, but he was very weak and I thought it best not to hang about too long. He thanked me for sticking by him over the years, sent his love to Rita and Kimmy and that was that really.

As we were leaving he said, "Joey, come and see me again. Don't ask, just come any time you want." I never saw him alive again, because when I went again some time after, I was turned away by the sister in charge who told me he was having a bad day. Fair enough. But on the way out I couldn't help noticing that a TV crew was laying cables everywhere and setting cameras up outside his room. So I have my thoughts about that.

I eventually watched the result of that filming that was obviously going on that day and was disgusted that my cousin's dying was turned into a peepshow for money and entertainment. Who on earth thought it was a good idea to show Reg as a shadow of what he used to be and then link together shots of him with filthy comments from Lenny Hamilton? Doesn't he have any respect for the dead or any decency toward us family left behind?

Them fellas like the Lambrianous and Freddie Foreman who served years and years in prison for the twins, have a right to say what's on their mind. But to give airtime to a man who wants to make a living out of being striped with a hot poker by Ron, is an insult to us. Stripe him? Ron should've stuck it down his fucking throat. Only time I ever heard the twins talk about him was when they were calling him a grass and a rat. Revenge – that's what he wants, but he's taking it out on the wrong people now because he didn't have the bottle to open his mouth when the boys were still alive.

Still, while I was getting all wound up about things that were being said, I still managed to have one chuckle to myself over something that Roberta come out with. What were they pumping into Reg while he was hospital? Because whatever it was, forget your Viagra, they want to put it on the market and make a fortune. Consummated his marriage? C'mon. None of that lark was on the cards all the time he was under arrest and by the time he was free he could hardly breath, could barely move too quick and was wired up to a morphine box. I could be wrong, of course, but who's to say any different?

Anyway, day after the knock-back in the hospital I got a call from Roberta saying that Reg wanted a word with me. He came on the line, but he sounded so rough I could hardly understand what he was saying. Basically, what he wanted to say was sorry for the misunderstanding the day before. I told him to forget it because I doubt he even knew I was there at the time. We talked for a bit and that was it. I put the phone down and said to Ann, "That's it, it's all over". And it was, because he was dead not too long after.

Counting the bird he did in the early years before the big one, he spent more than half his life in prison. Was it worth it? You tell me.

I've stood beside too many family graves over the years, and every one takes a little piece out of you. Me and my Ann often go to the cemetery in Upminster where my close family are buried just to walk round and pay our respects. My mum and sister Connie have been gone long enough for me to come to terms with losing them, but when I stand thinking about my father, I look down and can't believe that tough old man is laying there. I used to think he'd go on for ever.

Then perhaps once a month we'll slip over to Chingford Mount Cemetery for the same reason. Doesn't half make me think that, when I look round and see that most of the people that were such a big part of my life are laying under my feet. I don't think there'll ever be another family like them and give or take the ups and downs we've been through, I've got to say I've been proud to be part of them all. Yes proud – not proud of what those boys got up to, but of being connected to a strong loyal family stretching right back down the years.

I look at that big slab of black marble that says "Legend – Ronnie Kray", and I know it's only a matter of time before they get round to putting Reggie's name beside his. Same thought comes to me every time: "Well, boys, you never wanted anything else than to be famous, and you certainly got that – and a bit more. But you didn't half pay a heavy price for it."

Then I look to one side and there's my mate Charlie's little patch. Funny how something like a name can ruin a bloke's life. If he'd been a different sort of fella – maybe stronger and more forceful, whatever, I don't know – me and Rita wouldn't be putting this book together right now because the Kray name wouldn't mean nothing. If those twins had looked up to him a bit more and taken notice of what he said, which most of the time made a lot of sense, the three of them could've had a different life altogether. But as we all know he didn't stand a chance against that pair so he got sucked in time and time again. As for that last business that got him stuck away for twelve years – what can I say? I was going to say bit of a joke really, but it was nothing to laugh about when we all knew that once that door shut behind him he couldn't live long enough to walk out again. Nobody will ever convince me that it wasn't a fit-up. Someone up top marked his card and after that he'd got no chance.

He told me hand on heart that he never got involved in drugs and that he was innocent. If it was any different he would've said, knowing that it wouldn't go any further. He told me a lot more on those visits that I made to him when the end was near, but it won't do him any good now for me to start shouting my mouth off. It was an injustice, and I'll leave it at that.

He knew he didn't have long to go and I was pleased I was there for him as often as I could be in those last weeks. I've got a letter in front of me now that he wrote about twelve hours before he died, and by the time I got it he was already gone. He was too ill to get to the phone, yet he made an effort to say what he had to say to me and I'll always appreciate that.

He was always in the shadow of his brothers – always second best. And even now in death he's been overlooked because he hasn't even got a marker. Nothing that says he was a decent fella whose only real crime was looking out for those twins. Nothing that marks his coming or going. Says it all really.

10. They never saw

Rita Smith

Sentencing my cousin Charlie to ten years in prison was as criminal as the crimes he was supposed to have committed. What sort of justice is it that puts a man away because he has the same name as the guilty ones? I know he still had his life, but thinking about it, he was as much a victim of what the twins did as the men who died.

Reg and Ron both knew what they were doing when they did what they did, but I wonder if they ever considered the others who just happened to be there, or once they were in their cells, consider the hurt they left outside? I don't suppose they did for a minute – they had enough to think about with having to face thirty years minimum. Though, as I've already said, at first they did think they'd only get fifteen years as a maximum, but by the time the trial was coming to an end I'm sure they had both guessed that the outcome would be twice that, so of course they weren't surprised.

Unlike all of us at home. People always think of the prisoner. They wonder how can they get through ten, twenty or thirty years? But if you're a wife or husband, parents, grandparents or, like me, close cousin, when those gates bang shut you know that one way or another you're going to share every day of the same sentence – that's if you live long enough, and though we didn't know it then, Nanny and Grandad only had two years left.

They were both in their nineties, and like it does when you're old, the birth of their grandsons must have seemed like yesterday, and suddenly they know they'll never see them again. They loved the three of them but had idolized the twins since they brought the family back together all those years ago. Neither of them knew a fraction of what those boys got up to, though they knew enough to realize they weren't angels. But as far as the serious things went, none of us wanted to spell it out.

Their old television broke down so Ronnie told Grandad that he'd buy him a new one. Basically Grandad was proud and he was honest, so he said to Ronnie, "Nah, I don't want one of your effing knock-offs. I ain't having the law banging on my door." That was funny in itself because over the years the police had tramped through his front door on loads of occasions, but then that was looking for the twins, not him. Ronnie did buy the television, but he had to show the receipt before he was allowed to plug it in.

From being the strong man he'd been all his life, Grandad gradually deteriorated after he had a fall. He never ever took any notice when we told him to be careful or to leave certain jobs until Joe or Charlie called in. So he was well over ninety years old when he decided to climb on a chair, then balance on the table while he changed a light bulb. Nanny didn't even notice he was up there when she moved the chair while she was dusting round. So when he came to get down he stepped into mid-air. He hurt his leg quite badly and though he went on for a few more years I think it was down to that, that led toward him being taken into hospital with a chest complaint.

Even then he was funny without realizing it. An orderly came round with the menu card for dinner. All hospitals are the same – you choose from what's on offer in the morning for your meal later on.

So he's said, "What you got then, gel?" The woman must have noticed that he only had one tooth in his head so as a joke said, "We've got best sirloin steak". Well his eyes must have lit up at that because, like Uncle Joe, he really did enjoy his food.

When a plate of boiled fish and mash turned up at five o'clock he kicked up a terrible fuss. It was a different orderly and while she was telling him that the fish was on the form, he's telling her, "No, you've got it all wrong. I ordered steak." He sulked for days after that. Another time he caused a scene when the nurse brought him a glass of Guinness to build him up. He's shouting at the nurse, "Get that bleeding gut polish away from me. I won't have it near me."

When he was given a medical examination the doctor commented to him that he had the insides of a man half his age.

Grandad said, "An' I'll tell you why that is, I ain't never been with no other women."

Mum brought him home so that she could look after him, but when he got worse she had to take him back to the hospital to die. Nanny wouldn't have it that he was ill. She used to say, "Him? He's as strong as old iron," but he died on his birthday aged ninety-four, crying to come home and crying because he thought Nanny didn't love him any more because she wouldn't visit. He couldn't understand that with her suffering from thrombosis, as much as she wanted to, she wasn't able to travel.

I used to think what a lovely example they were to young people who get divorced after a couple of arguments. For seventy years they stuck together through all kinds of hardships. She effed and blinded at him every day and he'd shrug it off with a "Gerrout of it," but it never meant anything. He was loyal, proud and jealous, and I'll always carry a mental picture of him singing to Nanny "Beautiful picture in a beautiful golden frame". She always told him not to be so bleedin' daft, but she loved it and knew he meant it.

She went downhill after Grandad died, and was in poor health, but even so every now and then we'd see a spark of what she used to be. Like when she had an argument with a neighbour who was scrubbing her front doorstep at the time. Nanny picked up the bucket of dirty water and tipped it over the woman's head. They weren't parted for too long because she died within the year. A typical Lee, fighting to the end.

My dad used to pass her house every day on his way to work and just glance over to see that everything was in place. On this particular morning he noticed all the lights on and the door wide open, so he stopped, went inside and found her collapsed on the floor. She was conscious and saying, "He done it – that's him and his bleedin' armchair, tripped me over he did". Dad tried to tell her that Grandad was dead and buried but she wouldn't have it. "No, he pushed that chair right under my feet and down I went."

In the late 1800s when Nanny grew up one of the worst things that could happen to you was to die a pauper. There might not have been enough money for food or clothes, but that seemed to have been less of a worry than whether there would be enough money to pay for a respectable burial. I know Nanny worried about this because she told me often enough, and with that in mind whenever the twins gave her a few pounds she salted some of it away in her handbag. That was her insurance and in the later part of her life it was never out of her sight.

I really don't know how Auntie Violet coped with the loss of her boys and the constant visits she made to different prisons. Since then the twins have both publicly admitted that they killed her, and that thought couldn't have been easy for them because she was their world.

I think the real blame lay with the newspapers and cowardly people who wrote horrible letters to her saying things like she was guilty of giving birth to evil monsters, or it was her fault they turned out like they did. Time after time she would come over to my mum's clutching a letter or paper and breaking her heart. She couldn't understand why she was being personally attacked, and no matter how many times we told her that she couldn't have prevented what her sons did and that she'd been a good mother, nothing stopped the tears. One day after she'd read a letter in the papers from a woman saying that the twins' mother should've killed them at birth, she was so distraught she almost walked under a bus.

You see what I mean? The twins lived their lives exactly how they wanted. They did unspeakable things for their own satisfaction and never considered how it might affect anyone else. They never saw their tough old hero Grandad Lee with tears streaming down his face. They never saw the heartbreak caused right through our family and the families of the other men involved, and they never saw their mother hunched in a chair wracked with grief and sobbing uncontrollably.

They're seen as heroes by millions, but how heroic is it to inflict that sort of punishment on those you love. I'm not so sure they even considered or appreciated the efforts other people made in showing they weren't forgotten. In their minds they were the victims and visits from family and friends were taken as something to be expected. From their point of view these visitors magically appeared in the prison and disappeared after a couple of hours.

I wonder if they ever thought about what effort had gone on between the two? A journey of buses, trains or car might have started at five in the morning, and the same evening while they might be having a meal or watching television in the recreation room, their visitors were still trailing their way back to the East End in the rain or snow. I'm not saying any of us begrudged the time and we always looked forward to seeing them, but did they ever stop to think how all our lives had changed because of what they did?

While they were in Parkhurst we spent our holidays on the Isle of Wight, just to be near them. That's Mum, Dad, the kids and me. Blackpool or Margate might have made a change, but no – year after year we rented the same caravan and saw my cousins every day for the fortnight. It was our own decision to do it and my cousins would never have asked us to go to so much trouble for their benefit. We did it willingly but I doubt if the Isle of Wight would've been our first choice if they hadn't been in prison there. What we were doing wasn't normal visiting but we had an arrangement with the governor and knowing we were on holiday on the island he was kind enough to let us visit whenever we liked, within reason.

You might think that in over thirty years of regular visiting we would've learned every secret and every hidden thought of those boys. But each one of them was the same as the one before. A kiss, a cuddle, endless cups of tea. How was the journey? Meet this friend, meet that friend, and questions and answers about family and old friends. Why they were inside or anything to do with their past life of crime was never mentioned, but then that sort of thing had never been discussed with us women – or for that matter any woman.

Reg and Ron both had an uncanny knack of reading what was going on in your mind, and I suppose this sort of thing is less to do with clairvoyance and more to do with the dangerous atmosphere they lived in. I can remember asking Reg why he kept looking over his shoulder and he said, "Sorry, I didn't realize I was doing it. There's some funny people in here and it comes a habit to keep an eye on your back."

I've mentioned that Reg noticed that I was taking Valium, but another time, without saying what was on his mind in front of his

Mum and mine, he asked me to revisit on my own. When I did he held both my hands and asked me what my problem was, because he could see or sense things weren't as they should be. My problem was that my husband Ritchie was putting me through hell, but I couldn't say that to Reg in case he passed the word to friends outside and had him seriously hurt.

I hated Ritchie at that time for the way he was treating me, but I couldn't live with the thought that I might be responsible for having him hurt just because of my complaining. I made some excuse about being under the weather with a woman's complaint – something guaranteed to stop a man asking further questions, but I knew he didn't believe me. He said, "If it's money, don't worry because we won't be in here many more years, and when we come out we'll set up some little business. You and Kimmy will be with us and you'll both get a nice wage."

It was never going to happen but I thought it was nice he thought that way.

Another time when I took my David to see him he said, "David, I want you to promise your mother and your Uncle Reg that you'll never get into any trouble. Nothing's worth spending your life behind bars, so if you're ever tempted just think how I've ended up." In his own way he was saying that if he could turn the clock back he would've chosen another way of life – so even though it was too late he was more or less saying he did have regrets.

It was the same with Uncle Charlie. He was upset by the way Ritchie was behaving and went after him. Not to do anything physical because he was never a fighter, but just to try and talk some sense into him. When he caught up with him he told him, "You must be mad to treat your lovely wife and kids the way you do. You ought to be ashamed of yourself. The day will come when you'll regret it, then you'll be sorry. I am, and I know what I'm talking about. When I was younger I didn't treat my Violi nice at all. Now I want to make it up to her but she won't have it – she's turned against me; just don't want to know." He was so right. She'd turned against him so much that she wouldn't even accept a cup of tea if he made it for her. Perhaps in her own heart she blamed him for losing her boys. She never said as much, but seeing the way she looked at him most of the time, something was going through her mind.

At the end of 1981 Auntie Violet was seventy-two years of age, and looked ten years older. From what my Mum told me, up until the age of sixteen her sister was full of fun – always singing and laughing. Then she met Uncle Charlie and her life was never the same again. And looking at her over the last Christmas we'd spend together, I saw that she was frail and tired, with a sadness in her eyes. It seemed everything her husband and sons had put her through was etched in every line of her face.

Shortly after that she came to me complaining of stomach pains, and would I make an appointment for her to see my doctor as she didn't have one of her own. I told her that she might have to pay because she wasn't registered, but that didn't put her off so I could see she was quite worried. She'd always been a bit shy so one of her reasons for wanting to see my doctor was because she was a woman.

In the meantime she kept up her visits to the twins, and I don't know where she found the strength to travel all those miles, then put on a smile when she arrived at whatever prison, pretending everything was fine.

Eventually she was diagnosed as having a cancerous tumour in her stomach, and that it was only a matter of time. Mum and me visited her in hospital and she was very frightened. She didn't want us to leave but kept making excuses. "Don't go, stay and talk. Just a bit longer." I wished we had because we never saw her alive again – she died the following morning during an exploratory test.

The twins both cried on the telephone when I spoke to them. They never had a chance to say goodbye, to give her a last cuddle and say they were sorry for what they'd put her through, and I can only imagine that there was a touch of guilt among their genuine tears and grief.

Her funeral was a media circus and she would've hated it. Reg and Ron were out into the world for the first time in thirteen years, but I'm sure they would have given that up for the sake of knowing their beloved mother was still alive. On top of the sadness of that day, it brought a lump to my throat as I saw Reg tenderly place white roses on Frances' grave and kiss the marble headstone. Did he think it was worth being Britain's most famous gangster at a time like that?

When you think of how Uncle Charlie treated his wife most of their married life, it would've taken a heart of stone to hold that against him when you saw how he was affected by losing her. It was like he had no reason to carry on living and within six months he followed Auntie Violet, who in his own way he had loved, even though he had a strange way of showing it.

I seem to have criticized him a lot and there must be people out there who think I'm being unfair because they never saw any of the things I mentioned. And that was Uncle Charlie – without drink and in company he could be kind, charming and funny. But behind closed doors or in front of family that he didn't think he had to impress, he let his other side show, and I think that most of his behaviour was caused by insane jealousy.

First of all he was jealous of young Charlie, who came between them in the early days of their marriage, then later on it was the twins who took up every minute of Violet's time. And like too many men of his generation, outside the home he was jealous of any man who might look at her twice or talk to her for more than a few minutes. Which was sad really, because Auntie Violet never looked at another man in her whole life. All she ever wanted for herself was inside the walls of 178.

Uncle Charlie seemed to give up soon after the funeral, and eventually I took him to my doctor. In private Dr Phyllis told me she couldn't understand how he was alive and walking about because there were so many things wrong with him. As well as that she said that apart from his physical ailments, she didn't think he could go on much longer because he seemed to have lost the will to live.

After my cousin Charlie was divorced from Dolly, their son Gary had been brought up by Nanny. When she died he moved in with Auntie Violet. In the February of 1983 he came out of his bedroom and found Uncle Charlie lying dead on the stairs with his eyes wide open.

A lot of people think that Reg and Ron chose not to ask permission to attend their father's funeral because of the past, but that just wasn't true. They might not have had a great deal of time for him in life, but as often happens when someone dies, bad thoughts and old arguments get forgotten. The twins were no different, he was still their dad no matter what he'd done in the past and they were both upset at losing him.

If a few years had gone by between the deaths of their mum and dad, I'm sure it would have been different, but as it was, the shock of what should've been private being headline news only six months before was something they didn't feel they could go through again. So Charlie represented the three of them as their father was laid to rest.

Of his ten-year sentence, Charlie served seven and those years changed him from a generous man into an obsessed money-getter. Everything about him came down to taking cash off anyone who was gullible or caring enough to hand it over to him, and he didn't make any distinction between family, good friends or strangers.

My Ritchie, who was serving seventeen years for armed robbery, had given me a beautiful solitaire diamond ring. Only trouble was once I realized that he had become a criminal I was convinced this ring was part of the proceeds of some jewel theft, and I was frightened to wear it. I was talking about it to Charlie one day, and because he was in the business of buying and selling gold and what have you, he suggested he would sell it and get something else. It seemed the best thing to do, but I did make a point of telling him to make sure he traded it for something equal in value because I knew mine was worth a lot of money.

Weeks and weeks went by and every time I saw him I asked had he come up with anything yet, until getting fed up with me he produced this "jargoon" [fake ring] as Reg would've called it that must have come out of a Christmas cracker. I was horrified that my own cousin would trick me in that way, but I've always been too soft for my own good so I accepted it without a word.

When Ritchie heard what had happened he went mad and told me to dig out a box of his papers where I'd find the original receipt. I did and found that it never had been stolen and it had cost well over four figures from a well-known jeweller.

At one time my mum, Auntie Violet and my daughter Kimmy all worked part-time in the Blue Coat Boy in Bishopsgate. I think when the twins were outside they had some sort of interest in this pub, but whether that was a legal interest or not I've no idea. The landlord was a skinflint and every week without fail they had to chase him for their own wages. Yet when Charlie went to him for a loan of £2,000 he gave it to him on the strength of this family connection. Full of the flannel that had become his way by then, Charlie told him that within a few weeks he'd pack the place out with his friends – both faces and celebrities. It never happened and the money disappeared along with my cousin.

Auntie Violet was so embarrassed she wanted to pack the job in but the landlord wouldn't hear of it, saying the deal was between himself and her son and nothing to do with her.

Because he'd borrowed money from my dad in the past and never bothered to pay it back, Charlie was crafty and got his mother to ring my dad asking if he would lend him a hundred pounds. She said that he desperately needed the money because he was in trouble but had promised that without fail he would pay it back within two weeks. "In trouble" was all anyone had to say to my father and his hand would be in his pocket, so it was understandable that he was very hurt when Charlie never repaid him – yet always seemed to have plenty of cash, nice suits and gold dripping off his arms.

Only recently one of the old firm told me that when he was released after serving his sentence, a benefit was held for him in a local pub and it raised almost £3,000 – a nice sum to get him back on his feet again. Whether Charlie had set up this benefit night I don't know, but he collected the money from the landlord saying he'd take it personally to this man, and none of it was seen again.

It might seem as though I'm being disloyal but I can only say how things were and how nothing him or the twins did changed how I felt about them all. Whether it was violence, murder or simply confidence tricks, I never stopped loving any of them – but too often I found myself not liking them at different times.

Even young Gary picked up his father's ways. As a child he used to wind Grandad up over money. As compensation for not living with his parents, Charlie and Dolly slipped him money every time they saw him, so he always had a pocket full of cash. If he wasn't rattling it about like Ronnie used to, he was carefully counting it every five minutes. But he wouldn't part with a penny of it. Grandad used to say, "That Gary is a greedy little bastard".

As he got older, it's a sad thing to say but he couldn't be trusted. When my mum moved in with me from her flat upstairs, she left a cupboard full of spirits and other drink that had built up over the years. When I popped up there to get some for Christmas it was all gone. Gary and Charlie had sneaked in there and cleared the lot without saying a word.

Strange when you think that my dad took on the whole Lee family through marriage, yet looked upon every one of them as though they were blood relations. Any other in-law, if you like, would've said "Eff your family, they're not my problem," but he wasn't like that and helped out any of them that asked. He worried about the twins getting into trouble. He worried about his sister-in-law not having enough money for visiting the boys and he was always upset by Ronnie's mental state. All in all he cared for every one of the family.

The shock of Auntie Violet dying brought on his first stroke because he thought the world of her. Over the next two years he suffered more strokes and, as it always seems to in those cases, his personality changed as well. Mum couldn't understand why and she'd often say to me, "Why's he saying that? Why's he snapping at me? It's not like him." She never accepted he was as ill as he was. Not even at the end.

She got a phone call from the hospital saying that the end was coming, but she didn't go up there because in her mind if you ignore these things they might go away. It wasn't until I came in from shopping that I found out about the phone call. I immediately dropped everything and rushed to the hospital. He died just before I got there. My dad – my lovely dad had died without any of us holding his hand. I was crying as I stood by his bed, and so was the nurse who had looked after him. He was like that. Anyone who knew him saw what sort of man he was and took to him straight away.

Great Grandad Lee and Grandad Lee both had serious accidents as younger men by falling off of horse-drawn carriages. So had my father. Perhaps it was one of the risks of that kind of job. He was riding on what they called "the Dickey seat" when he fell down among the four horses, hurting his head. He recovered but lost most of his hair. Being vain, like most men of his generation, he wore a trilby hat for the rest of his life. I still have a small lock of his snow-white hair that the nurse cut off for me before he was covered up, but I don't need a memento to remind me of him. Every year of him being my dad is locked in my head.

This was something that the twins, locked in another world, never had to suffer. As family members were taken away one by one, they were upset by every death, but they didn't have to live with the slow deterioration that we did and in some ways that can be more painful than the final release.

I was lucky to have my mother for another three years after we lost dad, but if she hadn't had the Lee stubbornness I might have had her beside me for much longer. But none of the family had time for illness and she was no exception.

For a long time it was obvious she wasn't right. She was short of breath and had to keep stopping if we were out shopping, but no way would she admit anything was wrong or allow me to take her to the doctor. In fact in all seriousness she said that if I put her in hospital she'd put a curse on me. How was I to know she had angina? Something that even then could easily be kept under control with tablets. The end came quickly with a massive heart attack, but at least I was with her. On her death certificate the doctor wrote that she'd died of a heart attack, but to me she said, "It's not really an acknowledged medical condition, but I think she died of a broken heart". I thought the same because she never got over losing Dad.

She was the last and the most important to me, of the strong, funny, warm and caring women that I'd shared every day of my life with. The loss of anyone in the family is hard enough, but a mother is something special and suddenly I felt very alone. Though as always life goes on, but it would never be the same for me again.

So many people supported me at that time I couldn't begin to mention them all. There was a lovely wreath from the Kemp brothers that reminded me of the time they both came to my flat to meet Mum when they were making the Kray film. They arrived with an enormous bunch of flowers, which she was obviously pleased to get, but afterwards in her usual outspoken way she said to me, "I wish they'd brought chocolates instead – you can't eat flowers". Those two boys really did take to her and said that she reminded them of their own grandmother and family.

My Kimmy was so busy getting autographed photographs for her friends – who were big fans of Spandau Ballet – that she forgot to get one for herself. Something she always regretted, especially now that Martin is the heart-throb star of *EastEnders*.

Ronnie's wife, Elaine, came to pay her respects and ended up washing the dishes at the after-funeral tea. She was such a nice ordinary girl. I often wondered why she'd married Ron but she never said and I thought it might be rude to question her about such a thing. A year after that she was divorced and Kate Howard took her place.

When Ron rang to tell me what he was planning to do and I asked him what was so special about her, he said, "She's so funny, Rita. She makes me laugh every time I speak to her." In my opinion I doubt whether it was her humour that appealed to Reg when he introduced her to his brother. Unfortunately both my cousins had become just like Charlie, and would knock you over to take a shilling from you. Reg in particular began to look at everyone he met as a "mark" as they say in the con game. I can remember him commenting on the fact that this girl had her own business and her own personal letterheads, which seemed to impress him for some reason.

I can only imagine that his idea was to get her to invest money in one or another of his schemes, but that went all wrong when Ron took a real fancy to her. I've never spoken to Kate and I've never met her, but something about her personality must have appealed to Ron because he was never one to make friends very easily.

Reg brought them together and he split them apart in the end. Kate wrote a book suggesting that Ronnie condoned an "open marriage" – that he didn't mind if she saw other men. That might have been true, but when Reg saw it in print he took it as a personal insult to the family. He was furious when he rang me up. All he kept doing was shouting, "Ronnie's going to divorce her. He's got to get rid of her." When I calmed him down he told me about this story and that Ron would go mad when he read it, so I gathered that Reg had already made his mind up as to how it should be dealt with, even before he had consulted his brother.

Not long after, they were divorced so Reg, as usual, got his own way. Kate had the last laugh though. Reg might have thought she was just another fool he could squeeze money out of, but since Kate parted from Ron she's made a good living by writing books while trading on the Kray name – something Reg hated her for until the day he died.

He always made excuses for falling out with various people, but underneath what he was saying was the fact that he couldn't bear anyone making money out of the Kray name unless he was getting a percentage. He fell out with Charlie and other members of his firm when each of them wrote books to make money as compensation for what they'd been through. Reg rubbished them all because he was getting nothing out of them.

A story that shows he missed nothing was about a young boy who'd been writing to him for quite some time. As often happened with his special friends Reg had sent the boy a drawing he'd done. Whether the boy fell on hard times or simply wanted to buy a new bicycle, I don't know, but he auctioned this picture, and with it selling for something like £600 it was newsworthy enough to get written up in a local Leeds paper. In the next edition Reg wrote a piece saying the picture was a forgery and he'd never heard of this lad in his life.

Something that hurt me and perhaps showed a change of mental state of mind was when someone told him that I had the original film that had been found in either his or Ronnie's cine camera. To him that meant someone had something that was worth money and he didn't have control of it.

He rang my daughter, drunk and abusive, demanding that this film be handed over. When she told him that her Grandad had bought it and it now belonged to me, he got even more angry and screamed foul language down the phone. Kimmy doesn't take after her mother – she takes after my Auntie Rose, so although she's never said as much I'm sure she gave him as good as she got, but what I do know is she slammed the phone down. He rang back – she did the same again.

He rang an old friend of the family to get my telephone number but Kimmy had pre-warned him and he left his answering machine on until Reg sobered up and calmed down. He'd been telephoning me every week throughout the years of being in prison, yet he didn't have my number on that particular day? That's the only redeeming thing about that incident. He knew he was out of order and couldn't bring himself to verbally attack or upset me.

He might have been behind the walls but, as I say, he missed nothing.

A chance remark let him know that I still had the pair of shorts he wore when he won some championship as a boy – complete with silver badge. Next thing I had some young ex-prisoner knocking on my door saying Reg wanted them back. They were his so I didn't argue – just handed them over, but I don't think he ever got them, or if he did they were given away to some "friend" or other. I'll never be surprised to be told they are up for auction on the Internet.

In 1995 we suffered a double blow when first Gary died of cancer at the age of forty-four, then shortly afterwards, Ronnie.

We knew Gary was going to die because of the nature of his illness, and in another way knew that Ronnie was slowly killing himself with cigarettes. On the telephone he was always breathless, and I used to ask him when he was going to cut down or give up smoking. He'd always say, "Don't worry, Rita, there's nothing wrong with my lungs". And perhaps there wasn't but forty cigarettes smoked in two and a half hours wasn't doing his heart condition any favours and it finally stopped on the 17th of March.

Another media circus. I couldn't help thinking as we drove through thousands of people lining the streets of the East End, that 99.9 per cent of them had never known the real Ronnie Kray. Few of them were genuinely grieving for him. It was a spectacle to tell their children and grandchildren about, but more than that they wanted to see Reggie in the flesh. And he put on a show worthy of the Pope for them. His tears and his grief were genuine, and who but a twin could know what it was like to lose one half of yourself, but behind all this his mind was still scheming.

Photographs are for weddings and are very rarely taken at funerals, yet Reg had every moment filmed, then sold copies of the video at ten pounds each.

Once again he stopped at Frances' grave, kissed the headstone and laid white roses for her. Twenty-eight years and she was still in his heart.

By the time Charlie was sentenced to twelve years for being involved in a multi-million pound drugs deal, I was beyond being shocked by anything that happened within the family. When I look back to the pain and tears of when Ronnie was sent down for three, I found I couldn't relate the same to Charlie's sentence even though I knew I would never see him in the outside world again. At his age it just wasn't feasible. Perhaps I was numbed by the years and years of heartbreak.

He rang me from the prison and said, "Don't believe all you read in the papers, Rita. It's a fit-up and things are different from what they look." I did believe him, because knowing him like I did there was no other alternative. If he was involved in any way it could only have been on the very fringes where he thought he could earn a few pounds for doing very little. Mastermind? Up until then he was making a living by turning up in clubs and at parties as a celebrity – the Kray name was still enough to draw people in. In his seventies he was too old to be a threat to anyone, yet I can't help thinking someone up there wanted to show they could crush the Krays out of existence. Just as they had back in 1969.

He rang me one day in April and we had a nice talk about nothing in particular. As he was going he said, "Bye then, Rita," paused for a moment then added, "Love you". It was only after I put the phone down that I realized he'd never said that before and it gave me a very strange feeling. He died the next morning.

I'd criticized him, got upset over certain things he'd done, and sometimes been ashamed of his greedy ways. But underneath all that he was a gentle, nice man and, as with the others, I'd always loved him and would miss him. You can't help thinking that he would've had a better life if the twins hadn't been born. But when that same question was put to him on *The Richard and Judy Show* he thought about it, then said, "No. I never wished that, but my life would've taken a different path if they hadn't been around."

Little did I know that seven months later the whole story would come to an end. Reg hadn't been in the best of health for some years. He'd had a couple of operations that were surprisingly never given the usual publicity. Whenever he telephoned me or Kimmy he was always said, "Fine. Don't worry." Typical of the family, ill health wasn't something to be talked about. He kept it to himself the same as he did about anything to do with his wife, Roberta.

When he first met her I gathered from the way he spoke that he was very impressed by the fact she was "middle class" or "posh" as he put it. Other than that he said very little, almost as though he thought I might disapprove of this new relationship after what he'd said about Frances over the years.

Personally, I think he was looking for a new secretary and she happened to come along at the right time. For a lot of years I know he had a business relationship with an honest, caring woman who looked after his affairs for no reward, and knowing Reg at that time in his life, for little thanks. If tickets for some Kray function had to be sold, she was the one who made the phone calls. If celebrities had to be contacted for support in money-making schemes, she was the one who had to call them. From her front room she was the marketing director for such things as T-shirts, books, used Reg Kray phone-cards and signed drawings. Because she could be trusted, she made a large number of friends, but when Reg deliberately started to rip off these people or entice them into projects that were little more than scams, she drew the line; had a blazing row with him and walked away from helping him out.

A week later Roberta was on the scene. Where she came from or why she wanted to marry Reg I don't know. Maureen Flanagan, the very first page three girl, was very close to my three cousins (particularly Reg who at one time had asked her to marry him), told me that Roberta was just one of many gangster groupies. Knowing that Maureen was in daily contact with Reggie she pestered and pestered her for an introduction. Eventually she gave in and personally took Roberta to Maidstone prison to meet Reg – the rest is history.

Something that did make me laugh was when Maureen was being interviewed on television. She was asked "He's proposed to you a number of times but why would you want to marry Reg Kray" and she replied, "At least I'd know where he was every night".

Roberta never introduced herself to any of us who were left in the family, but that was her choice and really none of my business.

Only once did he ever let his guard down and admit that he felt a bit concerned about his health. Training and working out in the gym was what kept him going over the years and sometimes I thought he took it too far, but what else was there to do? I happened to make some remark about was he still doing a hundred press-ups every morning and he surprised me by saying, " No, Rita, I've cut right back on all that what with this stomach of mine". I said, "What, have you picked up a bug or something?" And he said, "I think it's a lot more than that. Wouldn't surprise me if I've got the same as Mum." I said, "Don't be silly, the doctors would've picked that up in no time". But he said, "That's the trouble. They won't take it seriously. I keep on to them but they just ignore everything I say."

I couldn't believe that even prison doctors would let someone suffer constant pain, so stopped myself worrying by thinking that they were right and it was just something and nothing. Reg was proved right in the end and if earlier treatment could've saved him but was denied, it's a terrible indictment of the prison service.

Joe went up to see Reg as soon as he was taken into hospital and when he rang me afterward he told me that it had been quite upsetting to see him looking so ill. He was even more upset when he wasn't allowed in the following time and he said to me, "Rita, you wouldn't believe it. Our Reg must be days away from dying and they're setting up cameras and what have you. Surely they're not going to film him in that state?" As it turned out they were, and I can only think that set the cash register tinkling again for someone.

It seemed to me as though there was a definite reluctance on the part of those around Reg for any of us family to visit. What was the problem? Did someone think that either Joe or myself would take a photograph of our dying cousin then sell it to the papers for thousands? Or did they think we might get some last words and again sell the story. I know it's only my opinion, but if that was the case, how sick some people's minds can be. Over the years I have seen the enormous amount of money newspapers have been prepared to pay out for any stories about the Krays and speaking for myself there have been times when a bit of extra would've been welcome. Yet not once have either Joe or myself been tempted to betray any of our cousins for reward. In fact over the years I know that Joe has dipped into his own pocket more times than can be counted just to help the boys out.

Thankfully the end wasn't long in coming. As usual it was a day out for sightseers and miles of copy for the newspapers. But what seems to have been forgotten was that for some of us we were burying another loved member of our family. None of them were ever famous gangsters to us; they were just Charlie, Reg and Ron – warts and all. And it's not hard to imagine what thoughts were going through my head as the funeral cars paused alongside the site in Vallance Road where we'd all grown up and spent happy years and sad years. If any good can come out of their wasted lives, it's that youngsters might reconsider following the same road. But in honesty it's unlikely the message will get across, so other families will end up suffering what ours did – and that's a shame.

Once we'd seen Reg reunited with Ron for ever, there was just one last gesture I had to make for him, and that was to place white roses on Frances' grave and kiss the headstone, just as he had done in life: a tribute from me to him and the only girl he'd ever loved.

Conclusion
Peter Gerrard

That two not very well-educated East End boys could take over London's underworld is more to do with the period during the 1950s and 1960s, when they were active, than that they were criminal masterminds. At that time London was wide open and ready to be taken. Key underworld figures were getting past their sell-by date. Police corruption was rife and the newspapers were hungry to replace the ageing underworld bosses Jack Spot and Billy Hill who, as time went on, were becoming less exciting copy than they had been.

So who better to replace them than the two apparently ruthless and charismatic twins? Once the headlines started to appear, it was self-perpetuating on both sides. In their quest for infamy the twins saw their gradually increasing column inches as public confirmation that they were indeed what they had always seen themselves as being. In the end the media and the twins fuelled each other – the legend had begun.

Violence was the key to everything they achieved. Yet what they did achieve was less organized crime than, as put to me by one of the firm, "disorganized crime". No long-term plans, no carefully executed robberies of the century, no tightly knit band of followers – simply, the firm was a loose bunch of Jack the Lads prepared to trade on the reputation of two men whose bargaining power lay in the fact that they were capable of vicious violence to get what they wanted.

Ronnie Kray was the key. He was the bogeyman – with his paranoid psychosis he was the ultimate threat that hung like a shadow over anyone who might think of getting in their way. If it were not for him the Kray legend would never have got off the ground.

As a team, Reg and Charlie should have ended up as millionaires running semi-legitimate enterprises. Charlie had the business acumen while Reg had a similar flair, with the added bonus of being willing to use controlled violence when needed – a necessary asset within the world they chose to operate in.

Ron never craved for wealth nor cared about figure-heading some vast criminal empire. All he wanted was to be seen as an all-powerful figure comparable to his heroes, General Gordon, Winston Churchill or Al Capone. That he gained side benefits from being seen as such was incidental to him.

I don't remember him ever being diagnosed as such, but his behaviour certainly points toward him being a sociopath; the definition being someone who has no concept of the consequences of their actions or any social conscience whatsoever.

When Reg killed Jack McVitie he was drunk, and if not physically goaded into the act by Ron he was at least driven by the mental bond that whatever his twin could do, he was man enough to do the same. When it was over he took great pains to cover up the murder, fully aware that he could eventually be brought to book.

Ron on the other hand slashed, stabbed and shot his way through many years, concluding his comparatively short career by publicly killing Cornell in cold blood. After every wounding or that single murder, he personally made little effort to disguise the fact that he was guilty – being quite happy to leave his mess to be cleared up by others. His sensitivity to slight or imagined insults was another symptom of his paranoia, and he spent a great deal of his time brooding over his very real "Death List" or planning revenge. He was a loose cannon and his mental instability would eventually sweep away everything else his brothers were working toward.

I first met Reg in Blundeston Prison while researching the background of an underworld executioner by the name of Alfie Gerrard – no connection to myself, but the name had grabbed my attention and I wrote to Reg for some information. Here was a man who received hundreds of letters a week, so I was impressed to get a reply almost by return. We corresponded for a short while, and then he sent me a visiting order inviting me to go and meet him.

I'm not sure what I expected when I arrived at the Norfolk prison. His letterheads carried a photograph of himself taken in 1968, and there had only ever been one picture in the newspapers taken while he was inside over the last twenty years. This was one of the reasons most people had a fixed mental picture of him and Ron as still being the men they were in their heyday. All my knowledge of him was from books and cuttings, and in the waiting room it was a strange feeling to think that in minutes I would be meeting one of the most feared gangsters of all time.

When he was finally allowed into the visiting room I was surprised by how small he was. With his short greying hair he appeared older than his years, though he looked fit and carried himself with confidence. His nose, heavily veined, gave away the fact that while alcohol is illegal in the prison system, somehow he'd managed to get his hands on a reasonable supply.

What surprised me more was his soft voice, his extreme politeness and the obvious pleasure with which he greeted me. Surely this was not the same man who could break a jaw with one punch and think nothing of it? But when I looked into those piercing eyes of his and then down to his fists, which seemed disproportionate to the rest of him, yes, I could see the man he must have been on the streets.

As we talked we were constantly interrupted by prisoners' wives and elderly mothers coming across to wish him well, and each one he received without any sign of exasperation. Each one got his full attention and a genuine enquiry after themselves or whoever they were visiting. An autograph, a hug, the occasional peck on the cheek, and he made fans for life.

At a prearranged signal from him I surreptitiously retrieved two miniature bottles of vodka from my inside pocket and poured them into a plastic cup of orange juice, under the cover of a large notebook. I did this on every visit for years and only once did I go empty handed. On this occasion I arrived in Maidstone too late for me to call into an off-licence, so I was unable to stock up on the usual spirits and as luck would have it that was the day they chose to give me a full body pat down. Normally, a body scanner passed over you with no contact was enough – anything further you had a choice: subject yourself to a full search or forget the visit. If I had been carrying contraband I would have refused and left the prison without being found out, so it was a good fail-safe in a way.

As often happened, Reg telephoned the night before and suggested I meet someone outside the gates and then take them in on my VO. Never a problem. This particular day it was a young girl who looked about twelve, but must have been older. Why she was going in God only knows, but it was none of my business to ask. I had not noticed she was carrying a handbag until we reached the scanner desk – too late to tell her that any bags are thoroughly searched. Not pockets, only bags or packages.

In complete innocence she gave the officer a little smile and placed her handbag on the desk. I could only watch in horror as with a Paul Daniels-like flourish the PO drew out half a bottle of brandy and held it above his head. I went weak at the knees for this girl and myself because I had the same tucked into my waistband. The chief PO came over and went absolutely ballistic. As I said, this girl appeared to be about twelve, and he towered over her screaming that he should have her arrested and did she know it was a serious crime, etc., etc. By this time she was frightened and in tears, and I think that softened him up because he said he'd overlook it this time, confiscate the alcohol, but if she ever tried it again he'd bring the full weight of the law down on her. Then it was my turn, and while I was being scanned the chief apologized to me for the noisy aggravation right under my nose, not realizing she was with me.

Only a week later, while this incident was still fresh in my mind, the same thing almost happened with a very well known actress. As before, my instructions from Reg were the same. Meet this lady outside the gates and bring her through on my VO. But having learned a lesson on the previous occasion and knowing that Reg asked all his visitors to bring a small token, I asked if she had any drink on her. She dug around in her shoulder bag and produced a small plastic bottle of gin. When I told her what would happen she said, "Oh, God. Now what shall I do?" Apart from her acting talents one of her popular assets was a Sabrina-like bust, so half-joking I nodded at her cleavage and said, "They won't dare look in there". So that's where she hid the bottle, and I couldn't help smiling as every PO in the reception area was mesmerized by this ample bust, and unaware that there was more in those double Ds than they were imagining.

On that first visit, though, two things struck me, one of them almost literally. Back then smoking was allowed on visits, and I must have given an unconscious signal that I was about to reach for my cigarettes on the table. Before I could, Reg picked up the packet, took out a cigarette and held it up to my face. As a reflex I opened my mouth to take it and Reggie's fist came flying up. As I jumped back he laughed and said, "Too late, I would've broken your jaw by now. That's my cigarette punch." A well-known trick but one he seemed to think was exclusively his and something he was obviously proud of. Again I looked at his hands thinking that I wouldn't like to be on the receiving end of them.

The other revelation was one that would be repeated on every visit thereafter. I was introduced to his "friend", a fresh-faced kid of no more than eighteen. I'm not homophobic and do not normally assume that male friendships are anything more than just that, but a certain closeness planted a seed that I found difficult to accept, bearing in mind that this was the notorious hard man Reg Kray, and ten years before he would publicly, though posthumously, admit to being gay.

As I said earlier, no recent photographs of Reg had been available for many years, so Lenny McLean and myself thought it would be quite a coup to get a picture for our book *The Guv'nor*. I got hold of a plastic camera to avoid the scanner, and Lenny managed to get a couple of shots while on a visit. When the film was developed I noticed that as well as Reg, Lenny had also caught this young man in the snap. They were always together so he was difficult to avoid

When I took the photograph in to Reg to ask his permission to use it he said, "Use me by all means, but not the two of us together". Then he fixed me with that look of his and said, "You writers take in everything you see. You've probably already worked out a situation in your head. What I'm saying to you is there are certain aspects of my private life that should stay private, so I'm trusting you to keep any thoughts about me inside these walls until I'm ready to say otherwise."

There was no threat in the way he spoke, and in fact nothing revelatory in the words he used, but I understood the implication. Why he felt he had to keep his sexuality a secret I do not know. Perhaps he was not aware how the outside world had moved on in terms of accepting gays, or perhaps it did not fit the image he had always portrayed. Either way it made no difference to me, nor would it to anyone else other than the Sunday newspapers, who would have had a field day.

As always with Reg, if he found you interesting the next thing to expect was a summons from Ron, and it wasn't long before I was invited to Broadmoor. At one time all any visitors had to do was arrive at the hospital, sign the book and they were in. Things had changed by the time I was going. First I had to telephone the doctor in charge of Ron, where I got the impression that I was being assessed during our conversation. Once past that hurdle, forms had to be filled in and a background check made before a laminated identity card was issued.

If I expected a gloomy crumbling mental asylum I was mistaken. The entrance would have graced a top hotel, with plush seats and potted plants. Once through the scanner I was escorted across a park-like expanse of brick paving and shrubbery into the small block where Ron lived out his life.

Unlike the generally surly and business-like manner of POs in the mainstream prisons, I found the staff here pleasant and helpful, even though they were serving the same function. I was shown into a brightly decorated, nicely furnished private room, where Ron was waiting for me. He gave me a hug, then pulled out a chair for me and asked what I would like to drink. I chose tea and he disappeared to get it.

It was only when we were settled that I could study this man who had been, was and still is thought of as the supposed epitome of evil. He was gaunt; pale faced but immaculately turned out in a grey suit, dark tie and highly polished shoes. But it was his eyes that held me.

Similar to Reggie's but much more piercing and giving me the impression that he was reading my thoughts. Like Reg too, he showed a great interest in what I did, where I lived and what family I had. This was not polite conversation, but what I took as genuine enquiry because he never took his eyes from mine and listened to every word. I thought I might have felt slightly uncomfortable; instead, it couldn't have been a more relaxed visit. In fact more so than with Reg because we could talk in private.

He spoke of his mother and of how much he missed her, his music, his prayers, and of how he would like to travel when he was released. He gave me the impression that while he had accepted his years behind locked doors, he had now reached a point in his life when he wanted to live in the outside world again.

After three hours it was time to go and as we walked down the passage to the main door, Peter Sutcliffe, the Yorkshire Ripper, came out of a side room. He and Ron ignored each other completely, and while he was still in earshot Ron said to me, "He's scum. I won't have anything to do with him."

Whenever my work took me to London I always stayed with my sister and her husband. And that is where I was that same evening when my police chief inspector brother-in-law took a phone call then passed the handset to me saying, "Ronnie Kray wants to speak to you". It was Ron thanking me for a nice visit. Twenty minutes later the same thing happened, but this time it was Reg thanking me for visiting his brother. Shortly after Charlie Kray called with the same message. The courtesy of all three might have been seemed old fashioned, but I was impressed that each one of them had taken the time to call me for no other reason than to be polite.

On subsequent visits to Ronnie over the years, not once did he ever ask for anything from me. I always took sixty cigarettes as a matter of course, but that was my choice, not his. In fact on one occasion, for no other reason than small talk, he showed me a heavy gold ring that had been given to him by one of the members of the Gambino family. I naturally admired it, so he took it off and said, "It's yours if you want it." Reluctantly but politely I turned down the offer knowing that our conversation would be relayed word for word to Reg, as it was after every visit. I knew that Reg would not have been very pleased, because by then I had become aware that unlike years previously, Reg had become the dominant twin.

As an example I arrived at Broadmoor one day and Ron had a sheaf of notes he had written concerning his marriage to Kate Kray. What he wanted me to do was use these notes to write an article that would refute certain allegations that she had published. He said, "Write something for the *News of the World*. Put my side of the story and tell them I'm not very happy with what's been said so far. Whatever they want to pay keep it for yourself."

The next morning at eight o'clock Reg rang me to say *he* didn't want me to pursue it – not Ron – *him!*

Regularly people ask me what Ron was like and I always tell them I can only answer that from my own personal perspective. I never saw madness, arrogance or anything of the vicious killer he might have been. I saw an interesting man with a very dry humour and a deep compassion for the less fortunate – something he often spoke about. And although he seemed to hold something of himself back he still came over as a friendly and caring man. In fact everything that was the opposite of his legend.

Something that often comes to mind when I read an article, a book or see a piece of film graphically describing insane murderer Ron Kray, is him reciting a child's prayer. He told me that he prayed every night, but one he had learned from his mother was his particular favourite – would I like to hear it? Then without any thought that his image might be lessened he quietly went into, "Now I lay me down to sleep, I pray the Lord my soul to keep" – and so on for a couple of verses. Coming from him I found it strangely moving.

It is academic now, but at that time his past was just that – a lifetime away. So it is a tragedy that he was not allowed to spend the last years of his life in freedom. It was a privilege to call him a friend and I felt a genuine sadness when he passed away.

Reg, so like his twin in younger years, was nothing like him in the latter part of his life. Up until Ron died Reg was equally caring. Nothing was too much trouble for him, and every request for help, or simply a signed photograph, was answered – and these ran into many hundreds. Even with this busy schedule he still found the time to write regularly to my young son Peter enquiring after his hobbies and schooling. And, always signing himself as Uncle Reg, he'd enclose drawings for our boy's amusement. This giving was something I had noticed from my first visit to him and on every subsequent visit. He had nothing that he perceived as of any value to give, but as a token of appreciation for a visit he always found some kind of gift: the pen he may have been writing with, a used phone-card, a crayon drawing – and at one time he shared out packets of smuggled-in cigarettes.

When he lost Ron he began to drink more heavily than usual, took to cannabis and became obsessed with scams to raise money. He had legions of young fans, each one a potential source of cash. He told me that if he sent out a dozen letters asking for money, nine or ten would reply to a given address sending cash, which would then be smuggled in. Or a hard-luck story to these same kinds of people about having no decent footwear would bring in a selection of expensive trainers.

Even myself and other good friends would find that almost overnight he'd turned into a "tapper". "Got a twenty on you?" "Got a fifty?" This would then mean a trip to the toilet, where I would fold the note up as small as it would go, wrap it up in cigarette-packet foil, then return to the room, where Reg could place it in his mouth before going through the usual after-visit search. Every now and again some young ex-con would knock on my door saying that Reg had sent him and, trotting out various reasons for asking, would try and borrow money. Unsuccessfully, I might add, after the first few times.

When a special friend was ghosted out of Maidstone Prison in the small hours, without even the chance of saying goodbye, Reg became distraught and his behaviour worsened. Then many of us would suffer early morning telephone calls, when he'd be drunk and incoherent or screaming abuse because some command had not been carried out to his liking.

Too many people were telling me that he was becoming a f—g nuisance, and he lost a number of friends when they changed their telephone numbers to avoid him.

Whatever he had become in those last years could never take away from the fact that against all the odds he had remained strong and intelligent for twenty-five or more years of his sentence. Perhaps because he never lost hope of being released one day.

The fact that it was obvious to him that politics would keep him inside for the rest of his life must have knocked the heart out of him. A psychiatric report put together for his last appeal stated that he was devious, manipulative and would not conform to certain prison programmes. Regardless of Reg publicly denying that any of this was true, it was in fact quite accurate.

Having said that, I personally felt that regardless of those facts they were pathetic reasons for denying him parole. He had more than fully paid his debt to society once he had served twenty years, so the fact that the Home Office kept him locked away until they were sure he would die within a short time, can only ever be classed as a miscarriage of justice.

The government papers that will explain why he could not be freed will not be made public in my lifetime, but one day the political reasons behind this decision will be known.

I have criticized Reg here, but as a final tribute I have to say that in the time I knew him he did me more good than otherwise. Without thought of profit or self-interest, he went out of his way to point my career in the right direction – and for that I can only thank him.

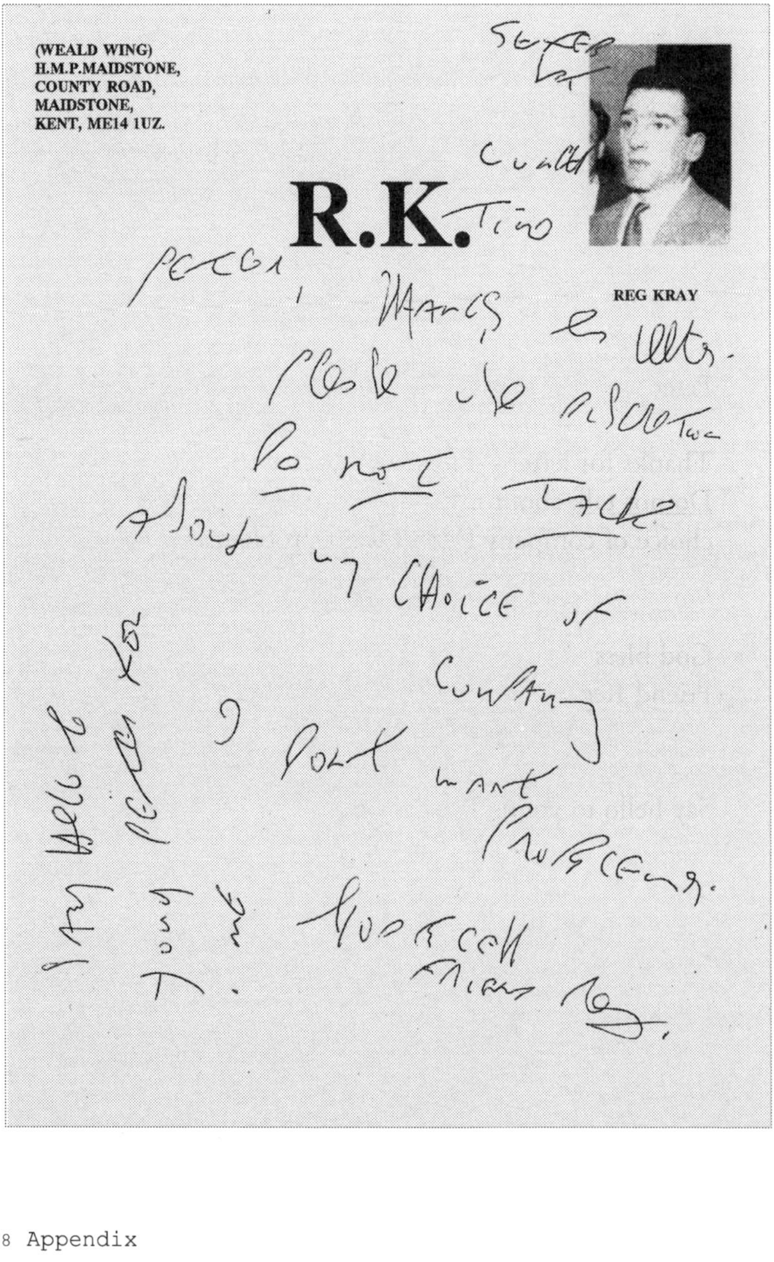

(WEALD WING)
H.M.P.MAIDSTONE,
COUNTY ROAD,
MAIDSTONE,
KENT, ME14 1UZ.

R.K.

REG KRAY

5th Feb

Peter

Thanks for letter – Please use discretion.
<u>Do not talk</u> about my
choice of company I don't want problems.

God bless
Friend Reg.

Say hello to young Peter for me.

(WEALD WING)
H.M.P.MAIDSTONE,
COUNTY ROAD,
MAIDSTONE,
KENT, ME14 1UZ.

R.K.

Peter

25th Sep
Sunday
4–40
a.m.

Words
Baileys Vange
Bottle of vodka

we give
you a lot to
work and
use plastic
top of
bottle because

Some times they use
a metal
detector.
Thanks
God Bless
Your friend
Ron

Clayton's here
to

25 Sep
Sunday
4-40 am

Dear Peter

Would you bring half a bottle of vodka in

Will give you a lot to work with
Use plastic top on bottle because sometimes they
use a metal detector

Thanks

God bless
Friend

Reg Kray

Index